The Ecological Heart
of Teaching

Studies in Criticality

Shirley R. Steinberg
General Editor

Vol. 478

The Counterpoints series is part of the Peter Lang Education list.
Every volume is peer reviewed and meets
the highest quality standards for content and production.

PETER LANG
New York • Bern • Frankfurt • Berlin
Brussels • Vienna • Oxford • Warsaw

The Ecological Heart of Teaching

Radical Tales of Refuge and Renewal for Classrooms and Communities

Edited by Jackie Seidel and David W. Jardine

PETER LANG
New York • Bern • Frankfurt • Berlin
Brussels • Vienna • Oxford • Warsaw

Library of Congress Cataloging-in-Publication Data

Names: Seidel, Jackie, editor. | Jardine, David William, editor.
Title: The ecological heart of teaching: radical tales of refuge and renewal
for classrooms and communities / edited by Jackie Seidel, David W. Jardine.
Description: New York : Peter Lang, 2016.
Series: Counterpoints: studies in criticality; vol. 478 | ISSN 1058-1634
Includes bibliographical references.
Identifiers: LCCN 2016021402 | ISBN 978-1-4331-3236-0 (hardcover: alk. paper)
ISBN 978-1-4331-3235-3 (paperback: alk. paper) | ISBN 978-1-4539-1733-6 (e-book)
Subjects: LCSH: Teaching—Philosophy.
Teaching—Moral and ethical aspects. | Teachers—Conduct of life.
Classification: LCC LB1025.3 .E3 2016 | DDC 371.102—dc23
LC record available at https://lccn.loc.gov/2016021402

Bibliographic information published by **Die Deutsche Nationalbibliothek**.
Die Deutsche Nationalbibliothek lists this publication in the "Deutsche
Nationalbibliografie"; detailed bibliographic data are available
on the Internet at http://dnb.d-nb.de/.

© 2016 Peter Lang Publishing, Inc., New York
29 Broadway, 18th floor, New York, NY 10006
www.peterlang.com

For the elders who left and the babies who arrived.

Acknowledgments

The authors would like to thank the following publishers for permission to reprint articles in this text:

Chapter 7 was originally published as Jardine, D. (1997). "All beings are your ancestors": A bear Sutra on ecology, Buddhism and pedagogy. *The Trumpeter: A Journal of Ecosophy*, *14*(3), 120–123.

Chapter 10 was originally published as Latremouille, J. (2015). A modern hunting tradition. *One World in Dialogue*, *3*(2), 9–11. Published by the Alberta Teachers' Association (ATA), Edmonton Alberta, Canada.

Chapter 11 was originally published as Jardine, D. (2015). In appreciation of modern hunting traditions and a grouse's life unwasted. *One World in Dialogue*, *3*(2), 7–8. Published by the Alberta Teachers' Association (ATA), Edmonton Alberta, Canada.

Chapter 21 was originally published as Seidel, J. (2014). Meditations on contemplative pedagogy as sanctuary. *Journal of Contemplative Inquiry*, *1*(1), 141–147.

Chapter 29 was originally published as Molnar, C. (2014). Life and mortality: A teacher's awakening. *In Education*, *20*(2), 90–102.

Chapter 52 was originally published as Jardine, D. (2014). Old dog. Same trick. *Journal of Applied Hermeneutics*. http://jah.journalhosting.ucalgary.ca/jah/index.php/jah/article/view/71/pdf

Table OF Contents

Foreword

Not Just as We Please, or by Choice: A Meditation on What It Means to Make a Difference

DAVID GEOFFREY SMITH

Insofar as one might have a historical materialist view of the human condition, and perhaps even if one doesn't, three points from Karl Marx (1852/1978) still bear consideration:

> [People] make their own history, but they do not make it just as they please; they do not make it under circumstances chosen by themselves, but under circumstances directly found, given and transmitted from the past. (p. 595)

In a way, the words serve as a warning. When it comes to meaningful and lasting personal, social, political or cultural change, don't indulge in any fantasies about pure autonomy or perfectly free action, because the real work to be done always entails dealing precisely with what one has been dealt, what one has received, be it from family, tribe, language or nation. Why? Because "[the] tradition of all dead generations weighs like a nightmare on the brain of the living" (p. 595), and unless one penetrates the veils of one's receipts, reproduction of the old life in new forms is the inevitable result. Marx took as his example the so-called French Revolution of Napoleon Bonaparte when land and property were divested from the monarchy, with its feudal social and political arrangements, and taken over by a new bourgeois class (> O.Fr. *borgois*, town dweller c.f. peasant) made up of new property owners, financiers, industrialists, the army, universities, churches, courts and the press, all of whom had become within one generation under Napoleon's nephew Louis the chief operatives of the new national republican state. In Marx's view, in a single generation the state had become a latent embodiment of fascism, since for most people (peasants, in the French case) "the duties of feudal obligation are replaced

XVI | DAVID GEOFFREY SMITH

by the mortgage," (p. 597) with people forced to sell themselves as labour to service their debts to the state. The new state was so confident of its revolutionary merit that it established a new calendar to mark the beginning of a new epoch starting on November 9, 1799, when Napoleon first seized power. November is the month of fog (Fr. *brumaire*), so Marx titled his essay from which the above quotes are taken as "The Eighteenth Brumaire of Napoleon Bonaparte." Unfortunately, this history is all but forgotten today, which of course was precisely Marx's point: forget the past, or better, just pick and choose what you like about it, and you'll simply repeat it with all of its blindnesses and forms of foolishness. Napoleon saw himself as a new Caesar, just as George W. Bush conceived the war on terror as a Crusade.

Another insight from Marx may be relevant here, one articulated in the book *Grundrisse*, a German word meaning "comprehensive outline," in this case Marx's *Outline of the Critique of Political Economy*, not published until 1939. It is estimated that originally only three or four copies of this book were ever made public in the West, and the work was not translated into English until 1973. Such is the fear in the West of a comprehensive critique of its own operating assumptions. In *Grundrisse*, Marx (1858/1993) described his fundamental method of analysis as involving an "ascent from the abstract to the concrete." There is something lovely in the image this phrase evokes, of a kind of clawing one's way up from the depths underneath the concrete, material world to eventually see that world as it actually is in all of its historical and existential depth through the traces that have brought it into being. But why "from the abstract"? Here Marx is employing the dialectical method of one of his earlier philosophical compatriots, G. F. Hegel, to note how our very ideas and abstractions of the world are created through the world itself. Ideas never exist in a vacuum, or on their own, so that people can "bounce ideas around" in a game of intellectual chess. Instead, when we take up our ideas, expressed primarily in language, as objects of contemplation we can begin to see the concrete world out of which they have arisen. Similarly, when we contemplate the material, concrete world right in front of us we can begin to see into the very shape and character of our intellects, of how it is we think about the world in the ways that we do. All this, in turn, can provide insight into the real work that needs to be done in order to live more freely and openly, no longer chained to the dead weights that have constructed us without our being aware of it. It is in this sense that the basic human project becomes a spiritual endeavor, one of emancipation from the endless rounds of personal, social and political reproduction that have haunted revolutionary movements in the past.

Finally, in the opening paragraph of his greatest work, *Capital*, Marx (1867/1990) addresses the question of where one should start in trying to understand the world in which one finds oneself. His answer was to look at "commodities," or even a single commodity. This is because all commodities are produced through *relations* of production and when we examine those relations, what

becomes apparent are the moral and ethical valences in them, their relative justice or injustice, and their connection to broader global orders. I was thinking
about this just the other day, while driving by a day-care centre close to my home.
Contemplating day-care as a commodity, I started to 'see' things that until then
had escaped my deeper consciousness. Children start arriving around seven in the
morning, usually brought by their mothers who drop them off on their way to
work. According to one of the day-care workers, most of the children come from
single-parent homes. Children are accepted at the centre at the age of two. On
some days, children are still at the day-care at six o'clock in the evening. I leave
it to the reader's imagination to 'deconstruct' this scenario through Marx's theory
of the relations of production, but here is a long starter question: What are the
relations that make this kind of child care 'necessary'—not just parent-child relations, but also proprietor-parent relations, proprietor relations to the owners of the
building from whom they need to purchase a lease, relations of building owners to
banks and financial institutions, relations of banks and financial institutions like
J.P. Morgan and Goldman Sachs to cultures of militarism and war—that in turn
produce immigrant and refugee populations who produce children needing special care as their parents desperately try to make a living in their new land? Wars
also necessitate higher taxes on citizens, so paychecks gradually decrease in value,
necessitating working longer and harder to make ends meet, to the neglect of one's
own children.

I was thinking about all of these things while reading the manuscript of this
book, which is a remarkable collection of writings from a remarkable gathering of
teachers brought together by Jackie Seidel and David Jardine. These are stories
and writings of people who are trying to heal themselves of the cultural maladies
of the neoliberal state, especially as those maladies find expression in the protocols
and practices of public education today. Here are teachers doing the hard philosophical and existential work of clawing up to the concrete of their material conditions from deep within the caverns of lives in the process of being reclaimed from
cultural and historical amnesia. It is very exciting to bear witness to this alternative
kind of pedagogical exploration, and credit for this must surely go to Jackie and
David, who have dared to claim that this kind of reclamation project is both possible and capable of bearing significant revolutionary fruit. I have seen this work
in action at one of their special retreats, with one of the most impressive features
being the degree to which the people involved had bonded together, across many
potentially difficult divides of race, gender, age and experience. By laying themselves open to a fully collaborative consideration of the problems we collectively
share as people living in deeply troubled and troubling times, this amazing group
provides an example of what can be produced when the relations of production
are based on mutual respect, patience, generosity, authentic listening and speaking,
and a certain kind of hope shining forth from nascent senses of empowerment.

My reading of the manuscript also took me back to my own earlier years as an undergraduate in the 1960s. Those were times too of new forms of gathering amongst people determined not to simply, mindlessly reproduce what they had inherited, especially in view of the pervasive, malignant war culture created by and through those inheritances. Perhaps the most fecund gathering place of the time was Greenwich Village in New York City. There, artists of all stripes—writers, painters, musicians, philosophers—would gather in coffeehouses and bars not just to present their work but also to discuss the world that was making their work seem a profound moral obligation. Poet Allen Ginsberg might read from his long poem *Howl!*, a deeply moving rant against the assumptions of the military corporate state. Bob Dylan might sing his revolutionary song *Blowin' in the Wind*. Joan Baez would inspire with her haunting rendition of the call to action, *We Shall Overcome*. All of this work fed the dreams and aspirations of a whole generation of young people, especially on college campuses even in Canada, which became centres of revolutionary ardour. We know how the story ended: police action. In the United States the National Guard shot students in cold blood.

As Stefan Halper and Jonathan Clarke (2004) have revealed in their book *America Alone: The Neo-conservatives and the Global Order*, when the neo-conservatives and their neoliberal siblings were plotting the takeover of the Anglo-American political system through the likes of Margaret Thatcher in England and Ronald Reagan in the United States, they vowed that never again would university campuses be allowed to become centres of political revolt and unrest. Such is the condition of our own time. Through strategies of surveillance, often masked as "accountability measures," professors and students who dare to question dominant narratives, narratives saturated with state propaganda, especially regarding the events of 9/11 and the War on Terror, face ridicule, censure and counter-accusation. A culture of fear has produced an erosion of intellectual courage; timidity has replaced honesty and forthrightness.

There is nothing new about all this, of course, as history tells us. However, each generation bears responsibility for upholding principles of justice, fairness, openness and hope in its own time, not for the past, nor for the future but for today, and the responsibility may fall in unique ways on the shoulders of educators. What will the enactment of such responsibility look like, and how shall it be cultivated? There is a hint of an answer in the ancient Greek term *parrhesia*, which literally means "to speak everything," implying speaking boldly, freely, frankly and without guile. It is the form of speech which characterized that of Socrates during his defense against charges of corrupting the youth of Athens by encouraging them to ask questions, and for his refusal to bow to local gods. One can read his speech in Plato's *Apology*. More recently, Cornel West (2015) in *Black Prophetic Fire* has invoked the term to describe the work of African American intellectuals like W. E. B. Du Bois, Ella Baker, Ida B. Wells, Martin Luther King Jr. and Malcolm X who directly and courageously confronted the systemic racism of American life, some-times at the cost of their own lives. Michel Foucault (2001) discussed *parrhesia* in his book *Fearless Speech*, making the important point that such speech is linked to truthfulness in one's own life, as well as in the taking of risk and the acceptance of moral duty. Again, I think one can glimpse nascent signs of all of these charac-teristics in the variegated writings of this book and for that I applaud Jackie and David's courage in making it possible.

In closing, I note two other aspects of *parrhesia*. One is that in Greek philoso-phy it is counterpointed to the use of *rhetoric* (Gk. *rhetor*). The teaching of rhetoric as the art and practice of *persuasive* speech, speech intended to persuade hearers to a particular point of view, was part of the core curriculum for students in classical Greece and it remained so in Europe generally until the late Middle Ages. Rhet-oric fell out of favour, however, because it was recognized that self-consciously mastering the techniques of persuasive speech easily led to the more craven arts of manipulation and verbal fraud. Today, rhetoric serves the lords of advertising and the macabre interests of propaganda. Conversely, *parrhesia* is unself-conscious speech, not a servant of the will or ego but simply the stating of the truth of things no matter what the cost.

In the ancient Hebrew tradition, the capacity for plain speaking was often linked to the word *dimus*, meaning "free inhabitants of the land." It shared an understanding with that of "the commons," understood as a kind of ownerless wilderness, an understanding to emerge from the early Israelite experience of wandering in the open deserts of the southeastern Mediterranean. In the true wilderness nobody owns anything because openness and sharing are the necessary conditions of survival. So it may be in our own time. Our capacity for new forma-tions of community based on honesty, openness and sharing may depend first and foremost on a recognition that indeed we are living in the midst of a wilderness, a cultural desert, a time of great moral corruption through the rule of Mammon. It is so easy to get lost. To survive, we must depend not only on one another but also on people who have journeyed through wildernesses in the past and lived to tell about it. Most principally, though, to acknowledge the moral desert of the times is to acknowledge, in the same breath, one's own freedom, the freedom to speak and act freely, without fear. There is nothing to fear because the essential truth of life simply is what it is, not a possession in any conceptual sense, or even possessable, only lived as a manner of being, and joyously too because it is indestructible. The gates of hell cannot prevail against it. Read the chapters in this book and you'll get a sense of what I mean.

CHAPTER ONE

Introduction

JACKIE SEIDEL AND DAVID W. JARDINE

Develop the following ideas with respect to your teachers. I have wandered for a long time through cyclic existence, and they search for me; I have been asleep, having been obscured by delusion for a long time, and they wake me; they pull me out of the depths of the ocean of existence; I have entered a bad path, and they reveal the good path to me; they release me from being bound in the prison of existence. I have been worn out by illness for a long time, and they are my doctors; they are the rain clouds that put out my blazing fire of attachment.

—TSONG-KHA-PA (2000, P. 83)

Everything is teaching you. Isn't this so? Can you just get up and walk away so easily now?

—AJAHN CHAH (2004, P. 5)

This book gathers together writings about and by teachers. It draws on three bodies of scholarly endeavor that fall outside of the purview of much educational literature: ecology, Buddhism and hermeneutics. These three lineages insist, each in its own way, that *our lived surroundings teach*, and that our attunement to these teachings is key to a thoughtful, sustainable and livable future. The writings in this text demonstrate how *everything* is teaching us—objects and school artifacts, children, illness, elders, texts, colleagues and friends and enemies, animals, bodies, places and their names, images housed in our shared and contested languages, our inner and outer afflictions and contemplations, conflicts and loves—the very Earth and our breathing of it seeks to *teach*.

Suggesting that everything is teaching you—that it has a *story* to tell if we are able to learn how to hear it—is a profoundly ecological, scholarly and contemplative act, and an act of refuge from the noisy surface clatter that defines contemporary life, especially, sad to say, much of the life of schools. The writing in this book is born of such a sense of refuge, contemplation and deep, difficult thinking about our circumstances and what stories have driven us, and what story we might tell about the stories we've told or simply fallen for, that would break this relentless, seemingly ever-accelerating spell that makes us believe that our exhaustion and panic are nothing but "the real world" and "just the way things are." It helps identify and interrupt current discourses of technical, managerial and efficiency obsessions in education (Callahan, 1964; Jardine, 2008b, 2013; Kanigel, 2005; Picciano & Spring, 2012; Seidel, 2006; Taylor, 1911) while at the same time vastly expanding our sense of where teaching resides and therefore what it means to be a teacher who finds oneself in the midst of a living world that is already full of lessons to be taught and learned. The scholarly lineages of hermeneutics, Buddhism and ecology provide not only critiques of our current circumstances but also new language, new insights and new possibilities for stepping into the practice of teaching in ways that are more livable for students and teachers and the world(s) of knowledge with which they have been entrusted.

As for the term "radical" in our title, we want to recover part of the meaning of this term that has, it seems, fallen from memory. "Radical" stems from the Latin *radix*, "rootedness" or, to use the Buddhist term, an experience of the "dependent co-arising," not only of myself and my teachers and students, but of any and all curriculum topics we consider. Each curriculum topic, properly and carefully considered, is, by its very nature, radical, rooted in living fields of ancestry, language, inheritance, shared and contested, new and ancient. Our learning to live in and with these living fields requires the radicality of teachers and students alike in questioning what these things might mean, given our current ecologically imminent circumstances.

The pieces in this book called on contributors to enact the old hermeneutic art (Gadamer, 1989) of mindfully and carefully unpacking the messages that are coming to us (to our students and to ourselves) in a way that itself has ecological echoes (Seidel & Jardine, 2014). It is an act of "learning your way around" (Bransford, Brown, & Cocking, 2000, p. 138) in these living fields of messages, of coming to "know one's way around" (Gadamer, 1989, p. 260) and not simply to be pushed and pulled around by stories that have lost their tell. These last images capture how this way of proceeding provides an *eminently practical image of the nature of teaching and learning itself*, one the authors have explored in great detail elsewhere (Friesen & Jardine, 2011; Jardine, 2011, 2013a; Jardine, Clifford, & Friesen, 2006, 2008; Seidel & Jardine, 2014). These are further elaborated by the many stories shared by teachers in this book.

This book emerged out of three years of intensive graduate-level study with a large group of practicing teachers in Calgary, Alberta, many of whom have contributed to this text (see the following chapter, "We Went Once Around the Sun," for more detail about these courses and about how this book is organized). Our classes were deliberately understood as a refuge from the regimes of distraction that surround schools, a chance to retell the tale of what good we are doing in the world, under its current ecologically and spiritually ominous circumstances. What happened was that teachers knew something was going on outside of the confines they seemed stuck in. Our collaborative study of the stories we are living out provided a way to begin to speak, to write, to enjoin each other in lineages of thought and study that provide release, relief and a deeper sense of being able to ask, along with farmer/philosopher Wendell Berry (Berry & Moyers, 2013): What is the right thing to do, here, now, in these circumstances of our living? As we asked such questions together, other work we had been studying of scholars, poets and philosophers, including Elliot Eisner, Philip Phenix, Maxine Greene, David G. Smith, Cynthia Chambers, Narcisse Blood, Dwayne Donald, bell hooks, Ashis Nandy, Hans-Georg Gadamer, William Doll, Joseph Campbell, David R. Loy, Thomas King, Thich Nhat Hanh, Ted Aoki, Don Domanski, Maria Montessori. All the referentialities that come with studying the work of these and many more scholars, poets and storytellers came cascading into their/our writing, weaving a story beyond the confines of where it first began.

Surroundings of ancestors, lineages, elders, voices, companions—this is what emerges in stories from the ecological, radical heart of curriculum, the heart of our common and contested "course," and our work felt increasingly surrounded, supported, rooted and encouraged by the lines of thinking that wove around us. During our courses, we heard many times that teachers often feel that they are alone in their suspicions about their circumstances, and often their only recourse is dis-ease, complaint and exhaustion. During our studies together, we examined how this isolation is a deliberate by-product of industrial and managerial schemes and how it is *profoundly anti-pedagogical* at its root. The refuge of our common work in this book was one of relief and commiseration, of realizing that with study one can fill the surroundings with tales of joy and hope. In this regard, this text draws on "life writing" (Chambers, Hasebe-Ludt, Leggo, & Sinner, 2012), "writing as research" (Richardson, 1994; Richardson & St. Pierre, 2005) and hermeneutic writing (see Jardine, 2013a, 2015c; Moules, McCaffrey, Field, & Laing, 2015; Seidel & Jardine, 2014). Many chapters will provide readers with rich examples of this sort of work.

In the end, this book has a double intent:

- It is designed and written to be a *refuge of encouragement for teachers and students in schools* who have sensed that there is something amiss and who are attempting to step away from our current circumstances.
- It designed and written to be *a scholarly and ancestral sourcebook for that refuge*, providing examples for those engaged in undergraduate, graduate, professional or personal study in and of education, curriculum and pedagogy.

Our book aims to reconnect readers to these rigorous and academically solid roots and to show the practical nature and importance of such reconnection—how it enlivens knowledge and engagement in teachers and students alike and provides a realistic and grounded sense of hope that neither ignores our current circumstances nor simply falls for them.

Thus, *The Ecological Heart of Teaching* is our storied offering: a refuge and a sourcebook that sees teaching as an ancient and radical art.

CHAPTER TWO

We Went Once Around THE Sun

Some Notes on the Origins and Organization of This Book

JACKIE SEIDEL AND DAVID W. JARDINE

While sitting in David's sun-filled office in the forests west of Calgary, finalizing the editing and reminiscing about how this book came to be, Jackie said: "It's because we went once around the sun!" We both laughed with pleasure at recognizing this to be true, that this long arc of time was one of our companions. We interrupted our editing to contemplate what it means and why it matters to remember, in these human and educational worlds, that we are gravitational travelers around that fiery star that makes all life possible.

In February 2015, we presented with a group of fifteen graduate students at the Provoking Curriculum Conference (Canadian Association for Curriculum Studies) at the University of British Columbia. The presentation was a forty-five-minute, multi-voice performance that included excerpts from many of the chapters in this book. When we finished, the audience was interested in understanding the context of the graduate courses in which this work had been made possible. In particular, some wanted to know how we had been able to create such rich, philosophical, performative scholarship within the contemporary confines of the market structures of universities, in particular the constraints of measurable course objectives, or having to assign grades. Indeed, these are constraining times. The chapters in this book written by graduate students, most of them educators, are existential responses to what it means to live in such a time. What afflicts the university is also afflicting the educational spaces of the young and those who teach them. In the graduate programs from which this book emerged, we were not free from such constraints; but rather than be limited by them, we made the conscious study of them part of our purpose together. We took seriously Robert Bly's (2005) admonishment in his poem "Advice from the Geese": "I don't want to frighten you, but not a stitch can be taken / in your quilt unless you study" (p. 29). And so, we studied with rigour and purpose, not for the purpose of achieving a grade or credential, but for the existential purpose of understanding our lives and this world together. And although we didn't answer those questions in this way at that time, our best, most genuine and heartfelt answer in retrospect to how we did this is that we went once around the sun!

In 2012, under the auspices of the Werklund School of Education's revised graduate programs, we created and offered a four-course graduate certificate called "Roots of Classroom Inquiry." A local school graciously hosted us and more than twenty graduate students each week for a year. During the first certificate, we decided to create a second one: "Storytelling in the Ecological Heart of Curriculum." In 2013, the same school welcomed us with about twenty-five graduate students to meet weekly, while another school offered hospitality for a second cohort of a re-imagined "Roots of Classroom Inquiry." In the beginning, our imaginations were bound by the technical confines of post-secondary organization: four courses of three credits each with distinct beginnings and endings. By the second year, we realized that it made more sense to imagine each certificate as one year-long course, even though we were required to provide four course outlines, each with its own readings, assignments, outcomes, objectives and, of course, final grades at the end of each term. By the time we offered "Storytelling" again in 2014, with again a local school offering a warm and peaceful space to gather, we had learned a new kind of rhythm for collaborative study with teachers and others interested in these topics. Together with the graduate students, we learned to push away and practiced purposefully pushing away the institutional structures which, in David Loy's (2010) words, were binding us "without a rope" (p. 42).

Because we went once around the sun.

In twelve-week or one-semester courses, most universities' usual offerings, a topic must necessarily be condensed and rushed. There may be time for a surface-level survey, or for a seed to be planted and begin sprouting, but not enough for it to fully *become itself* and take root. We learned that a year together allowed us to luxuriate in time, to wait for ideas to grow, to not feel bound by a twelve-week structure to meet predetermined outcomes; rather, we could plant seeds and then wait, we could be patient, we could see what might grow and perhaps even harvest.

And we could *eat*. At the beginning, we made time for a snack in the middle of our three-hour evening class. As time went on, both the nourishing quality and the amount of food that members of the community brought in increased, as did the time that we spent together enjoying this food. Eating together was no longer a "break" but a vital part of our study together, a revitalizing part of the rhythm of our evenings and our year. Nourishing our bodies was not separate from nourishing our minds which is not separate from our miraculous participation in this nearly five billion year old planetary cycling around this star. In such a body-space-time, we were able to start telling different stories about what our work is for and about with children, in schools, in this time. We were able to engage in different, new and multiple stories, perspectives and interpretations about what was happening around us, and pull ourselves out of the myriad panics that seem to inflict schools.

Because we went once around the sun.

Our certificate outcomes did not include publishing a book of writing by graduate students; yet, here it is. Our main learning activities included reading, and rereading, and talking about what we read, and writing, and sharing our writing. From these practices, and we understood them as *practices*, emerged several conference presentations that many students participated in, and then—this book. It couldn't have happened if we didn't go once around the sun. There wouldn't have been time. There wouldn't have been trust between us to share our writing, first with one another, and then with a broader audience in public, and then on paper in this book. There would have been no harvest.

Because we went once around the sun, ideas and stories began to circulate and take root in our scholarly community. One day in class, we were meditating together on a particularly challenging passage in David Loy's (2010) book *The World Is Made of Stories*. One of the students joked, "Can you imagine if we gave this book to a new teacher and told them this was the only guide book they needed?" We all laughed. And then we took that seriously. Several of the chapters in this book grew from that moment, and that idea, and are formed as letters or advice to beginning teachers inspired by David Loy's book. We are grateful to David Geoffrey Smith for inspiring us with an assignment he gave to his graduate classes at the University of Alberta: Curriculum Artifact Studies. We suggested this as a possible writing activity/practice to our students. In this book there are several studies of artifacts that are so commonplace, ubiquitous and normalized in school environments as to have become invisible to us. The work of studying them carefully and closely, of examining the unconscious power they have in these places as objects that shape school culture, reveals them to us as conscious and interpretable. It enables us to ask: Why is this here? How did it get here? What does it do? What power does it hold over us? How does it shape these educational spaces? What happens to our work if it is gone? David Geoffrey Smith's chapter as a contribution to this book, "Blossom Everlasting: A Meditation," is another example of how such artifact studies might serve as freeing and hermeneutic gestures that renew understandings of the invisible and everyday around us. By stopping, and contemplating, we learn to see anew, and different stories can be told, and therefore different lives can be lived.

There is another important sense, and double meaning, to this cycling nature of life to consider and that was important to our studies. David Loy (2010) writes, "*Samsara*—this world of suffering, according to Buddhism—literally means going around and around" (p. 23). As we studied together, and shared stories of schools and classrooms, our conversations often turned to the kinds of suffering that are experienced in schools and communities by children, young people and teachers. We studied the ways that schools and teachers try to escape suffering, and remembered that these efforts can often cause increased or repeated suffering. Many chapters in this book either reference or are directly focused on a very immediate and material example of this: the strong reappearance in schools of leveled readers along with the highly teacher-directed, corporate trademarked methodology of Guided Reading (even with commercialized furniture and storage methods to facilitate it!). Recognizing and understanding the storied nature of these "artifacts," and their entanglement in capitalism, colonialism and the history of schooling, helped us to understand more fully how it is also possible to un-story or refuse them, to put them in their place, and to tell a different narrative of our hopes and intentions for children and the world. It enabled us to understand how such practices in schools seem to return again and again, in response to fear and anxiety, and compound suffering upon suffering. It enabled us to understand that our work might not be able to escape this, while at the same time envisioning ways of stepping off the wheel of suffering, even for a moment, to participate in more life-giving and life-sustaining cycles of the earth. This included eating the most delicious and nourishing foods together—foods nourished by the sun, gifted by the earth, given by one another—while engaged in serious conversation about our most serious concerns.

Because the chapters grew from that space, this book is organized as a conversation. We imagined that a reader might experience a bit of what we experienced. In putting the book together, we tried other, more conventional organizational strategies such as sections or themes. We tried grouping the stories about elders, the stories about animals, the stories about children and so on, but as we read through the manuscript this did not feel right. Then, we spread the chapters around on large conference tables and realized that it was better to put the pieces in conversation with one another, as if they were sitting around a table and sharing a meal. They all belong together. They all intersect. They all grew from the same place. They share an affinity that goes beyond themes or sections.

Because we went once around the sun, babies were conceived and were born (and also, in grief, not born) during the time we spent together. Several of our elders died during our studies (Ted Aoki: 1919–2012; Maxine Greene: 1917–2014; Elliot Eisner: 1933–2014; Narcisse Blood: 1954–2015). We mourned them and read their words more heartfully and. they gave us courage for this work. In reading far beyond the educational research and literature, we explored what David Loy (2010) refers to as "fragile ecological niches" (p. 32). This matters, he says, because the common story plots that shape this world are "invasive species that promote the cargo cult of commodifying consumption" (p. 32). Practicing and learning to listen to and tell other kinds of stories, to protect and create spaces for these *fragile ecological niches* to survive became our work together. One cohort spent a weekend at the Banff Centre, studying with Dwayne Donald and David Geoffrey Smith, walking in the spring snow by the Bow River, one of the precious headwater sources of life for those of us who live in southern Alberta. We are grateful for their profound contributions to our learning, both in person and through their scholarship, and for their contributions to this book. Michael Derby traveled from the west coast of British Columbia for a visit, to commiserate about the challenges of graduate school, writing, about the work teachers do with young people, and the conditions and possibilities of that work. He generously contributed a chapter that includes some of the writing and conversation from the evening he shared with us. We've also included David Jardine's introduction ("How to Love Black Snow") to Michael's (Derby, 2015) book that was written during our sun turning.

The subtitle of this book, *Radical Tales of Refuge and Renewal for Classrooms and Communities*, signals an understanding that schools are in *a* place, and as such, that the ecological heart of teaching properly belongs in communities. This is where we learn together and from one another, the young from the old, the old from the young, parents and children and teachers together, the human from the non-human. We remember that we are gravity-bound Earthbeings, and that the roots that sustain us might be found in the life-giving and life-serving stories we can share as we travel together around our star. Its bountiful energy feeds our communities both literally and mythologically. It warms the pages of this book. "The truth about stories," writes Thomas King (2003), "is that's all we are" (p. 2).

We went once around the sun.

CHAPTER THREE

From What Does Ethical Relationality Flow?

An *Indian* Act in Three Artifacts

DWAYNE DONALD

As part of an ongoing effort to articulate new ways of living together that are not fully circumscribed by colonial frontier logics (Donald, 2009b, 2012a, 2012b), I have been increasingly inspired by the wisdom teachings of Cree Elders. In Cree teachings, ethical forms of relationality are emphasized as most important because doing so supports life and living for all perceptive beings in organically generative ways. The Cree wisdom concepts most central to this relational insight are wicihitowin and wahkohtowin. The term wicihitowin[1] refers to the life-giving energy that is generated when people face each other as relatives and build trusting relationships by connecting with others in respectful ways. In doing so, we demonstrate that we recognize one another as fellow human beings and work hard to put respect and love at the forefront of our interactions. The Elders teach that when wicihitowin is enacted in these ways—with the true spirit and intent of what it evokes—that there is much good that flows from it. The term wahkohtowin refers to kinship relations and teaches us to extend our relational network so that it also includes the more-than-human beings that live amongst us. Doing so helps us remain mindful that we human beings are fully enmeshed in a series of relationships that enable us to live. Thus, following the relational wisdom of wahkohtowin, we are called to repeatedly acknowledge and honour the fact that the sun, the land, the wind, the water, the animals and the trees (just to name a few) are quite literally our relatives; we carry parts of each of them inside our own bodies. We are fully reliant on them for our survival, and so the wise person works to ensure that those more-than-human relatives are kept healthy and treated with the deep respect that they deserve.

Taken together, wicihitowin and wahkohtowin can be understood as promoting ethical relationality. Ethical relationality is an ecological understanding of organic connectivity that becomes readily apparent to us as human beings when we honour the sacred ecology that supports all life and living. Thus, ethical relationality describes an enactment of ecological imagination wherein our thoughts and actions are guided by the wisdom of sacred ecology insights. Ethical relationality does not deny difference nor does it promote assimilation of it. Rather, ethical relationality supports the conceptualization of difference in ecological terms as necessary for life and living to continue. It guides us to seek deeper understandings of how our different histories, memories and experiences position us in relation to one another. It puts those differences at the forefront as necessary for wicihitowin and wahkohtowin to be enacted. So, ethical relationality is tied to a desire to acknowledge and honour the significance of the relationships we have with others, how our histories and experiences position us in relation to one another, and how our futures as people in the world are similarly tied together. It is an ethical imperative to remember that we as human beings live in the world together and also alongside our more-than-human relatives; we are called to constantly think and act with reference to those relationships.

The main insight that flows from these Cree wisdom teachings is that a purely human understanding of ethical relationality is a significantly impoverished version of those teachings in that it disregards sacred ecology. We need stories and mythologies that teach us how to be good relatives with all our relations—human and more-than-human. We need stories that guide us to honour wicihitowin and wahkohtowin. What follows is a series of textual engagements with three publically displayed mural artifacts that are intended to exemplify our ongoing struggles to enact ethical relationality.

THE GRANDIN MURAL

Inspired by the words of Tomson Highway (2003), I have become an apprentice to myth. Now, I don't mean myth as in an outlandish story made up by some misled person. Instead, I understand myths as insights into the lives of people and what really matters to them. The insights are manifestations of idealized versions of the past that are simplified and made coherent when people select particular events and characters which seem to embody important cultural values and then elevate them to the status of myth. Thus, myths can be understood as creation stories that articulate an originary dream of happiness and serve to provide guidance to people on how they should live their lives. In this sense, mythologies are templates of public dreams—a society's dream of and for itself. Following Highway (2003) and his Cree sensibilities, I understand these mythologies as neither truth stories nor webs of fiction; instead, mythologies are located at the exact halfway point between them. They are simultaneously truth and fiction.

Because I am also an apprentice to curriculum, I spend much time considering the intersections and overlaps of mythologies and curricula. If we can say that curricula are compilations of stories we tell children about the world and their relationships to it, then—following Herbert Spencer (Banks, 1980)—we can also say that particular stories are selected as curricula because they have been deemed most worth telling. Much of the work of curriculum inquirers is focused on clarifying the ways and means by which certain stories are selected over others as most worth telling. To better understand the ways and means by which particular curriculum stories are selected and promoted over others requires an inquiry that engages with the mythological networks that undergird the public dreams held by a society. These networks are often difficult to discern because such public dreams are usually framed and understood in commonsense logics that are perceived as uncontroversial. History and memory are often conceptualized in ways that perpetuate those commonsense logics. For many societies, there is a truth element given to their ways of being, knowing and remembering that is not considered mythological in character. Rather, it is usually understood as a naturalized state of affairs that need not be interrogated in any meaningful way. It is typically considered bad manners to engage in such interrogation because it is unsettling for those who have invested so much of themselves in these inherited truths. Like Roland Barthes (1957/1972), I have come to resent "seeing Nature and History confused at every turn, and I wanted to track down, in the decorative display of what-goes-without-saying, the ideological abuse which, in my view, is hidden there" (p. 11).

let me tell you one about grandin.[2] he's a holy man. bisop. he come from france long time ago. dem days you know not too many people here eh just us indians. he talk about god with people dere at st. albert. help us learn dem white man ways. only ting he take dose indian kids. the sisters dey do dat too. took dem away for school. pretty soon dey don't know deirselves. teach dem to be good white man i spose. it's a good story for dem. it's different our side. we tink about dem kids. how dey miss deir mamas. how much dey hurt from dat. it's like dat even today.

THE GLYDE MURAL

I have lately become preoccupied with prophesies and visions. This preoccupation is inspired by the reported visions and prophesies of mistahi maskwa—the Cree Chief also known as Big Bear—and how his attention to these had a profound influence on the decisions he made concerning his dealings with newcomers to Cree territory. mistahi maskwa had a powerful vision following his recovery from a bout of smallpox in 1838. His vision, almost forty years before Treaty 6 was negotiated, foretold of the arrival of many newcomers to Cree territory, the purchase of the land and the promise of bounteous presents from a Great Mother (Dempsey, 1984, p. 17). A later vision involved mistahi maskwa himself trying to cover with his hand a spring that was shooting up out of the ground. He was unable to stop the flow and the liquid spurted up between his fingers and covered the back of his hand. It was bright red blood (Dempsey, 1984, p. 85). mistahi maskwa had a rich mythological network to draw on when attempting to make sense of these visions. He saw them as warnings of terrible things to come for his people and did what he could to resist them. This decision resulted in mistahi maskwa going to jail where he became sick and eventually died an untimely death. His vision came true, as he knew it would.

I was thinking of these visions some time ago while sitting in on a meeting at the City of Edmonton's Aboriginal Relations Office. We were meeting with representatives of the Francophone community to discuss the removal of the so-called Grandin mural that has been on display at a downtown LRT station in Edmonton since 1989. Artist Sylvie Nadeau's creation commemorates the missionary work of Bishop Vital Grandin in the area and celebrates French Canadian contributions to the opening of the Canadian West to settlement (Nadeau, 2011). Nadeau drew on her understandings of the French Canadian mythological network to create the mural. In doing so, though, she offended many people who see the public display of the celebratory mural as an insult to the thousands of Aboriginal children who experienced multiple traumas while attending Indian residential schools. The controversy surrounding the Grandin mural and its proposed removal is just one more example of the rising problem in Canada concerning public representations of the relationships between Aboriginal peoples and Canadians. Whose mythologies do we follow when constructing these representations? Which mythologies would best enable us to overcome the "iron logic of immanence" (Hodson, 2004, p. 3), a form of public pedagogy that has taught for many years that an entity called the West has arisen as a kind of "moral success story" for the rest of the world to follow and imitate (Wolf, 1982, p. 5)? In this rendition, "history is thus converted into a tale about the furtherance of virtue, about how the virtuous win out over the bad guys" (Wolf, 1982, p. 5).

Mistahi maskwa saw it all coming. I wonder what visions he would have for us today.

dey talk about prayer dis one. us indians we listen. we know about prayer eh. we know about holy. it's our ways too. not just white man knows about dat. dese holy man dey want us to pray like dey do. pray dem words come from england and from french too. about jesus. we don't know how come dey talk like dat. dey tink we don't know prayer. don't know why dey tink dat. maybe dey don't like us indians. don't like our ways. dey can't listen when we pray our ways. dey can't listen for dat. just on deir side. us indians we listen holy man dere. white man he's with god. white man he wants his ways. amisk-waciywaskihikan³ only for dem now. it's his place. it's his ways. white man he's da boss dat time. he own everyting. it's for dem. pretty soon dere's no place for us. we got no place. no place for dem good stories.

SKY TALK⁴

For the most part, I would say that the field of curriculum has traditionally been conservative in character. Curricularists have generally attempted to identify a societal trend that is already in motion and address it in curriculum documents. The implied desire is to describe a status quo, stabilize it and normalize it to reduce dissonance. Take Aboriginal curricular initiatives as an example. For the most part, such initiatives are not radical or visionary. They are in response to obvious societal and demographic trends and predicated on helping Aboriginal students become more successful in mainstream schooling contexts. Success, in this example, is measured by how well Aboriginal topics and students can be swallowed into the larger corpus known as education. That corpus feeds on and digests what it swallows, and eventually poops out what it cannot otherwise process.

I'd like to think that curriculum can be better than that. I'd like to think that curricularists can be visionaries. This would mean that curricularists would provide thoughtful leadership concerning Aboriginal-Canadian relations and take responsibility for envisioning a fundamentally different kind of relationship. This envisioning process is not dedicated to the stabilization of a desired status quo, but is instead focused on promoting more ethical ways of living in relation to those who don't look like us.

What are the mythological networks that curricularists can draw on as sources of inspirations when doing such work? Joseph Campbell states that one of the problems that North American societies face is that mythologies particular to land and place have been ignored or denuded to the point that they now have no guiding ethos (Campbell, 1988, pp. 9–11). For the most part, the dominant mythologies that guide settler societies like Canada are characterized by notions of power and control perpetuated under the aegis of colonial power and the expansion of market capitalism (Donald, 2009a and b). These are the stories that children have been told in Canadian schools for many generations. While we certainly need to demythologize these stories and expose the colonial logics embedded within them, we also urgently need to remythologize ourselves. We need the guidance of those creation stories—those dreams of happiness that help us live good ethical lives alongside our many relations. Whose mythologies can provide such guidance?

that janvier from cold lake he make dis eh? well me I don't know deir ways. don't know da dene ways. but I see that she make a kind of prayer for us. for all da relation living here. all da relation. da water. dem mountains. da animals too, wawakesiw, mooswa, moostos.[5] da birds. askiy—it's for da land too. here land and sky it's one ting. how dey work together. hold hands. dey talk. we see how dey are relationship. us indians we come from da sky. it's for our stories and our songs. that's why we see sky talk dere. human being talk to da sky. sing to da sky. bring down dat sky. it's about us for good life again. find our place again. all dose relation come for dis prayer. that janvier he calls dem relation. asks dem to come. don't need dene words to hear dis. i see it. I hear her singing. it's holy song. it's for all of us you know. it's even da white man. maybe she hears the singing too. maybe it's for wicihitowin. wahkohtowin—good relation. that janvier he make a good prayer for us.

NOTES

1. Following the textual practices of McLeod (2007), I do not capitalize Cree words in this piece, even when they are names or appear at the beginning of sentences. This is an aesthetic choice intended to emphasize difference and make the point that Indigenous language use does not need to conform to conventions of English language use.
2. This commentary and the two that follow are inspired by the works of Halfe (1994) and Scofield (1993) and the provocative ways in which they both follow English and Cree linguistic sensibilities in their poetic texts. The particular character of the texts created in this piece is also informed by the speech patterns of Cree Elders and the poignant ways in which they can express complex understandings using an imposed language while simultaneously struggling to follow basic English language conventions such as consistency of gender designations.
3. The Cree name for Fort Edmonton translated into English as "Beaver Hills House."
4. This is the title of a painting by well-known Dene Suline and Saulteaux artist Alex Janvier.
5. In order as mentioned, these Cree words are translated as "elk," "moose," and "buffalo."

CHAPTER FOUR

Successful Assimilation

LESLEY TAIT

I first encountered the words "successful assimilation" while reading everything I could about the significant loss of lands for the Michel First Nation Band. Michel First Nation is where my family comes from. My great-grandfather was chief. My grandfather was chief after him. Trace it back far enough and I am a direct descendant of Michel Calihoo for whom the band was named. He himself was a signatory on the Treaty 6 documentation. This is not a loose association with Native people. This is something more.

Something significant.

Yet I would never be looked at by unknowing eyes as a Native person. I don't have the skin tone; I don't speak the language and colorful feathers are a fashion statement I have always shied away from.

In 1958, for the first and only time in Canadian history, the Canadian government involuntarily enfranchised the remaining and vastly depleted lands of the Michel Band as a whole and sold these lands to various parties. The Indian Act was changed in 1958 specifically for the "legal" enfranchisement of Michel lands, then immediately changed back in 1959 after the completion of land title transfer. Between 1880 and 1958, the entire 25,600 acres of Michel reserve were lost to enfranchisement and surrender.

We are now a scattered people. A people without a cultural and ancestral homeland. A people without our extended family around the next corner. A people with no land on which to share our stories with ourselves or with others. We, the Michel Nation, are disconnected and disjointed from each other and our heritage.

Would this be different if we were not "landless"? This landlessness and "enfranchisement" has many far-reaching implications. The stories are not as strong as they used to be. The traditions are beginning to fade, the understandings of the land are beginning to dwindle. And if we take an idea from Thomas King (2003) that all we are is our stories, where does that leave the people of Michel? We don't live with our relatives, in the same community like other bands, like other indigenous families. We don't have a place to come together, to celebrate, to mourn, to pass on knowledge and history. I would assert that the dispossession of our lands has led to the breakdown of my family and our connection to one another and our culture.

Or as others may view it: Successful assimilation.

So who am I? I do not speak our language, I do not drum or chant. I cannot hoop dance. And yet I choose to identify myself as aboriginal and as a member of Michel Nation.

Am I the "assimilated Indian" whom the government and Frank Oliver were looking for? Are we, the people of Michel, an example of successful enfranchising?

This year, I started a new teaching position. I am a literacy specialist, and 98 percent of my students are learning English and entering into a new culture for the first time. Yet, I also walked into a building where books exist at "levels" and are housed in plastic bags. These are objects removed from their "place." Literacy is thought to be successful if children move up the ladder from plastic-leveled bag to plastic-leveled bag. We continue to colonize these children through the good news of literacy. Learn to read and become civilized.

This school, as with many others, assumes its audience before teaching begins. It does not matter who walks through that door, the curriculum and the aim will be same. There is a constant low level of panic. What if they don't learn to read? What if we, as teachers, fail? Every aspect of curriculum has been disconnected from where it truly lives.

How do we step outside the panic? How do we slow down in a time of terrible trial when this is what we see every day in schools?

The current response to kids not reading is to give them books not worth reading. These plastic bags promise quick growth and increased phonemic awareness. They promise a year's growth in only six months. Follow the program and all will be okay. They, in fact, promise successful assimilation. These words now sit very heavily on my shoulders and they are uncomfortable.

CHAPTER FIVE

A Pedagogy OF Panic

CARLI MOLNAR

Global warming is threatening human life.
The dollar is falling. Your stocks are losing value.
Traffic is at a standstill. You will be late.
You'll never be able to pay off that loan.
Our forests are being destroyed.

There is much in the world to make us afraid. Our economy is anxious. This panic has penetrated the walls of schools and spreads like mold. The pulses of schools race.

Narrow, crowded hallways push masses of children along, shoving them towards the ever-important future.

Towering, forbidding steel fences surround the buildings, whispering the paranoia of school shootings, intruders and the anxiety that too much freedom would surely bring.

Sharp sounding bells deliberately induce panic, reminding the children that they are out of time, making their hearts race and their bodies jump.

The fluorescent lights hum, mimicking the panicked buzz of a trapped fly. Classrooms are filled with piercing rays of artificial light, installed to supplement the lack of real sunshine.

Sometimes the anxiety of the building I teach in tries to infuse its way into my classroom, trying to root itself within me and the children.

In those moments when this despair edges its way in, I feel threatened by the time constraints, mounds of paperwork and the dichotomy between curriculum-as-plan and curriculum-as-lived (Aoki, 2005, p. 159). These seemingly important pieces of education begin to steal my stillness and replace it with the lures of distraction.

Anxiety stabs at my mindfulness and suddenly it takes strength to pause and listen to the child who is telling me a story because I am distracted by planned curriculum. I feel myself rushing. If I'm rushing, the children must be rushing too.

I can feel the building poisoning my soul with a pedagogy of panic.

I must pause.

I breathe.

I recognize the panic that surrounds us, but I recognize the treatment too.

I search for reminders within me that inspire. The words of David Smith (1999) bring comfort:

> If we can be more at ease with things not immediately understood, more patient and more hungry for a simple love of the world itself as our earthly home, maybe we have a chance at taking one small step into the future (p. 24).

Breathe.

The words of Wendell Berry (2010, p. 13) offer serenity:

> The river is of the earth and it is free. It is rigorously embanked and bound, and yet it is free. "To hell with restraint," it says.

I listen to the reprieve within the words of Ajahn Chah (2002, p. 327):

> This isn't my business. It's impermanent, unsatisfactory and not-self.

Breathe.

This panic that tries to lure me in is not okay.

I seek the solace within the peaceful reminder that Thich Nhat Hanh (1991, p. 104) offers:

> Peace is present right here and now, in ourselves and in everything we do and see. Every breath we take, every step we take, can be filled with peace, joy, and serenity. We need only to be awake, alive in the present moment.

Exhale.

These reminders give me strength to recognize that this panic is not okay. The economy might be sick, but this disease has no place in our classroom. When I feel this anxiety creeping in, I must practice filling my soul with stillness and a pedagogy of peacefulness.

Global warming is threatening human life.
The dollar is falling. Your stocks are losing value.
Traffic is at a standstill. You will be late.
You'll never be able to pay off that loan.
Our forests are being destroyed.

CHAPTER SIX

A Better Place

SANDRA MCNEIL

Stephanie's hand shot up in the air, just as I was about to introduce a math lesson. I know she can take us on a tangent. She asks a lot of questions and when she speaks she is not always concise. But, her excitement and energy about life and new ideas always seem to draw me in. This day I hesitated long enough for her to say, "This is totally off topic, but I want to ask your opinion about something."

Opinion?!!!

Any time a student asks my opinion I find myself entering the tensioned space between the planned curriculum, which Aoki (2005) refers to as the curriculum guide or the mandated curriculum, that teachers are required to teach, and the lived curriculum, which Aoki denotes as the space in which teachers exist with their students; a place of complexity requiring decisions to be made in order to keep the class "alive and moving" (Aoki, 2005, p. 161).

Stephanie proceeded to tell me that she just had an eighty-minute debate in Humanities about the fact that Calgary's city hall is flying a rainbow flag during the Olympics and only seven students thought it was a good thing.

"Even our teacher disagreed!"

The fact that I didn't know about the rainbow flag was a surprise to me. I am an "out" teacher.

******

I didn't always want to be a teacher. At least I didn't think I wanted to. However, it is difficult to discern what I wanted from what I thought was actually possible. What I do know is that I was plagued by fear.

What would the students and parents think?

Will the parents even allow their children to be taught by a homosexual?

Will the parents assume that I will have a negative influence on their children, and "make them gay"?

"I can't possibly be a teacher if I want to be an out lesbian" was the chorus repeating in my mind. Thankfully, my desire to be a teacher was strong enough to counter this chorus with a belief that my sexuality should not play any part in my ability to be a good teacher.

As I went to school to become a teacher, and even in my first two years of teaching, I slowly came out to my peers, colleagues and administrators. I still didn't feel safe enough to talk about my life partner to my students and their parents. Instead, I allowed them to assume that I was single and straight, answering all questions about my life with evasive statements. I would see pictures of my colleagues' husbands and wives on their desks or witness them being picked up and randomly meeting students in the parking lot. Making brief mention of a husband or wife flowed freely from their lips without apprehension, fear or even a second thought. Each time I didn't tell the truth I felt myself become more and more bound by my fear, prompting me to evaluate whether this was the profession for me.

Outside of the school, I was in a loving relationship and with the legalization of gay marriage in Canada in 2005 we decided to get married. What did getting married mean to me? Despite my apprehension and deep-rooted fear of being an "out" teacher, I finally, for the first time in my life, felt confident and empowered to tell the truth … to be myself. I was now married, wearing a ring, recognized by the government of Canada as equal to a heterosexual marriage under the law, and I was not going to lie about my life anymore. I owed it to myself, to my wife, and to my students.

I was asked, "How are you going to tell your students?" I knew that I did not want to make an announcement. I didn't want to make it a big deal. I wanted to share my life in the same way any one of my colleagues might talk about their partner. I wanted it to simply roll off my tongue. I decided that when/if I was asked whether or not I was married I would tell the truth. In fact, I rehearsed my responses to many questions in order to make sure I got it "right."

Two and a half months passed without a question. I fell into the same routine I had in previous years. Speaking about my life through my relationships with my friends and my sisters but never once mentioning my wife. Then one day in the middle of November a student asked, "Ms. McNeil, are you married?" There it was. The question I had been waiting for. I could feel my face flush and my heart pound. Was I going to answer it "right"? I responded "yes" and then promptly changed the subject.

Facing my biggest fear was in my reach. The next day the questions continued, but this time, twenty-five students chimed in.

"I didn't know you were married."

"Who are you married to?"

"What's *his* name?"

"When did you get married?"

The only answer I could muster was: "Yes, I am married. Now you only have one hour for your Social Studies so you better get working."

My face felt hot; my heart was pounding; my hands were shaking. I was allowing the students to believe that I was married to a man and in essence I was lying.

As their teacher, my silence, my inability to be honest was teaching them to be afraid, to be silent themselves. Reminiscent of Elliot Eisner's (2002a) chapter "The Three Curricula That All Schools Teach" in which Eisner writes about the explicit, implicit and null curriculum, I found myself dancing within and between these spaces. Eisner suggests that there are two major considerations in the null curriculum, "the intellectual processes that schools emphasize and neglect" (p. 98) and "the content or subject areas that are present and absent in school curricula" (p. 98). There is no curriculum guide, especially in the province of Alberta, on how to engage students in topics involving sexual orientation. In fact, in 2009 the Alberta legislature passed Bill 44, which amended the Alberta Human Rights Act, forcing school boards and jurisdictions to provide notice to parents if any program involving religion, human sexuality and sexual orientation is taught in schools. As well, parents are able to make a written request that their child not be exposed to such programs.

What was I teaching my students by letting their assumptions stand? This certainly is not part of the planned curriculum. It became very apparent to me that my original plan was not working. Letting it roll off my tongue, answering questions openly and honestly was actually sending me into a frozen state and the only thing I could do was say, "Yes, I am married."

The number one reason I became a teacher was because I wanted to make a difference in students' lives. The reason I needed to tell my students the truth was based on the teacher I strive to be. I needed to face my fear.

I drove to school the next day feeling more gut-wrenching anxiety and anticipation than I have ever felt. First thing in the morning I said to my students, "I have a few things I want to talk about." I faced my fear and this is what I said:

"One of the reasons I became a teacher is because I want the students I work with to be confident individuals, I want you to believe in yourselves and to always feel like you can be yourself. I want you to stand up for what you believe in and live honestly in the world.

"Having said all this I know that many of you have noticed my ring and have recently discovered that I am married, you have a lot of questions and are quite curious. I wouldn't be the honest, sincere and confident person I want all of you to be if I continue to let you believe that I am married to a man, because I'm not. I am married to a woman."

I said it.

And the student response?

Followed by a few questions and some shocked faces was

… Applause.

I had anticipated the worst that could happen. I even made a list of all the negative repercussions that might follow the moment I was "out" to my students. What I didn't anticipate was the gratitude from my students for being honest. Or the comments from parents during interviews such as, "I think it is really good you could be honest with them, thank you," or the fact that I have never felt so free. I no longer look over my shoulder at the grocery store when I am with my wife.

My wife and I are now mothers and as I look back on my experience of becoming an "out" teacher, I could never have become a mom had I not conquered my fear. Each year following that first year was different. It didn't miraculously make everything easy. I made some assumptions of my own. I believed that if I came out once, I was done. Rather conceited of me now, as if this groundbreaking event in my life would be held with the same significance by anyone who knew of it. Word did travel and for the most part my students knew before they even entered my class. But every year I am still asked either about my husband or my child's father. Fortunately, the free-flowing roll-off-the-tongue responses that I once longed for actually happen. Eventually, I put a photo of my wife on my desk.

This year I decided to be proactive and in the first week of school my wife and daughter came in for a visit to meet my homeroom class.

Done.

No anticipation.

No assumptions.

No pointed questions.

Each year a new layer of homophobia has been shed. Each year I find myself closer and closer to the teacher I want to be, helping students become the people they want to be.

****

So, back to Stephanie asking about flying a rainbow flag at Calgary's city hall during the Olympics. Once again I could feel my face flush almost immediately. I wasn't certain that this particular group of students all knew I am a lesbian, but I was pretty sure that was why she wanted to know my opinion. The subsequent conversation entailed my "coming out" to some of them, or confirming rumours others had already heard, followed by my monologue (with a teacher's hat on) about how I realized there are multiple perspectives and I know some people believe the Olympics needs to be kept separate from politics and human rights. I made it very clear that when we speak about Russia's stance on gay rights, we need to speak of the Russian government and not Russians in general, as there are many Russians who do not feel the same way. I felt the need to represent all sides fairly. I made sure they knew I understood the complexity of the question posed to them.

I did, however, share with the class that my immediate and instinctual reaction to finding out that our city and several other cities were speaking out against Russia's anti-gay laws was "YES!!!" I shared a few stories of my own about homophobia I have confronted in my life, in hopes that they would understand why it means so much for our mayor to stand up and say, "It's the right thing to do" (Dormer, 2014). When I read that line, I immediately thought of Wendell Berry's words during an interview with Bill Moyers (2013): "We have to ask what is the right thing to do and go ahead and do it and take no thought for the morrow."

It became clear to me that the students didn't have enough information to offer an opinion or choose a side. On one hand, I am grateful that teachers are entering these conversations in their classrooms and are not afraid to have open dialogue about controversial topics. On the other hand, I needed to ask what the role of a teacher is when entering this kind of dialogue. Maxine Greene (2001) writes about aesthetic education and while she is speaking about art and literature, I think her words have significance in this encounter too.

> Whether we teach the very young or the adult, we obviously have to have some clear idea of what a developed capacity in a particular symbolic medium is like ... we have all come to realize the importance of some foundational understanding, some knowledge that can not always be totally specified. The kinds of knowledge that can be made available and feed into what we have called "tacit awareness" clearly have a good deal to do with the stage at which the learners involved arrive. (p. 27)

In this case the medium was a debate, a polarizing conversation about a "controversial topic." What knowledge did the students need in order to engage in this conversation from an informed place? How are we teachers perpetuating the dominant culture by asking students to weigh in on a controversial issue and choose a side without the capacity to experience the encounter? Debates are provocative, resulting in definite student engagement. I could tell the debate had been heated and had evoked a lot of emotion. But maybe what needed to happen was a focus on listening, understanding and elaboration versus defending one's position.

The arguments against teaching about sexual orientation in our schools supported by the likes of Bill 44 ring some truth. Gay/straight alliances will absolutely bring forth conversation in the schools. An inclusive curriculum means homosexuality will absolutely be talked about in the classroom, in the same way that heterosexuality already is. Students will be taught that you can fall in love with anyone regardless of gender; students will learn that their teachers are part of the LGBT community; students will learn that it is possible in our world to be honest and not hide from society with shame and guilt, unable to confront homophobia. Students will learn to be inclusive. Students will feel safe and supported regardless of their sexual orientation.

To the voices that are afraid of homosexual teachers, gay/straight alliances, gay marriage and dialogue about sexuality, ... you are right about your children in the schools ... and the world will be a better place, because it is the right thing to do.

CHAPTER SEVEN

All Beings ARE Your Ancestors

A Bear Sutra on Ecology, Buddhism and Pedagogy (1997)

DAVID W. JARDINE

Transforming according to circumstances, meet all beings as your ancestors.
—HONGZHI ZHENGJUE (1091–1157)

Just spotted a year-old black bear crossing HWY. 66 @ McLean Creek, heading north.

From a distance, struggling at first to resolve its colour and lowness and lopey canter into dog or cat likenesses as it stretched up to the side of the road and across and suddenly slowed into distinctive roundhumpness ... bear!

Stopped and watched him amble up the shalysteep creekedge. Wet. Green-glistening. Breath arriving plumey in the damp and cold after days of heat waves ... been 33 degrees C. and more for four days running in the foothills of the Rockies west of Calgary. Here, roaming in the edge between prairie and forest, between flatlands and hills and mountains—here, when summers break, they tend to break deeply.

Cold rain. Cold.

It is so thrilling to not be accustomed to this sort of experience, to have it still be so *pleasurable*. Bear. His presence almost unbelievable, making this whole place waver and tremble, making my assumptions and presumptions and thoughts and tales of experiences in this place suddenly wonderfully irrelevant and so much easier to write because of such irrelevance.

Bear's making this whole place show its fragility and momentariness and serendipities.

Bear's making my own fragility and momentariness show.

That is what is most shocking. This unforseeable happenstance of bear's arrival and my own happiness are oddly linked. This "hap" (Weinsheimer, 1987, pp. 7–8) hovering at the heart of the world.

My own life as serendipitous, despite my earnest plans. Giddy sensation, this.

Like little bellybreath tingles on downarcing childgiggle swingsets.

Felt in the *tanden* (Sekida, 1976, pp. 18–19, 66–67) in Walking Meditation (Nhat Hanh, 1995).

Breath's gutty basement. Nearby, the lowest Chakra tingles with an upspine burst to whitesparkle brilliance just overhead and out in front of the forehead.

In moments like this, something flutters *open*. Shifting fields of relations bloom. Wind stirs nothing. Not just my alertness and sudden attention, but the odd sensation of knowing that these trees, this creek, this bear, are all *already* alert to me in ways proper to each and despite my attention. Something flutters *open*, beyond this centered self.

With the presence of this ambly bear, the whole of things arrives, fluttered open.

All Beings are your Ancestors. The feary sight of him, teaching me, reminding me of forgotten shared ancestries, forgotten shared relations to Earth and Air and Fire and Water.

That strange little lesson having to be learned again: that he has been here all along, cleaving this shared ancestry, cleaving this shared Earth of ours, making and forming my life beyond my "wanting and doing," (Gadamer, 1989, p. xxviii), beyond my wakefulness and beyond my remembering.

It is not so much that this bear is an "other" (Shepard, 1996), but that it is a *relative*, which is most deeply transformative and alarming to my ecological somnolence and forgetfulness. It is not just that I might come awake and start to remember these deep, Earthy relations.

It is also that, even if I don't, they all still bear witness to my life.

Relations. Who would have thought? Coming across *one of us* that I had forgotten.

Coming, therefore, across myself *as also one of us*. Such a funny thing to be surprised about again. In the face of this Great Alert Being, I, again, become one of us!

Great Alert Being, this bear. Great Teacher. His and my meaty bodies both of the same "flesh of the [Earth]" (Abram, 1997, pp. 66–67 [see Abram & Jardine, 2000, for a later conversation]), rapt in silent conversations (Abram, 1996, p. 49).

Where, my god, have I been? And what have I been saying, betraying myself and my distraction?

This bear ambles in the middle of all its Earthly relations to wind and sky and rain and berries and roadsides and the eons of beings that helped hone that creek edge to just those small pebbly falls under the weight of his paws:

Even the very tiniest thing, to the extent that it "is," displays in its act of being the whole web of circuminsessional interpenetration that links all things together. (Nishitani, 1982, p. 150)

The whole Earth conspires to make just these simple events just exactly like this:

"Within each dust mote is vast abundance" (Hongzhi, 1991, p. 14).

This is the odd butterfly effect (Glieck, 1987, p. 17) fluttering in the stomach.

This, too, is the profound co-implication of all beings that is part of ecological mindfulness—that each being is implicated in the whole of things and, if we are able to experience it from the belly, from each being a deep relatedness to all beings can be unfolded, can be understood, can be felt, can be adored, can be praised in prayerful grace, a giving thanks (Snyder, 1990, pp. 175–185). Lovely intermingling of thinking and thanksgiving (Heidegger, 1968).

So the thrill of seeing this bear is, in part, the exhilarating rush felt in seeing it explode outwards, emptying itself into all its relations, and then retracting to just that black bear, now an exquisite still-spot ambling at the center of all things. And more!

The center is everywhere. Each and every thing becomes the center of all things and, in that sense, becomes an absolute center. This is the absolute uniqueness of things, their reality (Nishitani, 1982, p. 146).

Like breath exhaled outwards and then drawn in deep draughts. This inwardness and outwardness of emptiness (Sanskrit: *sunya*; Japanese: *ku*)—each thing *is* its relatedness to all things, reflecting each in each in Indra's Netted Jewels and yet each thing is always just itself, irreplaceable. Smells of the forests of mid-August and the sweetness of late summer wild flowers. Winey bloomy blush. Intoxicating.

All Beings are your Ancestors.

Hey, bear!

If we are to meet all beings as our ancestors, we must also meet all those very same beings as our descendants. This odd, fluid, difficult, shifting edge point between the ancestors and the descendants is where our humanity lives.

This is "the empty field" (Hongzhi, 1991) that opens and embraces.

It is also the lifespot of teaching and learning and transmission and transformation.

There are many Great Teachers.

All praise to bear and his subtle gift.

Bragg Creek, Alberta, August 8–10, 1997

CHAPTER EIGHT

Relearning Freedom

Advice to a New Teacher

MARGEAUX MONTGOMERY

Freedom results from understanding how stories construct and constrict my possibilities.
—DAVID LOY (2010, P. 33)

I remember thinking to myself early on in my career that eventually I would feel like I had it all figured out. Now, well into my journey, I am being taught and transformed by what I experience. Some days flow seamlessly and other days I feel like I am just beginning again. With that being said, here is the advice that I would give right now, in this moment, to you, new teacher.

There will be stories that will narrow your ideas, thoughts and choices. They will exist in places of normalcy; part of a larger master story, Loy (2010) explains as "revolving around fear and anxiety" (p. 31). These may be told to you by people in power about the powerless. You will also have your own stories that will encircle pressure on your ideas and pedagogy. Scripted to you over your own experiences of education and prevailing in social and cultural norms. These types of stories are powerful and sneaky, so watch out for them.

There will also be stories that build hope and create understanding. These will occur in glimpses and there will be gaps. You will fail and continue. You will remember an artefact from your past and think about how you have changed as a person and as a teacher. You will embarrass yourself and you will recover from it.

You will say things that you did not mean and you will learn from these.

There will be moments in which you will have ineffable experiences of understanding. Hold onto these moments so that you can identify those feelings again.

These moments occur organically and cannot be forced. Be patient and trust yourself. Your knowledge will continue to be shaped and shifted as you become more familiar and practiced in the place you are.

Breathe.

There will be joy, laughter and tears. You will be incredibly fortunate to spend days with adults and children who will challenge, educate, and enrich your life. They will also be there to offer support when the constricting possibilities arise around you. Know that you are not alone, as Catherine Keller (in Jensen, 1995) reminds us that by "simply existing, we make a difference" (p. 280).

I offer a passage by bell hooks (1994) that found me, before I started my own journey into teaching. It has helped me create my own story and see through others:

> Urging all of us to open our minds and hearts so that we can know beyond the boundaries of what is acceptable, so that we can think and rethink, so that we can create new visions, I celebrate teaching that enables transgressions—a movement against and beyond boundaries. It is that movement which makes education the practice of freedom. (p. 12).

CHAPTER NINE

Matches

DEIRDRE BAILEY

The excerpts below are from David Jardine's (2013b) article "Time Is [Not] Always Running Out," published in the *Journal of the American Association for the Advancement of Curriculum Studies*:

> With lights lowed, we all lean inwards in this circle of storytelling, and its arc goes far beyond just those gathered here. This wider feel of textured fabric is also a nebulous part of the story told:
>
> > Next to the hearth, by the bedside, on the back porch, round the cracker barrel, in the lap. Mouth to ear, mouth to ear, over and over and over again, grandmother and grandfather, uncle and aunt, mother and father, nanny and nurse were in turn listener and teller. (Yolen, 1988, p. 12)
>
> Migratory arcs come back round again. This temporal fabric is recurrent and intergenerational—an odd experience of going somewhere new and returning to somewhere old at the same time, and coming to (re)inhabit a place already inhabited.
>
> > These tales could be a short as the English ghost story reported by the venerable English collector Katharine Briggs: He woke up frightened and reached for the matches, and the matches were put into his hand. (Yolen, 1988, p. 2)
>
> (JARDINE, 2013b, P. 2)

A few weeks ago, media chatter condemning "new" math as fuzzy and ridiculous and calling for a return to memorization-driven pedagogy rose to a pitch that I found impossible to ignore. I waited and listened, hoping for a thoughtfully articulated clarification of the inquiry-based approach to perforate the constant criticism. None came. Finally, feeling quite literally compelled to offer a "voice of reason," I published a blog. I described the "new" approach to math from a teaching perspective and tried to qualify the difference between memorable and memorizable mathematics. I explained how thrilling it had been to watch my students come astonishingly alive with the opportunity to *think* and question in mathematics. I urged that proponents of "memorizing math facts" consider children to be equally worthy of more beautiful, complex learning opportunities and that these need not preclude computational proficiency. I tried to negate recent media reports that children were being "experimented on" with this "new" math curriculum and were being left with no understanding, no "skills," and no "ability."

It sounds ridiculous in hindsight, but although I had ultimately written a rebuttal of the dominant discourse, I didn't anticipate a negative backlash. The first angry accusation was a blow, and I found myself bewilderingly on the defense, backtracking and double-checking what I had written, struggling to maintain thoughtful ground. It was a diffcult and disconcerting couple of days, a bit like trying to play chess with someone who kept knocking the pieces over and pretending it was part of the game. I was fighting for something the "other side" seemed determined not to comprehend. Struggling to regain my footing in a space that felt suddenly hostile I lay awake most nights, planning my next point and mentally reviewing my defense. It was exhausting.

I arrived in class on Tuesday frustrated, angry and eager to commiserate with classmates. Instead, we began with Don Domanski (2013):

> here deep in the forest   in the stillness of ecocide
> in the quietude between spruce trees   when absence redeems you
> when the world is rising and leaving
>   when you've forgotten your name
> forgotten the wistful knot of air that is your spirit
> that's when the ancients say you'll reach the bottom of things
> and start upwards again (p. 91)

The inexplicable sense of comfort was so relieving I was almost in tears.

The space was transformed.

Domanski was followed by Joseph Campbell in conversation with Bill Moyers (Permutter & Konner, 2002). We were struck by Campbell's patience as he countered Moyers's pragmatic attempts at making myth "relatable" for the general public, his considerate refusal to articulate ancient mythological ideas "on the grounds of the other."

David said: "There's this surface story, and we get caught—banging back and forth in that … but there's another way this world can be experienced" (lecture notes, March 2014).

Then Wendell Berry (2000) arrived: "The fallibility of a human system of thought is always the result of incompleteness. In order to include some things, we invariably exclude others. We can't include everything because we don't know everything; we can't comprehend what comprehends us" (p. 34).

comprehend (v.)
mid–14c., from Latin comprehendere "to take together, to catch hold of; to seize." (n.d.)

David: "We can't catch a hold of what catches a hold of us. The question, then, is how do we prevent 'it' from catching a hold of us? … It's why I left the room. I need to take care of the spot that can stay composed" (lecture notes, March 2014).

The conversation reverberated and I began to recognize my story in the story. To find my footing.

The second half of the class brought David Suzuki and Thich Nhat Hanh in conversation with Suzuki Foundation chair Jim Hoggan (Hoggan Public Relations, 2011). As we contemplated their interchange, I recognized myself in Suzuki, up in arms because "what the public doesn't think is a problem, is a problem."

Thich Nhat Hanh spoke to Suzuki about the environment, and he spoke to me about teaching:

This civilization will be destroyed. It has already happened in the past. We have to accept this as it is. Acceptance like that can bring us peace. And with that peace we have force. To meditate, to look deeply, to gain insight … and with that insight you are free—from despair, from anger—and a better worker for the environment. [*me: for children*] (Hoggan Public Relations, 2011)

As Thich Nhat Hanh spoke, he radiated composure, not because it was going to be okay, or because anyone was going to "solve the problem," but because probably *no one* was going to solve the problem, and *it was going to be okay*.

Walking into class on Tuesday I had felt as though I was barely holding on. The argument I didn't mean to start had drawn me into a surface exchange filled with anger and frustration and despair. Our "storytelling" community handed that conversation back on a deeper, more authentic plane. The added presence of multiple echoing voices of scholars practiced in relating to the *real* collectively conspired to return my thinking to a place of composure, patience and calm.

As the class wound down, I mentioned that I felt as though it had been all been for *me*. There had been something familiar in all of the conversations, something that seemed to recognize my struggle and was present to help.

"That's why this class is a refuge," David said, "that's how the world is supposed to feel. You're supposed to run into your best friend, and know that the universe is all okay" (lecture notes, March 2014).

[I] woke up frightened and reached for the matches, and the matches were put into [my] hand. (Yolen, 1988, p. 2)

There is without a doubt a fabric to this world and I am finding myself in it. Thank you.

CHAPTER TEN

A Modern Hunting Tradition

JODI LATREMOUILLE

FINDING MYSELF IN THE MEASURE OF THINGS: INTRODUCTION TO "A MODERN HUNTING TRADITION"

My inspiration for "A Modern Hunting Tradition" came in the form of a quote by David Smith (2014), who wrote that:

> Furthermore, some things reveal themselves on their own terms, when they are ready, not simply under the duress of a formal curriculum requirement at 10:30 a.m. on Tuesday. This is now well understood in the realm of ecology, for example, and the study of (so-called) wildlife. The best way to see animals in their natural habitat is simply to sit still; then the animals will come out of hiding and show themselves. (p. 82)

I wanted to be reminded of what it feels like to sit still, to notice, to remember the more-than-human world (Abram, 1997). In conversations with colleagues, friends and students, I have come to notice that growing up "in the bush" is, for a growing number of humans, a story of foreign lands. Places like Rock Island Lake, the fishing camp that my parents operated where I spent my first five summers; Fox Farm Road, the log cabin on the mountainside; Paradise Lake; and Nicola Lake—these are my places, where I feel at home. Joe Sheridan and Dan "He Who Clears the Sky" Longboat (2006) explain that "settler culture" (Western society) has not yet "naturalized" to the land, in that it has yet to create myths that respect the possibilities of this place (p. 366). Finding myself *at home* in the bush, not the forest that "to most settlers remains a dark and evil spirit in need of exorcism or destruction"

(Sheridan, 2001, p. 196), but the stomping-hunting-fire-building-silent bush of bushmen and bushwomen, means finding myself in a place that *requires* something of me ... for my (earthly) survival.

I am mindful that "forgetting the animals leads to the animals forgetting about us" (Sheridan & Longboat, 2006, p. 377). Similarly, when I think of traditions passed down from elders to youth, I consider how they are constantly renewed in the attention given to them by each new generation. As youth coming into traditions, I hope that we may try to challenge and question everything that has been handed down to us, while our elders may wait patiently for us to sort things out, sometimes pushing back, other times conceding, always listening. If a balance is achieved, we find our tradition constantly renewed in the measure of things. What possibilities arise when we learn to walk softly, to entice the animals out of hiding, to spot cougar tracks in the snow? What does it mean, pedagogically, for our actions to find their proper measure (Gadamer, 2004, p. 251), and thus, their consequences (Jardine, 2008b, p. 4) in these wild places and elder traditions that story us? Our human isolation from the earthly landscape is a precarious ignorance. David Abram (1997) says, "We still *need* that which is other than ourselves and our own creations ... we are human only in contact, and conviviality, with what is not human" (p. ix).

An earthly tradition.

A MODERN HUNTING TRADITION

My father, Vern, is the hunter. My mother, Lorna is the cook
Traditional. Cozy. Comfortable
Predictable and grounded, stewed in the crock pot
Savoury, only slightly spicy, unless I get my hands on it
I like my stews the new-fashioned way,
Just a little more exotic

I am a strong, capable woman well-marinated in this tradition
People who know me well half expect me to be a hunter—
Even if only because it challenges my gender role

But I am not a hunter. Well, not anymore.

I learned how to shoot a '22 at the age of twelve,

and I once killed a grouse by stoning it to death

Shameful stoning

It was a loud and grisly scene, with me leading a wild pack of elementary-aged children across the barnyard and into the pine trees, hooting and screaming as we tortured and murdered that grouse.

The moment that cracked me was when it was lying on the ground, unable to move, yet still breathing, eyes half-closed. I knew that as the instigator, I had to take responsibility for what I had done. I killed it with the final stone. We left that grouse in the woods and we never told my parents.

We never spoke of that day again.

We knew that we had dishonoured the two codes that our hunting family lived by:

1. Do not cause unnecessary suffering.
2. Do not waste one ounce of a life given for your sustenance.

I can walk quietly in the woods. I can identify edible berries and see the signs of danger and promise in the earth. I can smell a campfire a kilometer away, tell time by the sun, and mark a path to return by. I know how to remove a tick embedded in my scalp, and I can build a shelter to keep the night away.

I know how to tie a fly and catch a fish. I can gut a fish and help skin a deer. I know how to pluck a chicken and use every last piece of its flesh and bones for a week of meals.

But I usually leave the killing to others.
Unless I was truly starving, of course, then I would do what I had to do.

I respect it. The killing.

I can observe it. I can participate in the ritual with sadness and gratitude.

But holding a warm animal, a squirming fish, in my hand as the final after-beat of life drains slowly from its body, is too much for me.

Yes, I am known as "the emotional one" in my family. What of it? Would you rather I be cold, dead-living? Let a gal cry!

So I participate in our family's modern-day hunting ritual. My husband, Jason, is not a hunter, either, but my young daughters are showing interest and I hope that their grandfather will take them one day. Grandpa Vern, achy-old and curling up at the fingers like his father did before him, but strong and bush-humping along, beautiful-functional, still has so many things to teach them and learn from them, us. Jason is the "professional venison transportation agent" (a.k.a. a healthy, young and strong body which happens to be willing and to live down the road from his father-in-law) and because he helps pack the kill, our freezer is stocked and re-stocked with moose, deer—and salmon, huckleberries and mushrooms—each fall.

Every fall, we wait for the call.

"Ya, I got a moose. He's a big old guy this time, should be good eating though, not too tough. No, he's not too far into the bush, only a couple hundred metres over a little ridge." In Vern-speak, that is about 3 kilometres scrambling over rocky shale, wading through a creek and climbing rope-assisted up a small mountainside.

Vern is no road hunter. To the authentic bushmen of the Nicola Valley, that's almost like cheating. Unless, of course, you were truly starving, then you would take what you could get where it stood.

So, we plan the picnic. These days, we ask, "Is this a kid-friendly moose-packing trip?" And we pack up the snowsuits, hot chocolate, toilet paper, extra socks, snacks, the until-the-next-snack snacks, sleds, campfire kettle, and a full change of clothes for each child, "just in case." It is a little more complicated than it used to be when you'd grab a sandwich and an apple and march off into the bush with your matches, knife and packboard. The bush has taught me what it means to be prepared—if you have the room in your truck, bring it because you never know when you might need it. If you don't have the room, hope for good weather.

The men march out. Vern loves his grandchildren and would sit for hours with them on an anthill talking about ants and clouds and how to braid wild grasses into a wreath to wrap around their curly-top heads, but, "Son, we are wasting daylight. You women can see the trail, it starts right here. We'll meet you there in a few." Usually our fit, happy, childlike-wise mom-grandmother Lorna wants to stay at the truck and build a fire. She likes to sit and visit and drink tea, then go for a little exercise-walk. But she knows me better than that—sigh, she knows—I need action, I need to help with the man-woman work, and without uttering a word, she starts to pack up the lunch and the little ones for our snow-trek in the man-tracks out over the hills to the hanging moose. There are some cougar pawprints right there, but they are not fresh, so we keep the dogs close and walk tall and loud. We wonder if the cougar got any of the meat, but Vern knows to hang it high in the trees out of reach, so we expect that it will be waiting there for us. We haul our babies in the sled to the kill tree, and this time it is only about a half-hour hike. Grandpa Vern wasn't exaggerating for once. When we arrive, the ritual has just begun. The skinning knife is scritch-scratch, scritch-scratching against the steel, and the tiny wisps of new campfire smoke are trailing up into the fir boughs above.

Gloves off, jackets put aside. We scatter to find larger pieces of wood as the little ones crouch over Jason's fire-building shoulder, helping.

The skinning. The anatomy lesson. The hide falling away. The familiarity of a human-moose body unveiled of its coat. The tendons, joints, muscles, hair. Bled, cold. Tongue, eyes, guts, heart.

Vern takes his hunkering place at the fire. "Wanna bite of moose heart?" As he slaps his stick-roasted slice into the middle of his cheese sandwich. Vern does the roasting for the little ones. They watch, eyes flame-shiny, as it browns and sizzles. He pulls it off the roasting stick and gently breaks it in two and hands it over. They sit on their kid-log in quiet reverence as the first mouthful satisfies their well-earned gnawing autumn hiking-hunger.

Sometimes I prefer not to be there, because I'd rather after-hear my home-safe, sweaty husband tell the laughing-horror tale of how he almost slipped and fell off a cliff under the weight of a 100-lb moose head. Yes, a moose's head alone can weigh 100 pounds. Imagine the rest of it. Five, sometimes six pieces if he is a big old Mr. Moose, sawed apart and sheathed in their white cheesecloth bag to keep them from getting dirty. Sometimes if you get a good hill, you can be a little bit crazy impractical and hop on to the moose-laden packboard, but be careful of hidden stumps and flailing hooves. When the terrain is right, and he can avoid strapping himself into the packboard under a hundred and fifty pounds of moose, Jason will do it the new-fashioned way—winding through the scrawny birch trees, dashing ahead of an out-of-control hindquarter as it plummets down the snowy mountainside. Vern shakes his head, and keeps plodding under his burden. We walk ahead and wait for him at the truck. When Grandpa bursts out of the trees a few minutes later, screaming, "Look out! Moose meat on the loose!" we laugh as we dive into the snowbanks. You can, in fact, teach an old dog new tricks. The question is, do you want to?

My daughter saw her first dead animal hanging in my father's shed when she was two years old.

She called it "deer parts."

And it bothered her much less than the disembodied deer head trophy that my dad displays in his office.

That says something, now doesn't it?

Mostly, it says to never to put dead animal heads on display in my house (They scare the kids—c'mon, grandpa!) But the kids, too, will learn.

I witness the trophy tradition

desecrated by sport hunters who have never eaten their kill
and maligned by activists who have never killed their food

But for my dad it is not a trophy
It is a single body of worship
Of participation in the world
A world that demands our respect

At one time, if our ancestors refused to respect
they would perish—remember that now
It's all one time
Our prey is watching over us

Every time I make a sandwich for a hike in the bush, or help haul a deer, or cook
a moose roast, I remember that grouse

That grouse suffered, yes I regret
But it did not go to waste
A coyote dragged it off, cleaned it down to bones and remnants
Some birds picked at the remains, and others used its feathers for a nest
The worms fed off the tiny, dark stain
I, too, will be sustained by the grouse
It will remind me of what I am
What am I, in the terrible and fragile?
I will be as noble as the worm
I will not waste that grouse's life

CHAPTER ELEVEN

"You Need Accuracy"

An Appreciation of a "Modern Hunting Tradition"

DAVID W. JARDINE

What am I, in the terrible and fragile?
Our prey is watching over us.

—JODI LATREMOUILLE, "A MODERN HUNTING TRADITION" (SEE CHAPTER 10)

The general patterns and shapes of the social world are part of our labour to understand and interpret, for ourselves and for and with our students. Such is a great part of Social Studies. Research into such grand patterns and shapes is a vital part of coming to know ourselves and how our lives have turned out thus and so. But there is another labour that is often occluded by such research, and this other labour is sometimes misunderstood.

The social life for which Social Studies is meant to provide an articulation is actually lived out in locales of great intimacy, particularity and grace. Families, practices, languages, roles both inherited and resisted, times, places, heartbreaks and joys, geographies known through the body and breath and the labor of hands, and, too, great arcs of reminiscence, ancestry, old ways barely recollected or inscribed in practices learned hand over hand, face-to-face, full of forgotten-ness. To be properly understood and articulated, these locales of intimacy don't lend themselves to forms of research that demand generalities or methodological anonymity as is proper to various social sciences. They demand a form of research that is proper to the object of its concern—an old Aristotelian idea that knowledge must "remain something adapted to the object, a *mensuratio ad rem*" (Gadamer, 1989, p. 261).

This wonderful piece of writing by Jodi Latremouille, "A Modern Hunting Tradition,"(see Chapter 10), is a strong and elegant example of remaining true to such measures. It is an example of how writing itself is a powerful, difficult and rigorous form of research (Richardson, 1994; Richardson & St. Pierre, 2005). It shows how a careful and poetic reflection on one's life can reveal truths about our living, and how such "life writing" (Chambers, Hasebe-Ludt, Leggo, & Sinner, 2012) stands firmly in the phenomenological and hermeneutic traditions of inquiry.

I mention all this because Jodi shared with me an e-mail she received from her father after she sent him an early version of this piece, and it points to something vital to the power of this writing. Included in brackets are Jodi's comments on how her writing was edited in response:

> Enjoyed your writing, not sure if you need accuracy but if you do:
> I never skid anything in the Cheesecloth Game bags, they are only when we put them on the packboard.
> *[I had originally written that my husband skids a piece of moose down the hill in the game bag. Edited as per this e-mail]*
> Small moose in five pieces, big one in six with the head attached to the neck making it a pretty good load as J. will attest. Ha Ha.
> *[I had originally written 3 pieces, 5 if very large. Edited as per this e-mail]*

Vital to the power of this writing is, again, that it must find its proper measure in the things that are its subject. I have found this, myself, in pursuing such writing, that it is not flimsy or subjective or random, but needs a terrible accuracy. Otherwise the whole thing deflates and becomes nothing but a self-referential, overly personal reminiscence. It loses its *beckoning*. Here, in this writing, we have profoundly personal reminiscence, but it is cast out into the world and its ways. This is why it is so effective for me as a reader. It is careful in its heeding of the life-world in all its meticulous detail. Part of its power to address us is in this accuracy. Without it, it betrays its object and betrays its own weakness. *This* is why, in heeding the demands of accuracy, such writing is legitimately deemed research and why and how such work should form part of the work of Social Studies in our schools.

So, in appreciation, I want to betray my age and what struck me most in Jodi's writing, that the lives of these Great Beings should not be wasted, and that, in understanding this, we understand something of ourselves and our own frail passings. Our lives, too, should not be wasted.

I end, therefore, with a wee bit more of that e-mail which betrays, as does Jodi's work, a great and trembling intimacy in the hunt:

> So far nothing to pack or skid yet this fall. Been close to two three point Bull Moose and got within 50 feet of a bedded Bull and cow. [The] bull … was up and gone before we could shoot, a big guy. The cow walked to within 30 feet of us. Mixed feelings on chasing a big productive guy like that this late in the season, could be tough. Probably leave him for another year and try for him early. He's probably getting old like me anyway and past his prime so will give him this last hurrah before we meet.

CHAPTER TWELVE

Advice TO New Teachers

SCOTT HASSETT

Do I contradict myself?
Very well then I contradict myself
I am large, I contain multitudes.

—WALT WHITMAN

First, Google Wendell Berry, listen, watch, think.

I still remember when I had it all figured out. When I knew what I was doing, and everything seemed so easy.

I remember when it all fell apart, those damn kids seemed to always get in the way.

I remember when I thought there was a difference between the two, that somehow I could get back to knowing. That it was possible to "teach the right way," to master the craft.

For me, my turning point, the moment where the weight of a thousand young lives was lifted came with a simple revelation, nothing's innocent, and hence nothing's not.

There are ways of being with children that honour the humanity of each child, the connectedness of the world, that tap into wisdom and feed the soul.

And sometimes these ways will be wrong.

There are ways that don't, that focus on efficiency and control, on power and jumping through hoops.

And sometimes these ways are necessary

No simple truth lasts, except maybe that no simple truth lasts.

Teaching isn't about doing things right, it's doing what's right, and I think that's a more accommodating space. Some days you can be too organized and structured, and that's okay, as long as it's not every day. Other days chaos will reign and there's something to be learned in that space, just not everything. The work isn't about keeping the train on the tracks but instead keeping the boat between the shores.

I struggled in my first year, in my last year, likely in my next year. I've found that when the stress of the day begins to overwhelm me, when external forces bear down, and my own inadequacies seem impossible to evade. I go outside, to supervise, to watch, to try and find peace. Outside, life is inescapable. The joy of children at play, the sounds of friendship, games and discovery flourish. Here joy is infectious, here the stress feels more manageable, the hurdles less daunting and the sharpness of my imperfections dull.

I realize that in this garden weeds grow, hidden amongst the games. I remain acutely aware that moments of unkindness, bullying, anger and resentment all lurk. That my own practices bear the scars of external blows, and my own imperfections. If I leave these weeds untended they will overrun the garden, they will destroy all the beauty and they cannot be ignored in a naive attempt to see only hope. Now when being in the garden it is my awareness, and attention to, the weeds that ensure that the garden can grow. But this attention must be careful, must not linger, the focus remains the garden itself, in its wholeness in all that it offers; otherwise, what reason would I have to tend it?

So if I can offer one piece of advice it's a more gentle accountability. This work requires you to be present, and honest, but also forgiving, of yourself and of them. Hold yourself up to a standard, not a simplistic measure of right and wrong, but one much more grand and forgiving, a standard of humanity.

Have I done right by kids today?

And if this fails, Google Wendell Berry again.

CHAPTER THIRTEEN

Beckoning

JENNIFER GRAY

Beckoning
a silent invitation to slow my stride.
No reason to stop for unaccountable time lacking proof of productivity,
wasteful passing of dashes on my watch
but I do.

I sit.
Slow my breath as thoughts transmute.
The rush diminishes, eliminating the static cacophony.
Swiftly harmonious, the liquid melody at the base of the ridge,
the swishing sway of the blades.
From the branch, a staccato call.
An alarm, allowing awareness to acknowledge the adjustment.
Guilt wanes,
I am recalibrated.

CHAPTER FOURTEEN

Remembering
Mr. Routhier

LESLEY TAIT

I have suggested that what seems urgent for us at this time in understanding what teaching more truly is, to undertake to reorient ourselves so that we overcome mere correctness so that we can see and hear our doings as teachers harbored within pedagogical being, so we can see and hear who we are as teachers.

—AOKI (2005, P. 197)

I knew his supervision days by heart. Tuesday and Thursday recess and Monday lunch. I counted down to those days as they meant a chance to wander the playground, a chance to hold his hand and be involved in a very personal conversation. I remember that hand. Slim and strong and always willing to be held or be placed on our shoulder. That hand comforted me in moments of sadness and congratulated me in moments of elation. It would provide high fives when difficult solutions were deduced and yet could instill a deep respect when wrong had been done. But it is the hand-holding at recess that I miss. He was able to make that time feel like my time. My time to ask questions, to tell him about my life and to feel important. Here was man possessed of strength and kindness. A man who found a way to make this classroom magical and full of wonder.

We were not allowed to sit idly with Mr. Routhier, but were instead required to engage in the world around us in a myriad of ways. We were encouraged to ask, to question as he made every attempt to interrupt our sense of "normal." Somehow this classroom, this space became ours. His and ours. And it was magical.

We would curl up on the floor in front of him and listen intently as he assumed the many voices of the characters in our books. Some kids would lie with their eyes closed, others on their knees trying to be as close to the words as possible. We would speak not a word as we were transfixed not only by the words on the page but by the characters brought to life by a man. Our imaginations created scenes and descriptions to match the voices we heard. Here was a man able to completely entrance his class with language and story. In fact, the first two books I bought upon graduating from education were *Owls in the Family* and *Jacob Two-Two Meets the Hooded Fang*. Mr. Routhier had read both to me. It was the first I remember being captivated by a book. It was in this way that we discovered worlds, places and people. The world was invited in and was, in turn, turned back out in our own stories and in our play.

Each book we read by ourselves earned us a brick. I would bring up stacks of books to his desk. There he would patiently ask me which books brought my imagination into bloom. We were required to learn words like "bloom," "exuberance," "captivated," "enthralled" and "wondrous" to answer his book questions. Each book, loved or not, was rewarded with a brick. These bricks were special and valued. While each was simply a piece of laminated paper, they represented so much more. The bricks were taped, glued and sometimes stapled across the classroom. We were not to keep these bricks, but were to proudly display them wherever we saw fit. Each classroom wall, window and door of that room ended up wallpapered with bricks. Some askew, some straight, some overlapping. The favorite places could have been excavated for multiple layers of bricks. Here we were, a classroom of readers. That foundation was evident.

Christmas of my grade two year, I asked Santa for the book *Two-Minute Mysteries*. I wanted one of my own. Each time that book was brought out of Mr. Routhier's desk, every student would squeal. Once again we would gather at his feet and try to turn our brains to their "smartest" setting. Hands to the side of our heads, we would turn imaginary knobs. Once we were at our "smartest" he would read. Each story was short but contained clues to solving the mystery presented at the end. How did Dr. Halendjian know that Elsie was lying? Or, how did Dr. Halendjian know that Bill had stolen the skates? We thought we were incredible sleuths. We would sit and debate or argue about possible clues. Sometimes heated, sometimes quietly we would try to get the others to see it our way. We became experts at explaining our thoughts and presenting our arguments. When it seemed too tough for even this group of sleuths, my friends and I would ask to stay in at recess and attempt to solve it. We would draw elaborate maps or diagrams attempting to find the solution. While likely never correct, we were sure we had devised Dr. Halendjian's solution. Mr. Routhier never once read the actual solution presented at the end of each mystery.

Mr. Routhier came to my First Communion. He and his family joined us at the church and returned to my home for celebration and cake. He was a part of our lives. He thought nothing of that line between "teacher" and teacher. He understood Ted Aoki: "Education that alienates must be considered 'miseducation' and education must be transformed by moving toward a reclaiming of the fullness of body and soul" (Aoki, 2005, p. 62).

I was a good student. Probably never once thought of as a genius by my teachers, but smart enough. I took pride in that. I could solve math problems, I could read books. Here was part of my identity. Part of who I thought I was. It was also in Mr. Routhier's classroom that I learned that I was not the smartest student in the history of the world. We had spent January exploring the idea of subtraction. We explored base ten blocks, we drew, we completed art projects, we invented our own algorithms, all to help the concept become firm in our minds. Near the end of our exploration, we were given one question. One question I could not solve. I tried drawing it out, used base ten blocks and was completely stumped. How could this be? Shane Krepakevich solved it. In fact, Shane was the only student to find the elusive solution to this question. I was crushed. I was smart and here was something that someone understood before I understood it. I remember the disbelief. My seven-year-old self had no understanding of not being the best. Somehow he knew.

Mr. Routhier told us about his son. He spoke quietly around this topic. His usual exuberance was replaced by a gentle quiet. He told us about his son's likes and dislikes. He told us of holding his hand in the hospital. He spoke of the fear and the worry. He spoke about loss. How he died I am not sure I ever knew. What I knew was there was sadness here, a deep and unabated sadness. He chose to share this close pain with children. He understood that these children were able to understand his pain and empathize. We knew this was a precious topic and yet we understood that its sharing somehow made him even more ours.

Attempting to separate out the threads of my being that have felt his influence is impossible. They are too numerous. Yet I recognize his guiding hand and its far reach.

CHAPTER FIFTEEN

Teaching Everything

KAREN SCHWEIGHARDT

Tricky, this living in Alberta.
Quite disorienting, really.
Heavy, black oil courses through my veins where life's blood used to be. It confuses me.
The machine needs to be fed. I watch the sad lady feed it with her credit card.
I become anaesthetized from the mind-numbing hum from the casino floor where I am working
in the middle of the night to help pay for my kid's education. This is where I need to be right
now, right?
Do you want to save the Earth? Make sure you write a mission statement and apply for the
grant. Fill out the form in its entirety and submit by the due date. Don't forget to display the logo
on all the material that goes home to parents.

I often think our society has lost its collective mind when it comes to the environment. This confusion was also written about by E. O. Wilson (2012):

> Humanity today is like a waking dreamer, caught between the fantasies of sleep and the chaos of the real world. The mind seeks but cannot find the precise place and hour. We have created a Star Wars civilization, with Stone Age emotions, medieval institutions, and godlike technology. We thrash about. We are terribly confused by the mere fact of our existence, and a danger to ourselves and to the rest of life.

It is important to listen to the voices of our environmental and educational archetypes that have gone before and added to the body of world wisdom. But it seems these important voices are drowned out by the powerful forces of capitalization and market economy.

In my graduate studies, I was influenced by Buddhist Zen monk Thich Nhat Hanh. In his book *The World We Have* (2008), the following question is posed: "A student asked me, 'There are so many urgent problems, what should I do?'; I said, 'Take one thing and do it very deeply and carefully, and you will be doing everything at the same time'" (p. 110).

Ask yourself, "What is my one thing?" Choose a focus.

My one thing is love for Earth. If I put that first in my teaching, I am teaching everything. By choosing a focus to guide my teaching, I can feel less panicked about living in a world that I don't agree with all the time. If I choose a focus and know my purpose, it will propel both me and my students forward. It is action based, and based on the needs of Earth. From there, my program can move forth with integrity.

CHAPTER SIXTEEN

Blossom Everlasting

A Meditation

DAVID GEOFFREY SMITH

Not far from where I live, a restaurant recently changed hands and the new own-ers planted some gorgeous Japanese cherry trees in front of the building. When I drove by earlier this spring, the blossoms were absolutely stunning—a beautiful radiant pink registering against the white backdrop of the restaurant. When I drove by a month later, the blossoms were still blooming madly, or so I thought until suddenly I realized I'd been 'had'; the blossoms are fake. Through the wiz-ardry of modern chemistry, fake flowers can be made to look so real, you'd swear they were. (A new secretary in a local office I know was found one day, in a desire to impress as a new employee, watering the fake office plants.)

Interestingly enough, plastic flowers are usually made from polymers, a form of chemical compound based in petroleum, so you can draw quite direct lines between plastic flowers and contemporary petroleum-based war culture. A nice irony, and relevant here, is the fact that many young people who took part in the anti-war movements of the 1960s and '70s were called "flower children" because of their love of flowers both for personal adornment and as a symbol of peace. Those were the days before plastic flowers.

As a teacher, I am always looking for the pedagogical messages in things, people and events of the world. What we can learn, humanly speaking, from plas-tic fake Japanese cherry blossoms? In purely economic terms, as a business you can save a lot of money using plastic flowers. They never need watering, pruning, culling, so you never need to pay anyone to do that work, nor do you have to do it yourself thus freeing up time to find other ways of making your business more efficient and wealth bearing. Your business is secured into the future, at least in this one small way, and you are momentarily freed from the fear of self-annihilation, which the great analyst of human nature, Sigmund Freud, declared is the most basic human fear.

So one lesson we might gain from meditating on plastic flowers could have something to do with our intrinsic fear of death, and a consequent seduction into those technologies that can preserve life at all costs. Extrapolate this small specific example to a wider political and cultural vision and we can see the same logic at work: to protect my/our national, tribal, ethnic existence, technologies are developed to ensure my/our survival above all others.

But then, what is the nature of the 'life' that is preserved through a presumed possibility of life everlasting, of 'life' without death? Boredom through endless rituals of repetition can be the only consequence; the endless need to keep reassuring oneself, one's people or culture, that not only is *this* the best there is, this is *all* there is. It is a deadly form of living and it takes many forms, whether in vain attempts to keep educational practices chained to rituals of the past, or in romantic theories of the environment that do not acknowledge the violent eruptions and destructions of Earth's origins.

But back to our beautiful but fake Japanese cherry tree. In Japan, the annual blossoming of cherry trees is understood as a bittersweet moment, recognizing that the beauty of this momentary radiance will not last. So we could say that what is lost under technologically induced renditions of beauty such as the fake cherry blossoms in front of the restaurant is the very condition of beauty itself, which paradoxically involves something we would rather not face, namely, the inevitability of its 'end.' As South African writer Doris Lessing once put it: "Sooner or later we're all ugly." I put 'end' in quotation marks because the 'end' of beauty signified in the dying of a once-radiant blossom is not really the End; it is simply the necessary condition for its continued existence within Life beyond our immediately conscious present 'life.' This is the Life of eternity, the Life after 'death,' the source of true and lasting joy, available even in this present moment if only we can learn to see it, gradually understand it, and accept its fundamental requirement. In the words of American poet Wallace Stevens (1990, p. 26):

Death is the mother of beauty; hence from her,
Alone, shall come fulfillment to our dreams
And our desires.

This is not a swoon into morbidity but a simple, practical recognition that there is a deep and everlasting balance at work in the world in the organic relation between birth and death. We become aware of this as we confront the necessity of letting our children grow apart from us, as we notice the once-vibrant skin on our arms losing its tensile strength and as we gradually accept that there are certain problems we cannot solve within the range of our current intelligence and maybe never will. The deeper point is that none of this is a problem if we can see it all within the range of a more universal wisdom. Then, any mourning of loss turns into a view of new possibilities embraceable within a deeper freedom, knowing better how this is the Way of Life and that we are part of something far more wonderful, indeed compelling, than we could ever previously have imagined.

CHAPTER SEVENTEEN

Timed Beings

KHATLEEN ALNAS

Early morning, day after day,
timed beings, awaken by sirens.
Armed with gears, hopes and fears,
they march down empty hallways.

The captain orders,
"Sit up straight, eyes forward, lips shut tight!"
Trembling bodies, wandering minds,
       but the hearts kept beating.
            Alive.
Trapped inside a deceiving ploy
       is a room full of souls seeking to escape.

Machines by day, creatures by night,
fooled by the urgency and ubiquity at plain sight.
What happens
       when the heart no longer exists with the mind,
       and the mind matters without a heart?
Living creatures turn to timed machines
       with nothing but gears, fuel, and expiry dates.

CHAPTER EIGHTEEN

In My Timid Voice

L. A. JAMES

(a.k.a. Lisa Menzies)

Part One
And my timid voice
that sounds of Winnie the Pooh in my mind
cried out
I am confused.
Where am I to write?
But how much should I write?
How do I know
what will be
Enough.

Surely I know.
Surely I know I can write
At least
6 pages of beautiful work
and those six pages will be painful
and I will lose sleep
and the joy I will feel when those
few words form together to create a coherent,
and even powerful thought
and that joy can keep me going for a while
pondering and replaying its merit
and my chest will puff.

but 6 pages can take days even weeks
what if they want more
how can I keep it beautiful

and meet the deadlines

never been good with deadlines.

and who am I
but a mum
but someone who cares for children
and likes to play in the woods
but who am I
who comes from a lineage
of factory workers
of farmers
of craftsmen
of those with entrepreneurial spirit
of the self-taught that think differently
and weren't built for schooling
but that struggle for the way
that weaves a grand story and
leaves threads for me to pull from
that leaves space for beautiful writing

if I can just figure out how much I am to write

and if I even answered the question.

Part Two
Because
half of the time my ideas seem to be slightly
To the left
of centre
Not the political left
To the left or to the right for that matter
of the others' way of thinking
So I am not always certain I answered the question
Or even understood the question

And isn't it okay if my ideas are to the left
Isn't that what we are meant to do
Disrupt
Value multiple perspectives
But if you are to the left you are out of the club and
You must be in the club to be worthy

Of course
I am worthy
I know I am worthy
Of course I am

Some else already decided that
I am worthy to be here
Otherwise I would not
Be here.

But yet I am
questioning
Why do I keep hearing that question

And why is it that
To be worthy to be here
I feel or have been made to feel
That I have to write
pages upon pages
20 pages of thoughts
that are supposed to be beautiful
and deep and provocative
but I can't
When a thought is over
It is just over
There is no more to say
At that time

Until it has sat for a time

And then maybe there is more to say

But by then
The deadline has passed.

Part Three
there usually is more to say
but I look more to the words of others to fill the pages
than to myself
because
I need to fill the pages
And I am running out of time

The question comes again

Aren't I,
afterall
Mum to twins
who weren't built for schooling
One labeled gifted
One labeled autistic
Left-of-centre thinkers

Beautiful, provocative thinkers

Aren't I,
afterall the one
That has struggled to find the way
Out of the rabbit hole
Of deficit thinking

Aren't I
afterall
The one who has questioned herself
The one that has fought the authorities
Rejected Skinner
The one who has felt responsible
The one who has been humbled
The one that sees herself for the first time.

More threads from which to pull

But how much am I to write

Part Four
Write as much as you can
As often as you can
Write beautifully
Thoughtfully
provocatively

Relief
Disbelief

Space has been opened up
Light peaks through

For the first time
a way
To write in a way that honours me
The possibly left-of-centre thinker
Who was not built for schooling
To weave a grand story
To write provocatively
Thoughtfully
Beautifully.

And meet the deadline.

Maybe.

CHAPTER NINETEEN

My Brother

SCOTT HASSETT

My approach to education would be like my approach to everything else. I'd change the standard. I would make the standard that of community health rather than the career of the student. You see if you make the standard the health of the community, that would change everything.
—WENDELL BERRY (2013, N.P.)

Craig is my brother
My brave, powerful, infinitely hopeful brother
My Mom says he has an old soul
She said he would teach me patience
I scoffed
"More like make me lose my patience"

There are a lot of words people have used to describe Craig, but none ever seemed to fit. Impossible to squeeze the essence of a life into even the most accommodating of words. All I knew as a kid was that Craig was different, different from me, from what my world told me was ordinary. A random shift of genetic material scattering illusions of normality. Craig was different, he was special, but most of all he was my brother, I suppose I never knew him as anything else.

My story without Craig's is empty, a hollow shadow of the truth. No journey occurs unattached, and the threads of my own experience always seem to circle back, attach to him. Paths that seemed to run separate but never really so. I've always been defined as Craig's brother, and him as mine. Our own individuality only finding life in reference to each other.

For a long time I tried to outrun this tie
Find my "own life"
A fight to become "my own person"
A lonely battle
I'm happier surrendered

I often wonder about the specifics of Craig's schooling. My own adolescent self-importance prevented me from ever really knowing the truth. How did they try to fit his multisided, awkwardly angled peg into the round hole?

A diversity so extreme that no amount of codes, papers and accommodations could make him fit into the institution, and so they had to create a new one. If Craig could not be taught to contribute to the market, what purpose could school possibly serve? A system left barren by the unsolvable puzzle, what role to play when the assumptions propping up understanding of 'success' were toppled. What to prepare for if not a career, why learn if not to consume? They used terms like "life" and "social" skills to reset the standard, and he was handed to aides, separated, segregated, sometimes in body, always in spirit. He spent time working at a bottle depot, helping the custodian around the school, the closest they could find to a vocational fit.

At some point it was mutually decided that Craig would never read, and then he never did. Curriculum broken into bits of knowledge had no place to attach, like setting a table on the celling, and so he was fenced off from the fields of human experience. "He doesn't need to know that" a refrain repeated over and over again, in quiet whispers and spoken word, in subtle and not so subtle decisions. Doesn't need to know of ancestors and lineages, doesn't need to understand connections and discovery, doesn't need to engage in the art of learning.

I looked up 'need' in the dictionary:

Something that is needed in order to live or succeed or be happy,
He's alive, and he's happy
They may have been right?
What does that say about the rest of us?

The saddest part of Craig's story, of the dissemination of the community, on the prioritization of knowledge and arbitrary decisions about what matters, is not how school failed him, but how it failed to realize the opportunity of his presence. His marginalization created a space where everyone was so busy trying to shape him, they never asked what could be shared.

Craig was always a problem in need of fixing
Always a question
Never an answer.
A consequence less of his circumstance,
More about the quality of the questions

No one ever asked, how can we become more empathetic? What does it mean to be truly brave? What is success? And perhaps most important, what is happiness:

Despite trial and tragedy
Despite imperfections and unplanned consequences
Despite all that seems wrong, broken, and beautifully imperfect
Craig knew the answers to these questions, the wisdom of a trialed life.
"He'll teach you patience"
An understated prophecy

He is the root of the parts of me I most treasure, that I cling to when my conscience rages and the guilt of an unsaved world lays siege to my walls of rationale and justification. What little wisdom I have has long been nourished by Craig's perfectly messy glow.

I think Craig taught me how to joke, how to laugh; joy by osmosis. Always smiling, a lived lightness that allowed him to soar high above where his clipped wings should have ever allowed. I quickly learned humour as a language that reawakens the heart's memory of joy yet to be discovered. A small gift I have clung to in my own stumbled journey. When the introvert in me bleeds shyness and creates masks that mark me as arrogant, apathetic, or simply a jerk, humour has always been my crutch. Regardless of its quality, simply the attempt of a joke seems to break down barriers I would otherwise be unable to scale. I don't know where I'd be without him.

Craig taught me the fallacy of fairness, that what I think I deserve or have earned is irrelevant, and that 'what should be' is a quicksand of self-pity, and distracted solutions. That the true currencies of a happy life are kindness and connection. That what I give, can never pay back the gifts of the living world, and was never meant to do so. My job is not to fix, simply to live in peace, do right, and cultivate my connected soul's best intentions.

Craig taught me this
And so much more
Craig's story screams questions at the very foundations of what we have created as reality. Why, why educate, and for whose ends? When did we put the myth of individuality ahead of the health of the community, and what price have we paid? What wisdom, what joy has been left as distraction on the side of the road to success? In the light of Craig's wake the pillars of the market institution, autonomy, individuality, consumption, industry are revealed and I wonder, who is it all for? What mechanism serves those whose purpose runs deeper than the reality we have created? And why have I always believed that all of this was somehow okay?

It's funny how quickly the extreme is labeled as the exception, stray too far from normal and it becomes something else entirely, not based on what it is but what it is in relation to defined reality. The typical classroom, the typical student, their special needs cousins, labels that create walls solidifying expectations as reality.

And so that which is different enough becomes separate, a completely different thing, this is this and that is that, and never the two shall meet. Universal lessons become trapped in niches, surface differences betraying connections, unseen, unread, un-understood.

Does Craig's journey offer no insight into my own? A criticism of his life quickly becomes an analysis of special education, how we can do it differently for them. Craig's life was full of kind teachers and loving aides, the moments of his story likely carry more joy than my own; no, the lessons are not found in the specifics, but in the universals. Is how the system failed him so different from how it failed me? What it failed to give, what it never asked from him, of him, is what it never asked of me. Extremes and labels aside, are our stories really all that different? We are brothers after all.

CHAPTER TWENTY

Advice TO A New Teacher

IAN WALSH

Young teacher, young teacher, you will never 'go teach.' You will always be at a place.

Meditations ON Contemplative Pedagogy AS Sanctuary

JACKIE SEIDEL

1

Western educational institutions are characterized by the ways they operate (consciously or unconsciously) by the culturally inherited logic and rules of *chronos*—chronological time. Eco-feminist theologian Catherine Keller (1996) names this violent timeline an unwinding "death-line" (p. 137). It is the time of erasing the present in favor of a mythical future that never arrives ("progress"). It is the time of colonization, of the market, of extinction, of war, and of frag-mentation. It separates humans from our own bodies, from one another, from other species, from the fragile and finite earth which sustains life. It enables and legitimates the continued perpetration of unspeakable ecological, economic, and cultural violence. In educational institutions chronological time is often individ-ually experienced as the suffering of interminable rushing, competition, fear, and lonely individualism.

2

Meditating on the meaning of invoking the words *contemplate* or *contemplative* in relation to schools, curriculum, and pedagogy reveals a spacious opening in language that might offer us some healing time, space, and rest from this rushing, distracting, and violent timeline.

3

Etymologically, *contemplate* derives from Latin *contemplari*, meaning "to gaze attentively" (Latin. *con*, "with" + *templum*, temple). A *temple* is a defined as space marked out for "observation," a "consecrated space," a "sanctuary," or a "sacred space" (ODEE, 1966, p. 908). Because they are not normally used in relation to the inherited institutions of secular, industrial society, words like *sanctuary* and *temple* have the potential to disrupt or deconstruct common images of school and pedagogy. To speak such words, then, in relation to pedagogy, curriculum, and schooling at all levels might summon forth a new kind of responsibility to this language.

4

What are pedagogical obligations to *these* images?
Contemplate.
Temple.
Sacred spaces.
Sanctuary.

5

What kind of space and time does pedagogy imagined as sanctuary open for us as teachers and learners? Pedagogy imagined as sanctuary might be characterized by the active and ethical creation of sacred space. Pedagogy imagined as sanctuary calls for the courageous resistance of ways of living, being together, and educating that engage in or promote social, ecological, cultural, and economic violence. Pedagogy imagined as sanctuary creates an active and mindful practice: awe and reverence for life itself. Pedagogy imagined as sanctuary enables us to recognize illusions and false promises, drawing our gaze away from the forces of shallowness and disembodiment and towards awareness of senses, existential experiences and meanings, and to what is actually before us: This world. This student. This life.

6

To imagine pedagogy, curriculum, or school as sanctuary invokes images, thoughts, or feelings of peace, sacredness, and non-violence.

7

To utter the word *sanctuary* invokes a sense of spaciousness of both place and time, the kind of place where one might become aware of breathing, of silence, of stillness, of the sensory and sensual body, of the bodies and being of others both human and non-human.

8

We wake up.

9

The sanctuary is a place and time of rest. The desire to move fast and rush around falls away. To create such *restful* spaces and times is necessary to focusing, to learning, to being well, and to doing good work in the world. It is a place of rest from the frenetic and meaningless activity and exhaustion of participation in the neoliberal, globalized economy and all that has meant for education in our time when so much of life's energy is being consumed for more production and *in the name* of the future.

10

French philosopher Jean-Luc Nancy (2003) called the 20th century the time of "expropriating from beings their conditions of existence" (p. 18). He describes the ways our strength, labour, bodies, senses, and even the space-time of our own singularity become objects of production. "Capital" and the "global market" only can endure and prosper by such massive expropriation and extermination. The result, he writes, is that we are "deported in advance from the here and now" (p. 19). A violence in the service of "progress" and of a future that is already known before it is lived. Educational institutions at all levels have and are participating in these processes. To invoke "contemplative," *the temple*, in relation to schooling and pedagogy calls forth then a spiritual obligation to face, name, and resist the historical and contemporary political and economic forces that have created these institutions. This is the difficult, heavy, and ethical work of imagining and creating *other* presents and possible futures that remain free and not-yet-known.

11

To contemplate pedagogy as the time, space, and place of the temple or sanctuary implies then not the places of production, accumulation or expropriation, or of the accompanying waste, destruction, and excess with which we are so deeply familiar, but rather *the cultivation of an aesthetic of not too much and not too fast.* An aesthetic of conservation.

12

The sanctuary is not a place of competition or of getting ahead. Nor is it the kind of place that fills us with the desire to reform or fix it with fancy new programs and methods. Our desire might be to let it be. To be with it.

13

To pause.

14

Stepping purposefully and with intention, into the sanctuary, into the space for contemplation, for even a moment out of the turmoil and confusion of the rushing stream is sometimes enough to draw our gaze towards what matters.

15

To enter the sanctuary is not an escape away from the so-called real world; rather, this intentional action represents the possibility, so necessary in this time of unprecedented and unsustainable ecological strain on the planet, of sensing the deep and infinite interconnections with the rest of life, of our own entanglement in all this, of the co-arising of all life and its going back into the world. In recognizing the interconnectedness of life, awareness of others including the non-human others sharing this space grows. There is no desire to harm them. We are not alone. We understand that we share the same breath that has always been.

16

Chronic stress and feelings of threat give rise to fear and anxiety responses that might provoke more competing, rushing, protecting, colonizing. Sanctuary invokes images of safety, of a place where body, heart, and mind might be protected, a place where violence might not occur. This kind of safety is necessary for doing good pedagogical work in the world.

17

As a teacher educator, I visit schools often with student teachers. I witness the rushing and panic. The fear. A friend talks about sitting in a school hallway during her PhD research and observing people in the hallways. Her impression was that everyone was running and running. The thought that came into her mind was, "Where are they all running to?" In the sanctuary, there is no pre-determined destination. It is the space for observation and inquiry into the world, into our selves, into our relations. It is a space and time for awakening, over and over again, to the unfolding world around us and to our complex participation in it.

18

In the contemporary neoliberal and ever more corporatized model of schooling, curriculum, and pedagogy at all levels, the destination is the future. This is not an indeterminate or open future that has yet to unfold; rather, it is the future that is known and colonized in advance. It is the future of competition for few resources, the future of competing to be the winner, to be on top, to be the best, to be excellent.

19

Yet, it might be in our time that it is *the future* that requires sanctuary. We know that many challenges face us and our descendants and the non-human life that share our and their space. It requires sanctuary from us and our activities, from our befouling and spoiling, from our colonizing it in advance. It requires that we leave it, and ourselves, and *all the others* some space and time to unfold.

20

Such unfolding requires a different timing. The sanctuary is characterized by *kairos* rather than *chronos*. *Chronos* is clock time, linear time, and necessary for both colonization and for capitalism to do their work.

21

Madeleine L'Engle (2001) calls *kairos* "real time" and "that time which breaks through *chronos* with a shock of joy" (p. 45). *Kairos* might be imagined as the time of love and compassion, of wonder, of open potential and unknown futures, and of yet unwritten rhythms and possibilities for all life on earth. *Kairos* is a qualitative and deconstructive timing which interrupts the line of chronos when we meditate, when we play unselfconsciously, and when we work creatively. It is an existential and ontological timing that might be consciously practiced in our pedagogy in the hopes of untangling ourselves from the strangling timeline of *chronos*. It is the time that faces the present with courage, compassion, and a peaceful heart and mind.

22

This is the time of the sanctuary.

23

Come in.

CHAPTER TWENTY-TWO

Thoughts AND Aspirations FOR A New Teacher

STEPHANIE BARTLETT

Dear New Teacher,

When I first began teaching sixteen years ago, I was young. I was proud that I had made it through university and was now about to embark on the career that I had dreamed of for so long. I loved children and the rhythm and energy that arose from the school day, each moment different from the next and impossible to predict. But I didn't truly understand. I wish someone had told me that I could do all the planning and prep work I wanted, but I couldn't truly know how my day would unfold until I looked into the eyes of my students. David Loy (2010) says, "I live multiple stories that overlap with other stories, others' stories. ... When class is more fluid, personal success stories jostle each other, like basketball players elbowing for the rebound" (Loy, p. 28). He is speaking about the class system, but I find the analogy transfers well over to a classroom environment. Please know that even though you may plan team building activities and lessons on how to respect each other, putting a group of new students in a room together calls for the teacher to use story to bridge the connections and find the story that makes each student unique. It is not so much about the content as how we as a community understand how to best use that content in a way that interests and sparks us as a group. Share your true self with your students: your accomplishments, your hobbies, your family and your funny little stories. Use that as the springboard for them to feel safe enough to trust and share their own stories. One of our longest, deepest inquiries came from the story of one student that sparked the rest of us.

To teach students "to examine ... life is to examine [their] more important stories" is essential (Loy, 2010, p. 25). One of the things that I find very empowering for both students and teachers is the documenting of student learning and the ability to set goals. The longer I teach and the older my own children become, the more I realize the importance of wisdom, patience and story in education. Some of that comes with life experience. Please remember that a child is a parent's most precious endeavor and to be careful when communicating with them. When I started, I didn't intimately understand that we can't "change" the complexities of a child in one school year. Some students will struggle for years with their reading despite all of the strategies, meetings and targeted mini-lessons and support that we have to offer ... then sometimes it clicks as late as grade six and they are off and running. We just don't *know* ... but we can create and provide the right environment of trust. We can honour ourselves and each other as members of a supportive community and learn that "meaning is improvised together" (Loy, 2010, p. 26). I realize now that the most important thing we can do as educators is to look closely at the gifts and stories of each individual student and then teach them to look closely at their learning stories and important moments, both positive and negative, so that they can reflect, set goals and feel successful.

New Teacher, "[i]t is not enough to have a story about what happens. It is necessary to story why I do what I do" (Loy, 2010, p. 37). A large part of the time I used to spend planning is now spent writing and reflecting on learning experiences to find out where I am in the development of my teaching practice and where the students are in terms of both skills and creative development. I can use these reflections to write my professional story, to show parents the deep learning that is happening in the classroom, and to figure out what my next steps are. In a world where there is so much going on and so many expectations, this writing exercise is both meditative and productive. I wish I had known to do that right from the beginning. Just as we love to find our old journals from school, how special would that be to read your developing story as an educator?

It is important that you know your curriculum inside out and backwards so that when a child asks a question or an opportunity arises, you are ready. When I plan now, I do so knowing that the outcome is unknown and the outline is most likely to change along the way. This way, you can embrace inquiry in the field and know that you will cover the outcomes. It is tempting to compartmentalize the subjects and make sure that everything is "covered." Once you know how your students learn best and what drives their motivation, try designing challenges or letting them create with their hands. Then, you will see the literacy and numeracy come from within as students are required to calculate, count, measure, read and write to accomplish their goal and also explain their thinking. When you go down a particular learning path, stay focused, knowing that you will guide students and uncover the curriculum.

In the world of education where we are pulled in so many directions, perhaps the most important piece of advice is to stay open, yet focused. Keep your mind open for the opportunities that will present themselves through different experiences and questions. Focus on the moment and revel in the possibilities when teachers and students engage in rich, deep learning together. The immense feeling of satisfaction and accomplishment will help to keep the worries and stress of whether you are "covering enough" at bay.

I wish you the best of luck in your career and I know that you are wiser than I was when I started out. Believe in the child. Stay anchored to your collective stories and new possibilities. Breathe. Enjoy the journey. You will do just fine.

CHAPTER TWENTY-THREE

Dear New Teacher

TOWANI DUCHSCHER

Congratulations on being hired for your first teaching job! As you prepare to embark on this part of your journey, consider this question from David Loy (2010): "What happens when I realize that my story is a story?" (p. 33)

For when you realize that your story is a story, you must also realize that, like you, each of your students is also in the midst of their own story of Becoming. We are all in the process of our own creation. We are each in the process of our own story development. While you may play only a bit part in a student's life story, it is a great privilege to participate in that student's story of becoming. You should always consider what role you are playing in their story.

Try to remember that your students' stories are just beginning, always. Each day could possibly be the "once upon a time" of their grand narrative, the introduction of their story of self. Feel filled with joy and honour that you get to be a part of that beginning. To be part of someone's beginning is magical. Try to remember the magic in it even on the days that start out with "a dark and stormy night." Try to remember that each day is a fluid moment in a larger story. It is an important detail, but it is not the story in its entirety. It is a fluid story of becoming. So try to remember that "once upon a time" does not start a fixed explanation of any one thing, but it is the start to a great adventure!

Try to remember that great adventures are not great because everything goes as planned. Your favorite stories would not be memorable without their challenges and conflicts. What if Romeo and Juliet just fell in love and got married? What if Jack had sold the cow at the market like his mother told him? What if Bilbo hadn't answered his door? Challenges are part of great stories, and they are part of our own great stories of becoming. Try to remember that "failure" is a social construct. We don't speak of failure when we talk about Romeo and Juliet, Jack, or Bilbo, or any of our great story characters. Maybe this is because we can read their whole story from a wider perspective. Each conflict is one part of a bigger story. Each conflict helps to shape our protagonists. This applies to our own stories too. You will make mistakes but do not let them be "failures" that define you. Your students will make mistakes, but do not let them be "failures" that define them. They are simply battles, internal and external, in the adventure story of becoming.

Try to remember that great stories are not contained in the end of the story. Don't skip to the end. Don't skim. Read thoroughly and relish each word, each moment. It is only the true experience of each word that gives the whole story meaning. Try to enjoy each moment in your teaching day as an important part of the story, even the crappy, frustrating, infuriating moments. Instead of wishing those moments away, enjoy them the way you would if they were in your favorite novel, remembering that your story continues beyond that moment.

Fall in love with your own story, and the story of each of your students, as you do your favorite novel.

Have a great year!
Love, Towani

CHAPTER TWENTY-FOUR

Henry

MIRANDA HECTOR

Arrogant ignorance makes war without a thought of peace.
—WENDELL BERRY (2005, P. 54)

A boy in my classroom is going to be fixed by his I[ndividualized] P[rogram] P[lan].
He cannot read. (Refer to long-term goal 1)
He cannot write. (Refer to long-term goal 1)
He cannot count to 10. (Refer to long-term goal 2)
He is in grade one for the second time. (Refer to psychologist's assessment and resulting diagnosis)
He cannot speak articulately. (Refer to long-term goal 3)
He cannot stand up straight or sit cross-legged. (Refer to long-term goal 4)
He cannot cut with scissors or hold a pencil long enough to resist chewing it. (Refer to long-term goal 5)

The limits of my stories are the limits of my world.
—DAVID LOY (2010, P. 5).

***

He knows how to build.
He knows cars.

He can turn a row of wax crayons into a conveyer belt.
(There is no appropriate place to include this in the IPP. It is considered irrelevant to include it in the strength section.)

***

He does not wear pants with pockets so he keeps toy cars in his socks. He is not trying to be secretive, rather it has become a logical storage solution.
He finds pictures of cars in magazines while the other children cling to toys and animals and familiar television characters.
His favourites are the silver Mercedes-Benz vehicles which he gleefully rips out. Using scissors he cannot cut with he carefully removes each Mercedes-Benz symbol from the pages and rushes them into his backpack.
When I ask what he is doing he says, "I'm cutting out all the peace signs!"

***

He is beauty.

CHAPTER TWENTY-FIVE

A Little Uprising

PAUL LE MARQUAND

"You had a little uprising in your class last week. How are you doing, Paul?" I remembered this greeting, which was offered one Monday morning late in the second term of junior high, when I learned about student protests occurring in Jefferson County, Colorado, at the beginning of the 2014 school year. The majority of the elected school board members proposed a review of the Advanced Placement (AP) history course following revisions to its framework by the College Board. To earn college credit in this AP elective, students would now be expected to demonstrate an ability to critically analyze American history, including its past grave injustices. The bloc of board members was concerned with the course's apparent lack of patriotism, stemming from a supposed focus on social change achieved via civil unrest. Student opposition galvanized around a board member's expressed belief that "I don't think we should encourage our kids to be little rebels." Leveraging social media tools including Twitter hashtags and Facebook groups, students expressed their dismay through walkouts and by attending school dressed as historical figures who engaged in civil disobedience. Teachers protested alongside students and staged a "sick-out"; some observers noted that teaching staff coincidently also faced the prospect of the legal revocation of their collective bargaining rights by the same school board.

To which uprising was my colleague now referring? There had actually been two in the past seven days. The first was based on the Grievance Memo. It was an "anonymous" electronic document shared amongst a handful of students and eventually with me. I was struggling to engage these students in the course content;

they were much more interested in describing their dislikes of particular classes and the allocation of school funds. Each time I listened to their concerns one-on-one or in a small group, I suggested that for conditions to change they should also speak directly to the corresponding staff member; much to my surprise, they were scared to do so. In an attempt to overcome this impasse while acknowledging their self-reflection, I suggested that they try expressing themselves using a different modality: writing a memo. Astonishingly, in front of their peers, they sought my permission to begin typing their grievances. I would not have predicted this response based on the variety of noneducational files that I have stumbled on when searching through a junior high student's virtual locker for a missing assignment. With this newly invested authority, I enacted a condition raised by a student not associated with the group: the memo must also propose practical solutions. There were some grievances listed with no new ideas provided; for example, why are students required to learn about the history of a subject? Others disclaimed individual responsibility: teachers should not be biased against certain talkative students when the whole class is behaving inappropriately. The accusation that the majority of school fund-raising was wasted on Popsicles™ was a bit naive; however, it was encouraging that improved water fountains, parks and woodworking and sewing materials were suggested in place of frozen treats and even computer technology. Finally, more student input, possibly collected via an online survey, was requested in the selection of activities other than presentations about volunteering for the weekly open community period.

With the group's permission, I attempted to address each of the raised issues in front of the couple of classes that had already heard about the memo. We spoke of analyzing the past to better understand how the shaping of ideas and narratives contributes to our present experiences; of how we can only control our own actions, but can be a model for others; of how there were no roadblocks to using educational technologies to solicit constructive feedback from students regarding their learning spaces; and of how relatively inexpensive a box of Freezies™ is.

The students also asked that I share the memo with other junior high teachers. I had already planned on doing so, though I did not anticipate some of their responses. The memo was viewed as a petition or list of demands. Student concerns should be deflected by verbally directing students to the appropriate staff member; having them written down might necessitate a response or action. The school would appear in an unflattering light if the document ended up being circulated amongst the wider school community. The names of the students in the group were recorded, and any further discussion in class would be ill advised, as it would only serve to exacerbate the situation. The best-case scenario would be that the students would forget all about it over the weekend.

Standing in stark juxtaposition was Lio, whose separate uprising seemed to grow by the day. The campaign was against the imposed seating plan. My suggestion of giving it a try as a way of being open to new opportunities did nothing to assuage the complaint accompanying Lio's daily greeting. I was presented with studies showing how students learned best when they had a choice of seat, a strategy with which I experimented for the first half of the year. Realizing that I was not yet persuaded, Lio then announced Students United. This association already had Lio as its leader and sole member, a custom logo and a manifesto urging students to rail against my tyrannical reign. I decided to enter into negotiations to determine the group's demands. It turns out that all Lio wanted was to sit at his old spot, which was now vacant. He enjoyed working with his current elbow partners, but had all his favorites and files saved locally on the previous computer workstation.

At the time of writing, the Jefferson County school board had abandoned its planned review of the AP history course; it released a vague statement that such action was no longer necessary. Unfortunately, my earlier two uprisings met a different fate. The Grievance Memo might have been a small step made by a group of students towards greater accountability for and meta-cognition about their learning. The freedom of the weekend prevailed and it was never mentioned again in class. Lio, who supposedly rarely spoke in other courses, had found an issue on which he wanted his voice heard. After I granted his request, Students United stopped trying to recruit new members. It may just be the naïveté of a teacher early in their career, but I hope that I can keep learning spaces fertile for future uprisings—maybe even medium-sized ones.

CHAPTER TWENTY-SIX

(Here Is) Where You Are Supposed To Be

JESSICA KELLY

Dear New Teacher,

> *We actualize reality, without ever completing it, with stories.*
> *Our stories are never finished; and therefore never unfinished.*
> *If reality itself is always incomplete, each moment becomes complete itself, lacking nothing.*
> —DAVID LOY (2010, P. 40)

This passage spoke to me, as I had always been a person who thought of life in chapters. Sections. Specific groupings of time.

In my first few years of teaching I kept waiting for things to "click" and make sense. "When will I feel that I have all the answers?" I thought.

Through my time spent studying in graduate school, I have been able to reflect on and appreciate the unknown. The unplanned. I can wait for things to come to me. I feel that I will never have everything make sense and know now that I don't want all the answers.

In your first few years of teaching, try to find a support system.

This person isn't someone to complain to. Discussing what you dislike most about work is toxic and simply not healthy to do all the time. Find a way to voice your questions and concerns about education and have people really listen to you. Don't look for answers but share and welcome the words of others that let you find comfort.

Being able to make peace with things and have some of the day-to-day roll off your back is a necessary skill.

Be in the classroom. Physically, mentally and emotionally.

Please don't worry about feeling as though things are complete.

Focus on the experience, not the lesson plan.

Appreciate the job you are doing and appreciate yourself.

It is easy to blame yourself and assume you're not doing enough.

Your story is being written each day and to want it to end is to want the journey and experience to come to a close also.

Knowing yourself and what lies ahead at each turn would make for a very boring life—and classroom.

You are where you are supposed to be.

CHAPTER TWENTY-SEVEN

River Otters AND Such

JUDSON INNES

Last winter I had the good fortune to watch a family of river otters play in the frigid onrushing waters of the Sliammon River, which flows through the Sliammon Reservation into the Salish Sea on the west coast of British Columbia.

So I watch the river otters for a while on this December day, as they chase and wrestle, tumble and intermittently intertwine over large rocks covered in thick, electric-green moss, into pools of smooth, fast running water, and onto the shoreline, dense with tangled vegetation. One otter, free from the group for a short time, and fully submerged, suspends itself midstream, neither progressing nor losing ground. Rather, this lone otter hovers within the water, just beneath the surface, adjusting to the speed of the rapids through the powerful whip action of its long and tapered tail. Of course it's not all fun and games for the otters as they attend to the business of staying alive, though it is hard to ascertain where the play stops and the work begins. Perhaps there is no difference.

The Sliammon People, whose land this river runs through, have occupied this area, according to myth, shell middens and the Simon Fraser University Archaeology Department, for at least eight thousand years. One would assume that as soon as the great sheets of ice that once covered and shaped these lands retreated, at the end of the most recent Ice Age, the people moved in. Otters too.

Europeans began exploring the coastline around here in earnest in the 1700s, the list of explorers including those famous and infamous: James Cook, George Vancouver and Francisco Quadra, to name just a few. In passing through, they often named places they visited, with many of these names remaining today: Nootka Sound, Cortez and Quadra Islands, as well as the city of Vancouver. Though, of course, these landscapes had already been given names by the very people who stood before them. A curious turn from mastery to domination, helped along by a collective mind closed like a clenched fist.

Just over a century ago, Europeans, primarily, returned to the traditional lands of the Sliammon People to stay. Quickly they set to work subduing the land, or more accurately the trees; the massive, towering hemlock, spruce, cypress, cedar and Douglas fir trees that sit watch over the coastal rain forest: nourishing and protecting the flora and fauna around them, often for a thousand years at a time. When the Sliammon People, by now dispossessed of most of their traditional land and moved onto the reservation, saw the destruction all around them, they warned, "This is all just short-term thinking." Few listened.

Now, eight months on from that cold December day on the banks of the Sliammon River, and at the leading edge of another school year, I am faced with the question of how to take up topics of ecology and the environment with my grade five students. I could start the year with another story of destruction and denial, and no doubt wouldn't have to look too far for examples.

The Mount Polley tailings pond breach is certainly a story that needs to be told. For those unfamiliar, Mount Polley is the site of a gold and copper mine in south-central British Columbia near the town of Quesnel. In August 2014, ten million cubic metres of toxic sludge containing elements such as arsenic, copper and mercury, to name a few, were released into Polley Lake and its surrounding waterways when an earthen dam gave way. Of course, after days of silence came the usual denial, with a host of BC government officials quickly pronouncing the area "safe for humans."

Perhaps, though, I could start the year with a different story. On a warm Sunday evening late in August, just a few weeks ago, I was alerted by a neighbor to a migrating pod of Orca whales she had spotted while out on her porch. Eager to see them, I hustled down the street and soon found myself at the edge of the bluff directly above the calm Salish Sea watching three Orcas feeding on a school of herring. By now, the sun had sunk behind the jagged peaks of the Vancouver Island's Beaufort Mountain Range directly to the west. As the light faded in a soft orange and yellow glow the crowd on the bluff swelled to well over a hundred: with people materializing out of the gathering darkness a few at a time.

Silenced, we watched the Orca repeatedly breach the surface, rise up and smash the water with their tails, disappear beneath a rush of foam and turmoil before returning a short while later to swallow the now-stunned herring one at a time. For over an hour the Orca, hard at work, continued their choreographed carousel. The crowd stood shoulder to shoulder entranced by this awesome display, vaguely aware of one another, though maybe each increasingly aware of our own insignificance.

Eventually, when the last rays of twilight had receded, the people seemingly faded away. Alone now in near darkness, guided only by the faint light emitted by the eternal stars overhead, I left the bluff behind and wandered home.

Perhaps this story of our beautiful, sacred world might be the place to start with my students. I will let them draw their own conclusions, now and later, about the proper place of humans within it.

CHAPTER TWENTY-EIGHT

My Teacher Supply List

KAREN SCHWEIGHARDT

These are the things I find useful, mostly.

Paper cutter—favourite tool. I love the strong
thud of the arm as it smashes down on the board. I once used it as a musical
instrument to the
Song "takin' care of business"—THUD—"every day!"
Works every time. Measure first! Not an OH&S problem
Fight to keep.

Overhead projector, good for demonstrating groups in math
—great for blowing up images for art projects, you can
Make great portraits of anything using this method.
—fantastic for demonstrating EVERYTHING in grade 4 light and
Shadow unit, we made digital and stop action stories from shadow figures
Placed on an overhead and projected on the wall
Make Feist-like displays for the hallway
Don't let the janitor take it to the WAREHOUSE.
Warehouse means you'll never see it again.

Stapler. Works 62%, put name on with masking tape, which
People can rip off. My school won't buy the good ones with
the swing arm anymore, which sucks for putting up kids' work

Masking tape. 100% chance of being stolen. I put name on
the edge with Sharpie.

Hole punch. Most reliable of the bunch
I love the happy accident of paper hole confetti
Label with Sharpie.
Gets "borrowed." Look for it in neighbouring rooms.

Large scissors—stolen, put name on with Sharpie,
Casually spy when you're in other rooms to see if
It "accidentally" got borrowed.

Pencil sharpener on wall. Stopped working in 1985
Always getting bumped and receptacle falls off 114
Times per day. Still miss it.

Electric pencil sharpener—doesn't work, never did
Throw it out.

Manual pencil sharpener, keep in desk drawer, mark
With a Sharpie.

Mr. Sketch. Simply the best art supply. Label with labels or Sharpies.

Sharpies. Indispensable. Buy 5000, 4000 black, rest coloured.
All thicknesses.

CHAPTER TWENTY-NINE

Hypoplastic Left Heart Syndrome

CARLI MOLNAR

I decided to become a teacher because I envisioned myself spending joy-filled days creatively living with children. Six years ago, I began my journey into teaching. Over time, I realized that my vision of education often lives in tension with the rigid confines of formal schooling. I experienced this discord in my first teaching practicum. There were many joyful experiences within my practicum, but with time, I began to feel inundated with workbooks, unit plans, reading intervention strategies, worksheets, behaviour management techniques, and so on. Seeing how dedicated many teachers around me were to this formulaic teaching regime, I began to feel that, despite my better judgment, this must be proper schooling. I began to believe that perhaps I needed to abandon, or at least scale back, my vision of creative and joyous living with children and adopt the mainstream attitudes that seemed to surround me.

So, like many beginning teachers, I latched onto what I was shown. Many of my first experiences in my practicums involved watching stand-and-deliver lessons that attempted to transmit general knowledge of targeted curricular outcomes from teacher to student. I mirrored this pedagogy and was praised. Despite how rigid and uninspiring it felt, I assumed I must be doing it right. Yet I knew this monotonous ritual of knowledge transmission couldn't be the world I put before children each day. I couldn't hop over the life world carelessly.

I began to study. I found reprieve within educational philosopher David Smith's book *Pedagon* (1999). In one piece, Smith's words awakened something within me: "Young people want to know, if under the cool and calm of efficient teaching and time on task ratios, life itself has a chance, or if the surface is all there is" (p. 27). Life itself. I need to live with children. We need to be together. To talk. To share. To mourn. To laugh.

I also found solace within a close network of colleagues who shared similar questions about and visions for education. By routinely connecting with this group of educators, I began to realize I was not alone outside of the dominant discourse.

In 2010, I graduated with my B.Ed. and officially began teaching. I found myself living in the tension between curriculum-as-plan and curriculum-as-lived (Aoki, 2005, p. 159). It was joy and a struggle. I did the best I could to create a place where learning was sustained by experiencing genuine life together, trying to remember what mattered and what didn't. I continued to study. Poet Ben Okri's (1997) words reminded me of what I needed to do each day:

> Learn some of the miracles. Survive. Weave your transformations in your life as well as in your work. Live. Stay alive. Don't go under, don't go mad, don't let them define you, or confine you, or buy your silence. If they do confine you, burst out of their prisons with wilder fatidical songs. Be a counter-antagonist, break their anti-myths. Where the enemies breed destructions, sow seeds of startling lights. Keep sowing. Time will reap. Weave your songs by whatever means you can. (p. 14)

In my third year of teaching, despite studying and networking with other educators in similar positions, I continued to grapple with the dichotomy between traditional schooling and what I wanted school to be for children. I decided to continue my education by taking some graduate courses. Now, through these graduate studies, I am gaining a richer understanding of the historical context of education, of how schools became the kinds of places they are, and also of many kinds of educational research that might inform curriculum and pedagogy, including interpretive methodologies such as hermeneutics, life writing, and poetic inquiry. I have studied the works of many educational philosophers and poets, such as Ted Aoki, Maxine Greene, Wendell Berry, David Smith, and Dwayne Donald. Writing about my practice as well as reading and engaging in these inquiries with other teachers have enriched my work as a teacher. So has Kole.

In 2012, I met Kole. I was told by his parents that he had a terminal illness and would likely not live past his 18th birthday. I had the honour and the immense responsibility of being his Grade Two teacher. I had no idea he would become my teacher, too.

The collection of stories that follow live within the tension between the stated aims and goals of schools in our society and our awareness of the fragile mortality of all of our lives. Kole illuminates a critical dilemma in our system of education: Why is it necessary that a young, terminally ill boy be required to go to school to learn how to become an efficient member of society? Why should he prepare for a future that he will not have?

This piece of poetic inquiry has emerged from the lessons that Kole taught me about life. I am drawn to expressing important topics through poetic inquiry because of the way it enables events and emotions to be explored in a non-rational, non-literal way. I have composed this piece for many of the same reasons that poet Carl Leggo (2012) writes:

> I write poetry in order to share questions and insights with others. I write in order to learn to be still … as a way to know the world, as a way to be and become in the world … to create, to know, to engage creatively with experience. (p. 380)

In this writing, I meditate on what Kole taught me about what truly matters in classrooms each day and in the lives of each delicate human being. Throughout this paper, Kole offers a reminder of the fragile hearts beating within each of us at this very moment.

beat.

Version One: Kole
Curious. Imaginative. Mindful. Wise beyond his years. Has an instantly contagious laugh. Loves vehicles, drawing, creating his own books, learning about outer space, painting and building. Takes time to do careful work. Has cultivated a breathtaking, slowed relationship with time. Inspired by wonder-filled questions and theories about the world around him.

beat.

Version Two: Kole's File
Student Number 45324. Six-year-old male. Multiple concerns. Behavioural and medical disorders. Sees an occupational therapist weekly at the school to assist with difficulty cutting with scissors and holding his pencil properly. Socialization concerns. Interacts well with adults but not with children. Often defiant and does not complete his work. Questions the rules and does not sit still for more than five minutes at a time. Speaks out of turn and disturbs others while they are working. Requires support to complete most classroom tasks. Reads and writes at pre-Kindergarten level. Has missed over 50 days of school.

The words of Smith (1999) offer deeper insight into Kole's file: "We speak of 'children' instead of Jane, Mary or John, so that John's particular reading problems are deflected into theories of reading difficulty rather than attending to the specifics of John's life" (p. 90).

Kole's file suggests that his academic and behavioural needs are critical while the specifics of his life do not affect his file nor do they matter enough to be noted.

beat.

Kole was born with a rare congenital heart defect known as Hypoplastic Left Heart Syndrome (HLHS). He has already had over 23 surgeries and has spent much of his life in the hospital. He is doing alright now, but his life expectancy is uncertain.

The doctors say his condition is terminal.

beat.

Kole's favourite part of our time together in Grade 2 was the start of each day, when the children would scatter throughout the classroom finding comfortable spots, each clutching a loved book from our classroom library. The children would settle into peaceful spots and transport themselves to the worlds within picture books.

Each morning, Kole would carefully scan the classroom, looking for one of the children in our class who was reading a book that he wanted to listen to. When he found the child with that special book, he would curl up beside them and listen intently. The child that Kole chose to read with would position the book in front of him and read to him lovingly.

The other children knew what Kole needed. They knew that he was only beginning to learn to read. They knew he had a hard time making friends. They knew he needed their love, so that's what the children did: They loved him. They didn't try to "fix" him, or rush to teach him how to read. They were patient. They simply read to him. And inadvertently, these children helped Kole learn to read, by nurturing in him a love of books, by spending time cuddled in close reading to him, loving him into a reader.

Put children and their natural curiosity together with a competent reader with the time and inclination to watch over the children as they come into contact with books and almost unaware, youngsters will confidently declare: "I can read." "Like any other form of learning, learning to read is a relational activity—it depends upon a relationship" (Smith, 1999, p. 71).

beat.

Individual Program Plan Goals:

Kole will remain seated for 10 minutes while completing a given task 4/5 times a week.

Kole will raise his hand before he speaks 80% of the time.

Kole will correctly identify 50 pre-primer sight words with 100% accuracy.

beat.

When a child is not reading in Grade 2, alarms go off. Intervention is established. Children are pulled from their classrooms for help because educators fear they will fall behind if they do not catch up. A routine of flash cards, phonics worksheets, and guided reading programs are implemented. Panicked teachers breathe a sigh of relief. With lots of rigorous practice and repetitive drills these children might be alright by Grade 3. They can be fixed.

But perhaps, as Smith (1999) suggests, "If we can become more at ease with things not immediately understood, more patient in dealing with life's essential difficulties and more hungry for a simple love of the world itself as our earthly home, maybe we have a chance for taking one small creative step into the future" (p. 23). Maybe intervention needs to be replaced with time, love, patience and exploring together amidst beautiful books.

Poet John J. Guiney Yallop (2012) reminds us, "What's important becomes part of us, part of who we are, part of how we live with ourselves and with others— how we live in the world" (p. 106). Children and teachers deserve more important work than phonics drills and sight word recognition activities. They deserve to engage in thoughtful learning that has the potential to become rooted within them and alter the way they live in the world each day.

beat.

December. It was Kole's turn to bring something to share with the class. He began by standing up and confidently lifting his shirt, showing everyone his chest. Some of the children gasped. Scars covered his chest, stomach, and even his back. "These are my scars from all my surgeries," he explained.

He told everyone about a helicopter ride he took when he was a baby to rush him to the hospital, and he shared stories of his most loved nurses from some of his hospital trips. He explained how he was fed juice through a feeding tube in his stomach and that he almost died during two different surgeries.

The intimate conversation that was invited into our classroom after Kole's sharing was one of sadness, joy, suffering, existential wonder, and love.

beat.

What matters each day in a classroom where a young child's days are limited? Or even in a classroom where mortality is (seemingly) distant for all?

What work calls to us?

How might teachers take up the careful, delicate work of life? Life that is concerned with stories, memories, grieving, joy and creativity. Life where we are not devoured by busy work, preparation for the future, consumerism and lethal promises.

Philosopher Ludwig Wittgenstein (as cited in Klagge, 2001) reminds us: "For life in the present there is no death. Death is not an event in life. It is not a fact in the world. Our life is endless, in just the same way that our field of vision has no boundaries" (p. 114).

beat.

"Cut along the zigzag line on this paper, Kole."
"Why? What am I making?"
"Nothing. We're just practicing cutting on different lines."
"Why?"
"So that you improve your cutting skills."
"For what? (pause) Can I be done now?"
"We need to finish this, Kole. It's important."
"Children in today's classrooms have virtually no time to simply dream, wait, think, ponder or learn to be still. There is so little opportunity to find one's original face, because every space is seen to require some sort of instructional intervention." (Smith, 1999, p. 24)

beat.

Are we inspiring children to be sustained by imagining, creating, pausing, being joyful, peaceful, filled with wonder, love, and life?

Or are we forcing them to become driven by competition, progress, the future, globalization, consumerism, accountability, and fear?

Who are we inviting into our classrooms each day?

Who are each of these children who wait for us in single-file lines as the bell rings each morning?

Are we letting every part of every child come to school each day?

Or are we trampling these naturally curious, imaginative beings, brainwashing them with narrow worksheets and mundane, autonomous tasks that systematically teach children how to be efficient workers so that they can one day achieve some utopian sense of adulthood?

What does the institution of schooling tell children? It says, today doesn't matter. We're working for the future. Today you're just a student, in the future you can be more.

Maxine Greene (1995) asks us to consider: How many things do we do each day that contribute to our non-being (p. 23)? Filling in worksheets. Mindlessly regurgitating mathematical formulas. Surely children do not exist well in the world while participating in unauthentic activities meant to prepare them for tomorrow.

How can we enhance our lives so that we do not exist only to cycle through the mundane tasks of day-to-day life?

As Annie Dillard (1990) reminds us, "How we spend our days is, of course, how we spend our lives" (p. 32), making the moments we spend truly present in this world of utmost importance.

There isn't a set plan that we need to follow each day. It is within this unmapped space that "we are free to move, to breathe fresh air, to understand this life, to live with one another and with ourselves. To imagine life differently. To be reinvented. To fall in" (Seidel, 1999, p. 13).

beat.

Time is neither young nor old,
but simply new,
always counting,
the only apocalypse. (Berry, 2010, p. 40)

beat.

I wonder how fast trains go.
I wonder what's inside the middle of the earth.
I wonder how our eyes work.
I wonder what I will be when I grow up.
I wonder what a star feels like to touch.
I wonder why we dream.
I wonder what heaven looks like.
−Kole

beat.

Kole has his own rhythm of time. I noticed throughout our time together in Grade 2 that his peaceful nature constantly clashed with the formalities of the institution of schooling.

During recess, Kole usually skipped into the school five minutes after the bell, usually followed by an irritated recess supervisor reminding him of the need to stop playing and line up when the bell rings.

Kole missed the bus a few times while in Grade 2 because he would take his time getting there, stopping to enjoy simple moments. One day he missed the bus because he found a fresh pile of snow along the way and decided to leap into the pile and play.

Another day, Kole was missing during lunch time. He was found playing outside when the children were all supposed to be in the gym eating. "I wasn't hungry so I wanted to go play outside early," he explained, not understanding why the lunchroom supervisor was so concerned.

Kole was always the last one out of our classroom when we went anywhere. He liked to take his time when we walked through the hallways, stopping to talk to other children or teachers, or simply to enjoy pieces of art displayed on the walls along the way.

Kole is deeply attuned to a slowed pace in the world and I watched his peaceful nature colliding with the rushed nature of formal schooling. Many times, Kole ended up in trouble with teachers or administrators because of his slowed relationship with time.

One can learn from the stillness with which Kole experiences life. He taught me that in order "to be attuned to life where grace may appear, one needs to learn a poetic pattern of attention to the surroundings of those lives, attention that turns and turns again" (Fidyk, 2012, p. 349).

Kole mindfully enjoys each moment of his fragile life. The structure of school, on the other hand, rushes him along, trying to rob him of these moments of simple joy.

beat.

If we knew the number of days we have to live, would we plan our days differently?

beat.

Jumping in a pile of brittle, autumn leaves.
Sharing a well-loved book.
Finger painting.
Catching an icy snowflake on your tongue.

"These moments might be appreciated differently were we not accustomed to sacrifice them to the future" (Loy, 2010, p. 19).

beat.

It was a bright June morning. Kole slowly walked into the classroom a few minutes after the other children, delicately carrying something in his hands. He slowly opened his hands and whispered excitedly, "A black beetle! I found him before school! I named him Todd!" The children gathered around, curious. The morning's plans were instantly replaced by this invitation to wonder.

Together, we spent the morning observing Todd's smooth shell, admiring his long antennae, sketching his shiny body and learning numerous beetle facts from Kole. Can we keep him in our classroom? the children wanted to know. Before I could answer, Kole's voice called out: "If we keep Todd, he won't have a fair life, trapped in a jar, walking around in circles. He needs to be free. We have to let him go so he can live like he wants to."

The children nodded. They knew what was right. We followed as Kole carefully carried the fragile beetle outside, thoughtfully placing him at the base of a tree, watching as his new friend returned to the earth.

beat.

Kole loves to make imaginative and original books. At the beginning of Grade 2, he would draw intricate pictures that told magical and detailed tales. Once he had filled a book with careful, involved drawings, he would rush over to tell me the stories within his wordless books.

One day, not out of the ordinary, I felt Kole's gentle but persistent finger tapping at my side. He was eager to share his book with me, perhaps more fervent than usual: This time, accompanied by his detailed pictures, carefully sounded-out words filled the pages.

He explained. "I have been realizing that if people want to know my important stories forever, I have to write the words down, because maybe I won't always be here to tell them how my story is supposed to go."

beat.

"The distracting, distancing vision of preparing for the future, of rushing ever forward, may create a sense that our own mortality will never come and can always be postponed, we can behave as if we, and those we teach, are immortal" (Seidel, 2014, p. 134)

Life cannot be postponed.
Mortality is nearer than we think.

beat.

Kole is now in Grade 4. Every time I see him bound through the hallways, I am reminded of the fluidity of life. With inspiration from Kole, I am able to see what is important each day. We are not immortal. Our time on this earth is uncertain. We have an obligation to time and to the difficult, important work of living well today. Canadian poet Don Domanski (2002) echoes the transformative life lesson that Kole taught me in his writing about "the slender sadness:"

> [It] runs through every moment of existence, about the fleetingness of lives lived in a world where nothing can be saved. [It is] entering that state of being with a joy and wonder that comes from that very impermanency, from the absolute dispossession of everything we love and cherish. The wonder is that anything at all exists. The joy is that it does, even if it is as momentary as a human life. We can live this as a mode of attention, we can live within its movements, its cycles and treasure the phases, the round of it. (p. 246)

beat.

My Promises
Inspired by Kole

I promise
to breathe

to dwell on the important
to be absolved of the unimportant
and to be still

I promise to remain in open spaces with children
where we can create beautiful things
that are worthwhile(ing) over

I will
play explore create imagine

I promise to plan for each day
creative and joyful experiences

I promise to question
Is there life here?

I will listen

I promise to let every part
of every child
come to school each day

I promise to cut the carrot
when I'm cutting a carrot

I will pause
I will wonder
I will meditate

I promise to trust the journey
and to live well
today

beat.

"And this is when I see that this life is a miracle, absolutely worth having, absolutely worth saving" (Berry, 2001, p. 85).

beat.

CHAPTER THIRTY

Echolocations

JACKIE SEIDEL, DAVID W. JARDINE, DEIRDRE BAILEY,
HOLLY GRAY, MIRANDA HECTOR, JUDSON INNES,
CAROLE JONES, TANYA KOWALCHUK, NEELAM MAL,
JENNIFER MEREDITH, CARLI MOLNAR, PETER RILSTONE,
TRISH SAVILL, KARI SIRUP, LESLEY TAIT, LISA TAYLOR,
AND DARREN VAAST

THE TRUE NAMES OF BIRDS

There are more ways to abandon a child
than to leave them at the mouth of the woods.
Sometimes by the time you find them, they've made up names
for all the birds and constellations, and they've broken
their reflections in the lake with sticks.

With my daughter came promises and vows
that unfolded through time like a roadmap and led me
to myself as a child, filled with wonder for my father
who could make sound from a wide blade of grass

and his breath. Here in the stillness of forest,
the sun columning before me temple-ancient,
that wonder is what I regret losing most; that wonder
and the true names of birds.
                              Sue Goyette (1998, p. 11)

This chapter was originally composed as an oral presentation at the Eighth International Imagination in Education Research Conference in Vancouver, British Columbia, July 2013. We begin with Sue Goyette's lovely poem that inspired our work and was one of our texts.

In the middle of a set of four graduate courses that we undertook from May 2012 to April 2013, and in which we explored the hermeneutic and ecological roots of rich inquiry in the classroom, Neelam Mal brought in a book entitled *Nightsong* (2012) by Ari Berk and illustrator Loren Long.

Its immediate appeal was in a particular passage that seems to echo the experiences we were now starting to have repeatedly as our explorations continued:

> The sun had set, and the shadows clinging to the walls of the cave began to wake and whisper.
>
> "Chiro? Little wing?" the bat-mother said to her child. "Tonight you must fly out into the world, and I will wait here for you."
>
> "But the night is dark, Momma … darker than the moth's dark eyes … darker even than the water before dawn," the little bat exclaimed, twitching his ears this way and that.
>
> "I know," whispered his mother.
>
> "And when it is that dark outside, I cannot always see," Chiro admitted, stretching his wings.
>
> "There are other ways to see," she told him, "other ways to help you make your way in the world"
>
> "How?"
>
> "Use your good sense."
>
> "What is sense?" the little bat asked.
>
> His mother folded him in her wings and whispered into his waiting ears, "Sense is the song you sing out into the world, and the song the world sings back to you. Sing, and the world will answer. That is how you'll see."
>
> … And then she let him go. (n.p.)

We'd all started to experience something of this, of reading out a passage in our class from David Smith or Cynthia Chambers or videos and writings of Maxine Greene, or of Thich Nhat Hanh speaking with David Suzuki, or Edward Espe Brown speaking of Buddhism and bread making, or instructions on how to make a mandala, or Sue Goyette's and Don Domanski's poetry, and in each gestural move, hearing these things echo off memories of previous classes, turning into small classroom experiments that someone documented online of their grade two children's mandala work, or a story of mornings and families and birds in the backyard, or an anecdote or thread of family history, years ago, or meditating on Styrofoam cups, or a poem whose authorship had faded. The longer our class went on, the richer became these echoes until, near the end of that phase of our work together, vast echoing silences often overtook our gatherings as the voices of "responding and summoning" (Gadamer, 1989, p. 458) gaped open and drew us in. Just as often, gales of laughter or gasps of deep recognition erupted, and we spent ever-increasing time with each other over food and the most lovely commiserations. Teachers, kids, hard work, and finding deeper and deeper soils as we went. Finding that the seeming "radicalness" of what we were pursuing actually linked back, etymologically, to a sense of "rootedness" (Latin: *radix*).

Like radishes!

From 1650 onwards, "going to the origin, essential" (Online Etymology Dictionary, 2014b).

Jackie Seidel told us about new research being conducted on whales and their echoing songs and it became clear, once again, not that "'this is that' but this is a story about that, this is *like* that" (Clifford & Marcus, 1986, p. 100). We heard this tale as a great allegory to our work with students and with fellow teachers, an allegory to our developing and newfound refuge in echo-proximity to each other. We aren't crazy, and our seeming radicalism is not against the grain of things but with a grain deeper and more sustaining than the shiny false promises of much of our profession.

These whales not only locate each other in a vast three-dimensional space, but also can locate the locating of other whales locating each other. An e-mail from Jackie to David:

> I think the "location" part is interesting because it hints towards how much it matters that we know *where* we are and what the contours of that space are and who is sharing it with us. There is a kind of present-ness to it all that relates to what we've been talking about in our class ... to be 'in' time and 'in' place requires a different kind of echoing learning/knowing. When the whales (or bats) are echolocating themselves, it is for right now, to learn their way about the place they are actually in, not some other place. Scientists who study whales say they know so little about how any of this works, or what the whales are actually experiencing. They know they can "hear" distant pods and are probably collecting information from them as well ... they don't know if the entire ocean is one huge echo communication space for cetaceans. They haven't evolved at all for something like 50 million years since they went back into the water from land. It's so amazing. They have highly developed senses and social abilities, possibly greater than humans. There are so few of them left compared to 100 years ago. But whales live a very long time so there would be whales alive who probably "remember" when they were abundant. The emotion part of the whale brain is at least as developed as humans. I wonder how they think about what has happened to them?

"Their echoes, it seems, can reach right into the flesh of other whales" (Warren, 2012).

... ...

Shut eyes
    Take breath
        Breathe ...
            ... Pause ...

Open, move
Sway,
    Poised,
        with grace.
          Miranda Hector

... ...

Something happens to you as you read the words written by others. They become intertwined with the fabric of you. They carefully wrap themselves around your neurons, heart muscles and bones of your body, ensuring their survival with you.

As I read my grandmother's words, I find a way to visit the echoes she has left behind. I become the precocious child who found herself at odds with her mother's Victorian understandings. I am she and she is I. I am the immigrant to Canada traveling by train alone, pregnant and full of both fear and excitement. I am the new mother in a new country who writes home with feelings of adventure mixed with a touch of regret. I am the old women who has maintained her spirit and still finds herself involved in the occasional mischief. She, for a brief time, is at home within me.

Her words and her being will continue to reside and echo within me.

Watching Maxine Greene on the screen created a deep wish within me. I want her to be my grandmother. Could her spirit and essence help guide me? With time and thought, I realized, she already was.

Lesley Tait

... ...

Themes develop, overlap, expand and repeat
Experiences multiply and perspectives change while the soul remains undisturbed.
paraphrasing Maxine Greene (2001, p. x)

As I consider the underlined and fervently starred passages from years ago, I am reminded of a former self. A self changed by experience. Made different for the better and in many ways, worse.

The passages beckon. They call me back to a time that was simple. Idyllic. As a new teacher, I knew little and held on to those passages with the desperation that inexperience brings. They were all I had. I did not know curriculum, rubrics or competencies. I was not ruined by instructional minutes, outcomes or benchmarks. Ignorant of the science of teaching, I was free to lose myself in the art of being with children in unmeasured moments.

Still, to share what we notice, free from the strings of accountability. That was all I had. That was all I knew.

The longer I teach, the more I realize what is unimportant.

Kari Sirup

... ...

"Sense is the song you sing out into the world, and the song the world sings back to you"
Ari Berk & Loren Long (2012, n.p.)

... ...

My children have been waking up early lately and it has been driving my husband, Chad, and me a bit crazy, well a lot crazy. We've been taking turns getting up with them while the other stays dozing and warm for a little bit longer. This morning was my turn to stay in bed and sleep. We live in a small house, so I can hear everything being said down the hall. It went something like this:

Chad: Buddy, why are you up so early?
Jake: The birds are singing to me, dad.
Chad: Hmm, let's get something to eat.
Jake: Why are the birds singing to us, dad?
Chad: I don't know. Let's get some breakfast.
Jake: I love when the birds sing to me, dad.
Chad: What do you want to eat for breakfast?
Jake: Can we look and see if we can see the birds that are singing to us, dad?

Lisa Taylor

... ...

We have completely forgotten that the trivialization of joy in learning isn't the real world. In our rush for scholarship and superficial memorization of out-of-context data, we unthinkingly absorb the message that this just is the way things are. It isn't the way things are, it's the way we've made them. History has handed us over to a way of living and learning that doesn't allow us the opportunity to know things properly.

Deirdre Bailey

... ...

Our topic is echolocation. The process of navigating our way in the world by sending out pulses of sound and interpreting the returning echo. If you do this by yourself, then what you get reflected back is only a measure of your own perspective alone ...

Darren Vaast

... ...

Catch only what you've thrown yourself and all is mere skill and little gain. But when you're suddenly the catcher of a ball, thrown towards you, towards your center ...
Rainer Maria Rilke, from the frontispiece of
Hans-Georg Gadamer's *Truth and Method* (1989)

... ...

... when you are in a community of others all on the same journey then your sonic senses are amplified, modified and shaped by the perceptions of others around you. You get a clearer view of the world around you—a more three-dimensional understanding, if you will. As teachers, we experience this every year.

Darren Vaast

... ...

We read Jackie Seidel's "A Curriculum for Miracles": "With more breath. I learned to expect miracles and also to create space for miracles to happen. I learned that life itself is a miracle and that we are miracles, each of us."

...

BREATH

... ...

Jake: Can we look and see if we can see the birds that are singing to us, dad?
(This was the miracle. "Expect miracles and create space for miracles.")

In the end, all four of us wrapped ourselves in blankets, and sat quietly in the middle of the lawn, looking for the birds that were singing to us.

Our next step is to name them and to recognize their songs.

Lisa Taylor

... ...

"... they've made up names
for all the birds ..."

Susan Goyette (1998, p. 11)

... ...

Shut eyes
    Take breath
        Breathe ...
           ... Pause ...
Open, move
Sway,
    Poised,
        with grace.

Miranda Hector

... ...

A Simple Snowstorm:
It was April 11th, an ordinary day that the children called magical.

The children were working at their desks on a task that neither I nor the students can remember now. I think it was math. Outside our classroom windows, April snow was falling steadily. Giant, delicate flakes of snow were dancing through the open sky, seeming to mock our still, rigid bodies, stifled by hard desks. It had been one of those dreaded indoor recess days, not because of cold, but because of how wet and puddly it was outside. Something about not wanting the children to get wet in the puddles.

The snow was now falling more heavily, almost blizzard-like. We quietly got our jackets on and snuck outside the back door of the school.

Together, we ran outside, breathing in the crisp air and instantly feeling the soft blizzard powder tickling our faces and covering our hair. The children opened their mouths to catch the wet flakes on their tongues. We laughed at how silly we looked covered in the snow, lay on our backs and watched the snow falling towards us and we darted through the snowflakes chasing one another.

We became soaked.

"It's like we're having a shower with heaven water!" one child remarked joyfully.

"That was the best day of my life!" one boy announced when we arrived back in our classroom.

Carli Molnar

··· ···

Let's consider an ecological analogy to these isolated, deliberately unsurrounded, worldless, school activities. Consider this Styrofoam cup I'm just about to throw away. Any relations of it or to it cannot be cultivated, chosen, cared for, remembered, enjoyed, either by us or anything else that surrounds it. I cannot easily become composed around such a thing and it does not ask this of me [consider Lesley Tait's favourite passage that echoed in our class again and again, from a text composed by Tsong-kha-pa in 1406 in Tibet: "I compose this in order to condition my own mind" (2000, p. 111)]. There will be no mourning at its loss or destruction. It is not something to be saved or savoured. It does not show its having-ar-rived-here and we have no need to try to remember such an arrival. All trace of relations and endurance are seemingly gone. It appears, and then disappears, and its appearance is geared to not being noticed.

This Styrofoam cup does not *endure*. It does not age and become becoming in such aging. It breaks.

It cannot learn from its surroundings and show the wear of such learning on its aging face. And therefore, in its presence, the prospect of pedagogy is turned away.

In fact, it is produced *deliberately* in order to *not* last, *not* hold attention, *not* take on character, *not* arouse any sense or possibility of care or concern. *It is deliberately produced in order to not be remembered.*

It is deliberately produced of forgetting. It is *Lethe*. It is lethal.

David Jardine (2012, p. 139), from "Figures in Hell"

··· ···

One day, Trish asked: "What is the Styrofoam cup in the classroom?" We all stopped still.

A Styrofoam cup is disposable, yet permanent, like the worksheets and the fragmented activities so many children do in classrooms. The worksheets, the spelling tests, the unimportant tasks are disposable, yet the effect they have on children is often permanent. As the Styrofoam cups stack up, our ability to imagine, invent and create dwindles and the world as black and white becomes reality.

We can't care for Styrofoam cups and children can't care for disposable work.

Carli Molnar

... ...

When I find a crossword puzzle or a Sudoku that has been partially filled in, I am left with an empty feeling inside. The puzzle is ruined. It's fouled. It is a single use, a one-time thing and when others have been there first, it ruins it for me. The mystery of self-discovery is gone. There is no more life in it anymore.
They are over even before you begin.

Darren Vaast

... ...

Styrofoam Cup
Conference rooms to birthday parties
Hot tea, lukewarm juice
So small, never enough.
Stark white, light and airy
Statically charged,
Buoyantly held.
Sipping, nibbling, chewing
Squeaky, hollow
Broken pieces
Fingernails scratching, imprinting.
Imprinting the cup
Imprinting the planet
Biodegradable? No, degraded.
Chemicals leeching into us
Cancer

Holly Gray

... ...

It "cannot weather or age. [Its] existence is hurried by the push of obsolescence as one generation succeeds the next within a few months. [Its] suffering is written on [its] face" (Hillman, 2006, p. 39). This is no longer the gentle, heart-breaking suffering of being left in peace to impermanently become (de)composed in the embrace of the world. It is a deeper suffering produced of illusion, one that conceals this difficult, convivial peace that comes with the experience of impermanence. Hillman (p. 39) says that this image of an object that has "no way back to the Gods" is precisely an image of a "figure in Hell."

Ecologically and pedagogically understood, an image of a hellish figure cut off from what ought to be there for it *to be* its convivial, earthly self.

This is something worse than mere illness.

It is evil.

"Evil is the absence of what ought to be there" (Hardon, 1985, p. 136).

David Jardine (2012, pp. 143–144), from "Figures in Hell"

... ...

Cynthia Chambers, "Spelling and Other Illiteracies" (2012, p. 188):

Divorced from knowledge and tradition and imagination, literacy becomes a technology instead of a practiced craft.

Education is such a busy place. There is allure to the notion that a shiny, packaged program with laminated colour-coded flash cards could maybe help ... maybe take something off our VERY full plates. I see colleagues reach for these things in faith that if the school, the board, the system bought it, it must have value, it must nourish our children.

Assignments are uncomplicated, assessment is easier, answers are clearer. But it's like candy ... so sweet and easy and then suddenly your teeth are full of holes.

Neelam Mal

... ...

Throwaway stuff that never goes away.

Jennifer Meredith

... ...

This Styrofoam cup makes me awkward and uncomfortable because now that I've touched it—I am connected to its permanent presence in this world. A presence that cannot be undone and will not fit with what is. My complaisance is a crime which is knowledge's fault because now that I know about Styrofoam I have this responsibility to live up to.

Or:

A purpose?

How many of us bustle through purposelessness, lamenting that reason for existence has been lost? What a blessing to have found such an evident purpose in this cup. Be uncomfortable. Conscious. Careful.

Learn, react, repeat.

Deirdre Bailey

... ...

Lately, I've been spending time with the cup. Writing report cards, purchasing Dollar Store items, debating on what brand handbag to buy next, planning for Chemistry, dining with "friends."

I sit with friends over wine and dinner talking about life. About downtown Calgary. About their new Lexus. About their upcoming trip to Hawaii. About the unethical deal that in the end turned out "okay" and made him thousands.

Styrofoam.

Lisa Taylor

... ...

Eternal Death
Pure white. Pristine smoothness. Seemingly innocent. Cloned sameness. Collective indifference. Impermanent permanence. Wasteful convenience. Eternal Death.

Darren Vaast

... ...

One of our reliable companions in this echolocation venture was the Canadian poet Don Domanski. He told us of:

> ... what the Japanese refer to as "the slender sadness," that runs through every moment of existence, about the fleetingness of lives lived in a world where nothing can be saved. [It is] entering that state of being with a joy and wonder that comes from that very impermanency, from the absolute dispossession of everything we love and cherish. The wonder is that anything at all exists. The joy is that it does, even if it is as momentary as a human life. We can live this as a mode of attention, we can live within its movements, its cycles and treasure the phases, the round of it. (2002, p. 246)

> At poetry's centre there's the silence of a world turning. This is also found at the centre of a stone or the axis of a tree. To my way of thinking, that silence is the main importance. Out if it comes the manifestations, all the beings we call words. (Domanski, 2002, p. 245)

One of our "required textbooks" was Don Domanski's beautiful *All Our Wonder Unavenged* (2010).

As our time together increased, so, too, did the silences, where the smallest of gestures or the slightest of words arrived so full as to need larger and larger spaces of silence to work out its echoing returns.

And then at the end of such a silence, someone would say, "So *that's* why David Smith used that phrase!" and their words would arrive as a benediction for all we had been through, each one of us hearing and feeling and understanding this "*that's* why ..." as a hint of some intimate, unutterable secret that held us together.

David Jardine

... ...

A Pocket of Darkness

The comfort of timely darkness is banished
by artificial, unearthly glow.
On the extremes of the city the eternal, held off, awaits.

In the coulee a pocket of darkness.
Marbled pairs of reflected light,
briefly glow, then shimmer and fade out.
Alone now, they wind through tangles, relentless,
and re-emerge into one.
Call up to the creators; we are here, we are here.

What of those who occupy the spaces in between,
and linger along the precipice.
Outlines given vague shape by the fleeting;
ephemeral and haunting.
Await the familiar, an echo emerging from below.

Judson Innes

... ...

Part way through our last class together, we sat listening to the laughter and the lovely blurs of conversations after coming back to the classroom from our break for food.

"Listen. They *love* each other."

Jackie Seidel & David Jardine

... ...

Shut eyes
Take breath
Breathe ...
... Pause ...

Open, move
Sway,
Poised,
with grace.

Miranda Hector

... ...

Big flakes of snow meander from the gray sky on this spectacular winter day, the perfect time. We walk slowly through the deep snow. This grade one group assures me that this is the best way to uncover the secrets of their new classroom.

They are startled when birds fly so close we can feel the air beneath their wings. The sun peeks through the grayness, radiating bright streams that tickle our faces with warmth and make the snow sparkle like gems.

We stop to feel its power. Our quiet conversation is interrupted by strange movement in the bushes.

We are serenaded by the music of the ducks.

… to be part of this peaceful classroom.

They have interrupted the rush.

Trish Savill

… …

After all the brightwhite thoughts of disposable Styrofoam cups that deflect and reject our love and care, objects that cannot age with our own aging, objects that provide no surroundings, no housing of memory … Jackie Seidel brought in Don Domanski's *All Our Wonder Unavenged* (2010) and we read, aloud, several times, his "Disposing of a Broken Clock." He has graciously granted us permission to include this wondrous poem:

… …

Disposing of a Broken Clock

I put two final drops of oil in the mechanism
which is placing a word on either side of time

I anoint it twice   bless it in a proper manner
to pay homage to those cogs and gears
that held the hours in a drop of oil for so long
like dark wine that settled on an altarpiece
of moveable stirrups
                   coiled springs and mandibles

I carefully removed the screw that controlled
the weightlessness of the future and the one
that counterchecked the heaviness of the past

I wipe its face clean of hands and numbers
so it looks like the moon sighted through
longing   what the eyes have to endure

I remove the mainspring which shivers once
in my palm and then is still   the stillness of harm
done harm's way straining to be silent

finally at its centre I build a small campfire
to warm the ones who will come much later

those migrants those small beasts who circle
us endlessly   who follow the ticking of the grass
and the straw that overtakes the wind
who know only that an essential time lives on after us
who bow to the timepieces lowered onto their hearts
the continuum of water and the laze of stones.

Don Domanski (2010, p. 67)

··· ···

Peter Rilstone helped us linger over the images of anointing with oil, of penances and patience over the dead body, clean and clarified and let go into its proper disposition. Peter has recently retired from the local school board, but not from teaching. He provided exactly what our class needed—the great lesson that now, retired from the day-to-day work of schooling, the best thing to do was to learn Latin.

We ate up Domanski's words again and again. Something cared for that is properly let go back outwards into all its relations. All the slow words of giving up this thing in the world that had lasted, that had gathered memory and care and love around its face.

Over time gathered and not rushing.

There is one image in particular in "Disposing of a Broken Clock," of wiping the face of the clock clean of hands and numbers, that sent an unexpected shock through the class, an image of a young child come up close to have their face wiped cool and fresh and clean in summer heat, but then the child, too, who has died whose face is wiped and anointed for burial, with all our thoughts arced back to Jackie's "Curriculum for Miracles."

So Domanski's old and broken clock is properly taken care of, properly ushered back to the gods that made it, back to "the continuum of water and the laze of stones."

We are miracles, each of us.

David Jardine & Jackie Seidel

··· ···

For a thousand years scholars have esteemed the biblical commentaries of the theologian Rabbi Rashi (1040–1105). His work amalgamated his approach to interpreting Jewish scriptures with one of his teaching practices. Of the former, he reflected that for every biblical passage there are a dozen interpretations. Of the latter, he usually responded to a student's query by posing another question. And thereby he produced his timeless work, which was a compendium of his students' and his own reflections.

During our course "Ecological Consciousness and Inquiry in the Classroom," Jackie and David introduced our class to the poetry of Don Domanski. On the first reading of each of Don Domanski's poems, his writing made no sense to my classmates and me. Troubled by the apparent incomprehensibility of the assigned readings, when we requested a key to interpreting the poetry our teachers sent us back to the drawing board with questions such as Rashi might have asked: "What does it say to you? What do you think it means?"

While a colleague and I drove to and from classes, we exchanged our interpretations of Domanski's poems. Invariably we shared common thoughts, but each of us also had different insights based on our unique life experiences and bodies of knowledge. The mingling of our differences opened entirely new inroads to appreciate the richness of what we had read, which led to further understanding of ourselves and our human condition. It is remarkable that the car survived our spirited dialogues (distracted driving!) during the weekly trips between home and class.

My first readings of Domanski's "Disposing of a Broken Clock," in which he eulogized a cherished timepiece, struck me as the account of a rather senseless act:

> I put two final drops of oil in the mechanism ...
> I anoint it twice   bless it in a proper manner
> to pay homage to those cogs and gears
> that held the hours in a drop of oil for so long
> like dark wine that settled on an altarpiece ...

This poem reminded me of former possessions which I sorely missed when they were broken, lost or cast away, such as a medal, which my grandfather had given to me, that mysteriously disappeared when I was in grade four; and in adulthood, each of my Mazdas, in which I sat, before trading them in, and recalled memories of passengers, some no longer alive, with whom I had shared trips near and far. But never had I 'wasted' oil upon an object that I was about to discard. I puzzled, "Why did Domanski lubricate his irreparable clock's mechanism before disposing of it?" Like many of his images, their seeming incomprehensibility during the first readings struck me, and did not let go.

But sometimes time transforms what seems immediately illogical by striking chords of deep realities below and within. Domanski's words "anoint," "bless," "homage," "wine," "altarpiece" seemed to set apart and elevate to a sacred place his worn-out, no-longer-functional clock. These words evoked a connection between his 'wasting' oil and a similar accusation leveled against a woman who poured precious nard upon Jesus before he died (Mark 14:3). And *christus* means "one who has been anointed"—that word burst a floodgate of thoughts and questions, sent me to books and Google, roused ripples of connotations, connected heretofore disparate bits of knowledge and ideas, and discharged a surge of adrenaline. Ah, the delights and highs of learning, and sharing insights with others!

Domanski's words "anoint" and "oiled" seem inextricably linked. Traditionally, priests have anointed the sick before they die. Bishops have anointed monarchs with oil. The common word for "oil" in Latin is *oleum*—that which we pour on salad. But Latin has a second term, *unguentum*, from which comes our word "unguent," a word that beautifully, even onomatopoetically, falls upon the ear. *Unguentum* refers to a precious oil, and also means "salve," "ointment," "perfume." Moses anointed the first Jewish high priest with precious *unguentum* (Exodus 30:22–32). Psalm 133 reflects about this event: "Behold, how good and joyful a thing it is, wherever people dwell together in unity! It is like precious ointment [*unguentum*] upon the head, that ran down unto the beard, even unto Aaron's beard. … For there God gives His Blessing, and life for ever." The unguent or salve used for anointing or making sacred a monarch and persons on the threshold of death has a psychic and spiritual, if not physical, property of healing. Christianity has traditionally taught that the baptismal anointing of carnal flesh with water heals body and mind of their hereditary fate of falling short of a human's potential and ideal.

Through repeated reading and reflecting on "Disposing of a Broken Clock," my first reaction that Domanski had wasted oil metamorphosed into admiration for a symbolic act of ecological stewardship. This poet is one who does not unconsciously discard the shabbily old for the fashionable fad.

Peter Rilstone

… …

My thoughts turn to moments in time that could use a little bit of oiling. When time sticks and grinds, creaks and chugs, a little metal pot of oil at hand might smooth the gears. Not to move time more quickly. Time marches on quickly enough. Metal pots of oil with which to oil time; to ease a difficult time of waiting, to bring peace to a time of worry, to soothe a person's angst over the passage of another year—a little drop of slick oil to lubricate their troubles.

When the passing of time causes pain or sorrow for someone a wee drop of oil may soften their furrowed brow, ease their heart, slow their racing pulse.

Be where you are. Be mindful of giving time its proper due. Oil the passage of time to "countercheck the heaviness of the past" (Domanski, 2010, p. 67).

Edited May 6, 2013
Warm sunny evening after a hot blue-sky day

Carole Jones

… …

Now Domanski's reverence for his clock begs questions: Did those drops of oil express merely a marvel for the craftsmanship and aesthetics of an object? An awe of human ingenuity and invention? An apostrophic homage and nostalgic gratitude for a timepiece whose reliability he had trusted for ordering his life for decades? A gesture of healing or thankful dedication of an object before relinquishing it, in all its parts, to whence it came? An animistic empathy and unity (to use the descriptor in Psalm 133) with a treasured inanimate object? Or his oneness with not just the clock, but with our entire universe? A memorial of others, some may be no longer alive, whose times this clock had similarly measured? A nostalgic tribute to significant moments and events in his own and others' lives? An awed honouring of time itself? A wonder at the mystery of our vast, incomprehensibly complex universe beyond the small measure of order and sense and control that we humans presume to instill upon it? And so forth.

Beyond our interpretations of the readings in our course, a greater significance lies in how we were able, together, to approach and engage with the texts. How do we teachers mediate our charges' encounters with what at first may seem to them counterintuitive, incomprehensible, even impossible challenges? How do we prepare and open ourselves to make opportunities and spaces in which students share their life experiences, knowledge and concepts, and in which we learn from our students, even about topics that we have taught many times? How can we take up the mandated curricula in ways that honour and respond most effectively to what our students ask and articulate?

In harmony with Rashi a millennium ago, Northrop Frye explained that whenever he answered a student's question, he posed another in its wake, because queries raise us up, whereas statements lower. In this class, with this poem, and now with this chapter, we experienced ways which are as ancient as the earliest conversations among elders and young.

Peter Rilstone

… …

We don't become experienced through the application of a method because a method, properly taken up, must be taken up as if I could be anyone. [But] none of us is everyone. None of us is cut out for living just any life, and none of us will live forever. We are not perspectiveless. … I am defined but what I can thus remember, what necessarily exclusive and incomplete host of voices haunts my inner life and work and therefore haunts the world that is open in front of me. This composed and cultivated memory constitutes my openness to what comes to meet me from the world.

Deidre Bailey paraphrasing *David Jardine*, to his great surprise and delight (an inside joke)

… …

This is another gentle reminder that slowing down doesn't mean losing time. When else do you hear the faint, papery rattle of a dragonfly? Or smell the soil under your feet as you walk? Let us be mindful of this truth.

Neelam Mal

… …

We watched clips of a documentary film of Zen chef Edward Espe Brown called *How to Cook Your Life* (Dorrie, 2007):

> "It's not so simple, to do what you're doing," he tells us.

We mulled over how what you're doing, done well, cooks you. Careful and loving work composes me as much as I compose it (remember Lesley Tait's favourite passage from Tsong-kha-pa [2000, p. 111]: "I compose this in order to condition my own mind").

And how we watched a little video, together in class, called "How to Grow a Mandala" (Rodé, 2012), quietly drawing in our own journals. And how Jennifer Meredith and Carli Molnar did this with their own students (grades six and two, respectively).

And how Darren Vaast and David Jardine both got "cooked" in their own ways by this activity, frustrated with it being imperfect or rendering it asymmetrical on purpose.

"It's not so simple, to do what you're doing."

When you do, it cooks you.

"Towards you, towards your center."

· · · · · ·

I promise to cut the carrot,
When I'm cutting the carrot.

Carli Molnar

· · · · · ·

When I was a child I thought that maybe I'd be a teacher. It seemed fun. They had the answers to the workbook and occasionally took us on field trips. My mom was a teacher, I liked going with her up to the big high school, to the photocopy room, being in her classroom, writing on the chalkboard, pretending I was a teacher, too.

> "To read a place means you are able to dwell within it, to inhabit it, to gather from it the knowledge that makes life there possible, as well as intelligible and meaningful." (Chambers, 2012, p. 187)

I believe that this is what my mom did for her students. They didn't all appreciate what it was she was doing, but many of them did. She still sometimes runs into some of them at the post office back home. They share stories with her about their work, their families, and their lives.

The original intention of my writing was not to talk about my mom, but here I am with tears in my eyes writing about her.

Jennifer Meredith

· · · · · ·

Time

Tender parting and elegant flow,
a silent passing above the forest floor.
Wings raised up to gain favour,
and soften the looming perch.

Triggered now, firm thrust and smooth unfolding,
fell swoop and talon strike.
A mere moment swept away, devoured.
Echoed perhaps in a ripple of air,
or brief shrug of robust bough.

Judson Innes

... ...

Shut eyes
    Take breath
        Breathe ...
            ... Pause ...

Open, move
Sway,
    Poised,
        with grace.

Miranda Hector

... ...

the disposability of time
of time misused

letting it go as the river streams
it sits on my shoulders
heavy and waiting

an expectation of more, of wanting
calling to me to give it a name

the greeting of the two sides
    meeting in happy remembrance and sorrow
    of the expectation unfulfilled

letting it go, staying there for a while
awareness of more and of less
as shoulders sag

the open breath
sending away all that sits in opposite grain
recognition of what true names may join me.

Lesley Tait

... ...

"... and then she let him go."
Ari Berk (2012)

CHAPTER THIRTY-ONE

Chasing Calmness

LORI BONANNO

Dear New Teacher,

With every day you have an opportunity to learn from your students. Take the time to learn with them and to help them on their journey … on your journey. You hear their voices yet you feel "bound without a rope" (Loy, 2010, p. 42). There is nothing holding you back but your self-doubt. We have all felt this way. Overwhelmed! Needing more time … Time to plan. Time to mark. Time to sit and think deeply about a topic. Time is holding you back yet pushing you forward. So much accomplished yet so much to do.

"It is not enough to have a story about what happens. It is necessary to story *why* I do what I do" (Loy, 2010, p. 37). Think about it. Why are you on this journey? Why are you in such a rush? Why are you asking them to finish the whole page? Make them all complete the same assignment? Why are you doing what you do? Is it what *you* want to do? Are you wrestling with an idea of a set path you must follow? What is your story? Their story? You do not need to "accept the world we story together as 'the way things are'" (Loy, 2010, p. 17). When you think about teaching and learning, it's about taking the time to sit with a topic: to explore and play, to relax and breathe, to think deeply. It is not a race. Take the time to enjoy what you do. Breathe in … Breath out. Enjoy the present moment. Savor it. Your students will feel the space you are creating is about learning and not just getting it done. The journey *is* the story!

Don't feel overwhelmed by the work! When searching for the perfect way to solve a problem, manage a classroom, design a task, create a lesson there is no simple answer. Instead, know that there is a multitude of ways, infinite possibilities.

That it is why it is so hard to choose and to choose the 'right' one. We cannot "discover the master-story, the one true meta story that includes and explains all other stories" (Loy, 2010, p. 7). So don't panic! Choose a path, take a chance and see what unfolds. Take a risk! Your students will join in, create new paths and all the while you will be intertwined in the fabric of one another's stories and experiences.

The Nature of Things (Suzuki, 2014) aired an episode, "Chasing Snowflakes," which looks at snow and its character. In the documentary, physicist Ken Libbrecht, who grows snowflakes in his lab, answers the question: Why can't two snowflakes be exactly alike? His response:

> It's complicated and it's like seeing two trees that are exactly … exactly the same. Every branch, every leaf, it just can't happen because there is just too many possibilities for the different ways to make a tree and the same is true for a snowflake. And on some level you can calculate how many possible ways there are to make a large snowflake and the total number is larger than the number of atoms in the universe.

Teaching is complicated! We cannot replicate a classroom, an experience or a program. You can be inspired but you cannot replicate it. Our classrooms are like the tree and the snowflake: each one is different, unique and shaped by nature and the experiences of its journey. Our classrooms and the people within it all have experiences and stories to share. There are so many possibilities, so many topics and so many ways to get there. So amidst these possibilities, these unknowns, embrace that there are possibilities. How lucky are we to have all these choices? Take the time to sit still, connect with what you want to do with the children in front of you. Listen to their voices, their directions, their experiences and together focus on the learning and exploring of these topics.

When you feel overwhelmed—find a group of people that will help you, share in the work and find a refuge. But remember to stay calm—breathe. Avoid the complaint and negativity. It will eat at you, and for some it will consume us. Instead be calm. Embrace the work. Connect with it.

> When you are calm, when you are still, you see things as they truly are. You don't distort things. When you are not calm, it's easy to get confused and angry. All of us make a lot of mistakes and create a lot of suffering when we are not calm. Each human being should have enough tranquility to be truly happy. (Nhat Hanh, 2012, p. 12)

CHAPTER THIRTY-TWO

Tortuga

DEIRDRE BAILEY

I've got a turtle in my classroom named Tortuga. She's twenty-five years old and likes to climb things. It's pretty difficult with her short legs and an inflexible shell and we've watched her fall a lot but it never stops her. Tortuga's got some damage to her shell because once, earlier in her life, someone tried to drill a hole in it. Once, I overheard the children discussing it during recess ...

"That must have hurt her a lot."

"They probably thought she couldn't feel it. They didn't understand."

"People just forget to pay attention sometimes."

"They mustn't have been really looking at her. Sometimes people look at things but they don't really *see*."

Occasionally the children forget that she can't see them coming and they reach in suddenly to pat her face. It's probably terrifying. She always comes back out though. Ready to forgive, adapt and continue with her investigations, carefully negotiating her next obstacle; balanced, diligent, determined.

This turtle in my classroom is the perfect teacher. She's forgiving, resilient, optimistic. She invites imagination and lives in a place of possibility. She's got no ulterior motives and you can't help but trust her because she keeps trusting you. Tortuga is a portal to the more-than-human world and all its beauty. She's an outlet for our fundamental need to care for something. Her easy presence has changed our lives.

CHAPTER THIRTY-THREE

Conversation

STEPHANIE BARTLETT

A group of five-year-olds gathers together for a conversation. The sun streams through the windows into our happy classroom. Some children are lying down, others are leaning on each other, and I catch a couple looking dreamily out the window on the uncharacteristically mild January day. An effect of global warming? We don't know.

We have been looking closely at the globe for the past week and talking about what it means to *us*. Some students drew parts of the world that they have visited, or the country where their family originated. There was a heated discussion about the Arctic and the North Pole that spanned two days.

"Is the ice melting?" they wondered.

"What animals live there?"

"Santa lives there." (This fact was not up for debate!)

"There are chemicals in the water that are killing the animals."

Today, we have gathered around the globe, under the protective span of our class tree to see what makes sense to us and what we can *do*. There is no question that these children are passionately ready to save our world. As their teacher, I am here to listen and put the skills in their hands that will cause our community to wake up and take notice.

The Fire Sermon is an ancient text from the Buddha, written far before globalization, capitalism and technology (Bodhi, 2012). The message is powerful and urgent and in the text, Samyutta Nikaya says that the Buddha proclaims, "Monks, all is burning … burning with the fire of greed, with the fire of hatred, with the fire of delusion" (Samyutta Nikaya, Chapter 35, sutta 28). The word "delusion" has crossed my path often of late. In his essay "'The Farthest West Is but the Farthest East,'" David Smith (2008) says that "the purpose of education is to learn how to live well, to be free of delusion, and to be attuned to the deepest rhythms of life so that one is living life according to its fundamental nature" (p. 7). As a society, we are not doing that. We are distracted: the constant checking of smartphones, multi-tasking, rushing, focusing on the lives of others and a preoccupation with material goods and money.

In my own efforts to find this deep rhythm that is so essential to our collective well-being, I am grateful for the environment that we have created together in our classroom. There is no rushing. We have *time*. Time to play, time to learn, and time to talk. In his "Reflections on the Fire Sermon," Ven. Bhikkhu Bodhi (2012) wonders "whether we refuse to look at our global crises because they are too overwhelming or because other things with more glitter capture our attention (p. 86). It is easy to look this real threat in the eye, squeeze your own eyes shut in denial and turn away because of the sheer magnitude of what could go wrong. But … there is hope, and we as educators hold that hope gently in our hands and spirit and in the stories that we tell.

This work starts with compassion and the purposeful creation of a classroom where we live gently in a space of deep inquiry. We live meaningfully. We laugh. We listen. When we care for that space and build our collective community on trust, then we become able to look at the world and do our small part to divert us from potential crisis.

David Jardine said that the work of our school is the work of the world. So here we are, back in our warm, sunny classroom. Voices are raised with enthusiasm and we have to work hard to listen to each other. An important summit meeting in its own right.

CHAPTER THIRTY-FOUR

Dear New Teacher

DEREK LAWSON

You have stepped into the breach. There's no turning back now. All those years of school, the two university degrees, the ups and downs of your practicums; all these experiences have led you to this point. No amount of preparation is going to steel you for those feelings niggling at you somewhere in the recesses of your mind: Can I do this? Am I prepared? What if it all goes wrong? Will I have to dream it up all over again?

You will be pulled in directions that you are going to have to learn how to navigate: How to compromise your personal beliefs for the good of your nascent practice, how to satisfy the leviathan of "the system," how to negotiate your professional relationships. I could go on, but you already know these things. You may not know the specifics, but you sense that there may be choppy waters ahead.

There are really only two things that I think you need to consider as a new teacher: authenticity and discovering what is worthwhile. Be warned. Authenticity is powerful, as you will be exposing your weaknesses, biases and personal shortcomings. The glorious beauty is that your students will respond to your authenticity. They will feel a deep personal connection to you, and your (Gk.) *nous*, your soul as a teacher. They are the reason you are reading this letter: Be the one they have been waiting for. The real one.

What is worthwhile? Only you will be able to understand how to answer that question. Just know that what is worthwhile will sometimes feel dangerous, risky, rebellious and, at the extreme, foolhardy. Good! There is a rather cryptic passage in "Story-Time Lessons From a Dog Named Fideles" (Jardine, 2014b, p. 87) and I think it tackles this issue with a cryptic lyrical beauty that I cannot at the moment reproduce or mimic:

> "Who is to say what is worthwhile?" cannot be genuinely asked from a cynical distance by a self that is full of self-consciousness and who always wants to be first and who refuses the risk, refuses to let themselves enter the fray, the *Spiel*.

Get in the fray and ask questions. Find out what is worthwhile.

And it begins …

Nani

NEELAM MAL

My grandmother had twelve children. Eleven boys and one girl, my mother. We three are the only ones out of her twenty-five grandchildren that don't call her Bebe. Be-be is heavy, it sits with greater weight on your lips and tongue before being pushed out with your breath. Anita, Ajay and I get Nani. Na-ni starts heavy but then is lifted by the lightness of the second syllable. Easier to sing "Nani" and make her playful.

There is nothing delicate or graceful about my Nani. She is a woman who started working and never stopped—as a child, as a young bride, as a mother and as a widow. Nobody knows when she was born, either the date or the year. Her doctor suspects she's in her mid-eighties based on bone density tests (carbon dating?). She was born into poverty in India, married young and eventually moved to England. Her husband, my Nana, died when their twelfth child was still a baby. She speaks very little English. She doesn't read or write any language. She has already buried half of her children. Ours is not the sweet gentle granny rocking in her chair, knitting. This woman is tough—it shows on her face, in her words, in her very breath. She is our strong and unyielding matriarch.

Nani has thick, heavy hands. She once tried to teach me how to make *maki di roti*—a flat bread made from corn flour. You have to massage it into a ball and then flatten it by throwing it carefully, but with force, from one hand to the other until it is the right size and thickness. Her hands are perfect for the job. Years of practice and stored strength in her short fingers make the job look easy. It's not. I worked and massaged, pinched and flattened. I was unable to make my roti look like hers. They were lopsided and definitely not round. Weird flaps of folded-over dough and skinny, cracked edges infuriated Nani. How could her grandchild, the daughter of her daughter, have no skill at this centuries-old task? In her frustration, she reached for the rolling pin with those thick, heavy hands and chased me out of the kitchen.

My grandmother has never hesitated to hit her children. My mom and my uncles sit together and recount story after story of being walloped by Nani. All of my cousins have stories of her rage resulting in some sort of a bruise. Her temper is rivaled by no one. (She once hit a neighbour with a shovel because he was calling her racist names and swearing at her. She wasn't entirely certain what he was saying but knew she couldn't let it go. He never bothered her again.) I have always taken refuge in the fact that because I am hers through her daughter she will never hit me. My dad is her son-in-law. She doesn't feel she has the right to hit his children. Thank God.

Because of this, unlike the others, we sometimes get to see a glimmer of her hidden gentleness. She cuddles with us. She lets us play with her hair while she watches *Wheel of Fortune* (this is where she learned the alphabet). She giggles with us about Alanis Morissette "Thanking India" while naked in a music video. She lets me pinch the baggy skin on the tops of her hands over and over and watch it slowly recede from a mountain to a plain. She cracks jokes in broken English and sings nursery rhymes. She kisses us.

In the past ten years, Nani's age has started to show. Her skin is thinner and looser. Her eyes are milky. She is hunched from osteoporosis and in pain from arthritis. Her muscles have atrophied and she is always out of breath. She coughs and wheezes and rarely walks anymore. This powerful woman is watching her body deteriorate and it is making her crazy. She swings from apathy about her surroundings to flashes of volatile irritation. She looks fragile.

Six years ago, my uncle Peter, her baby, was hospitalized with pneumonia. He was thirty-nine years old and lying in a coma in his hospital bed. His lungs were failing and he was being kept alive by a respirator. My family flew out to Vancouver to see him. No one told Nani how sick he was. They all decided that it would be too much for her to bear. They all thought she would shatter. Finally, one of my uncles brought her on the ferry from Victoria to the hospital. They wheeled her on to the ward in a wheelchair. My tiny, hunched Nani was being asked whether they should remove Peter from the ventilator, to let him go.

For the rest of my life I will never forget my grandmother in these moments. Without a breath of hesitation she made the decision. Her face was soft and her heart was surely breaking. "I can't leave him in pain." And it was decided.

In those few moments of my Nani's heartbreak, when she was cracked open with grief, we were allowed to see her grace. Grace hidden beneath her tired, aching body and her prickly words. Her armour broken and we saw a side part of her that usually lay hidden. When it really mattered, she showed her grace—not in body, but in her spirit.

CHAPTER THIRTY-SIX

On Witches AND Kites

HANNAH BLADES

If in the twilight of memory we should meet once more
We shall speak again together and
You shall sing to me a deeper song.

—KHALIL GIBRAN (1923)

A hand-me-down box for my daughter arrived this weekend with a picture book in it that I hadn't laid eyes on or thought about since I was a child myself: *Witches Four* (Brown, 1980). Not really a classic, certainly not well known, but so well loved by my four-year-old self that when I pulled it out I was overwhelmed for a moment by that quiet, heavy-bottomed feeling that comes from long-forgotten memories called back. *What is it about?* asked my daughter when I gleefully presented the book to her. And I realized that I couldn't say beyond what the front cover artwork conveyed, which was, of course, four witches. Couldn't remember what the story was about, but clearly remembered the feeling. Remembered that I loved it, that I asked for it to be read to me again and again. So my much older self read it again, aloud, at bedtime. Four witches, with four hats, find four cats. Nice tidy story, proper rhyming, but not terribly profound, which is why I wondered why it struck such a chord. I didn't even remember the story, but there was something important about it that I couldn't quite put my finger on.

***

E-mail edu-spam recently produced a political cartoon in which a self-esteem fairy was depicted "making it all better" for a student receiving poor grades on standardized tests: Tests that were designed under the societal structures of the last century—a century characterized by competition and dominance, wherein hierarchical power structures maintained a strong foothold in all areas of society. In schools, the smartest kids were the ones who could memorize and regurgitate the most information, the ones who could prove that they had learned what they were supposed to learn, and still remembered it. Although there has been movement in pockets, the kinds of assessments that most teachers still use are based on these principles. And the movement, of course, has produced its share of backlash. Like the cartoon.

Assessment in general is a highly controversial topic, with stakeholders holding firm and often emotionally charged beliefs about what is right and wrong when it comes to school assessment and reporting. A 2009 provincial report found that feelings on the subject of student assessment amongst stakeholders ranged from "confidence in the system" to "mistrust" and even "paranoia" (Alberta Education, 2009). In 2013 a teacher in Edmonton went to the media after being suspended for insubordination when he refused to stop giving students zeroes for work that was not handed in. The public outcry supported both sides of the issue, and though the majority of media frenzy missed the point entirely (that tinkering with existing inauthentic grading systems does nothing to improve teaching or learning), the flurry of opinion and controversy was illustrative of the emotional response stakeholders have in relation to assessment reform.

I became familiar with Richard Lavoie's (1997) work as a day camp counselor for the Learning Disabilities Association many moons ago. His message was that adults who work with children have the great responsibility of creating experiences for children that can be very positive, or very negative. He talks about poker chips—experiences collected throughout a day, throughout a life, which contribute to a cache of confidence and self-esteem. Children who have consistently positive experiences get more poker chips, more self-esteem. Having more, they can afford to take greater risks with those chips, which often leads to the accumulation of more chips, more self-esteem, and the cycle continues. Conversely, children who have negative experiences accumulate few chips, can afford to take few risks, lose more when they try and fail and never get the chance to build their sense of self-worth. The negative experiences continue to tear them down, day after day.

This is similar to the idea of children belonging to one of two categories: *assessment winners* and *assessment losers* (Stiggins, 2007). We all need to be challenged, and I am a great believer in the value of living in the struggle of learning. But traditional assessment can, for some students, create experiences of continual failure, which in turn fosters feelings of confusion, embarrassment, avoidance, self-defeat, stress, boredom and hopelessness (Stiggins, 2007). As teachers and administrators, we talk a good talk about helping every student achieve, but somewhere from the back of my brain shouts that anecdote that children who make Cs in grade two, make Cs in grade twelve. What this points to is that poor grades are simply not a motivator for improvement (Kohn, 2012). The current system of assessment in schools does nothing but reward the winners and punish the losers, year after year after year, and to continue to support a system of assessment that makes children, if only just some of them, feel worthless is simply unethical.

As I was writing this piece one morning my step-daughter asked what it was about, and when I told her, she said that her own report card was coming out soon. When I asked what she was thinking about that, she said:

> When you get a 1, 2, 3, the teacher is really just saying you suck at this, you suck at that, but the kid might actually feel like they are pretty good at some of those things, in their own way.

She's eight years old, in grade three, and it breaks my heart a little that her teacher has the power to make her feel like she sucks at anything. For many of us, it's counter-intuitive to hand out an assessment that is perceived as being negative to kids who are trying their best and maybe even improving in their own way. What I feel uncomfortable about is the fact that there are students who consistently perform poorly and are beaten down by school over and over again. And as much as we try to make these students feel valued in the classroom and proud of their achievements, we simply don't have control over how they interpret themselves in relation to other students who get higher marks, or how those students who get higher marks treat the kids who don't. If we are truly meaning to celebrate multiple intelligences and strive for inclusive classrooms, I have difficulty seeing how the grading system we are currently using is going to help us achieve those goals.

***

Back to the witches and the wondering: Why could I not recall the plotline of a story I loved so dearly? Several days later I realized I was missing the point: *what* the story was about wasn't relevant, what was important was the *why* and the *how*. What was important was all the witches that came after those four—a lifelong interest that I would say at times verged on obsession: Roald Dahl, *The Witches of Worm, Blackbird Pond*, later Anne Rice and reruns of *Bewitched*. The fabulous Cher in *The Witches of Eastwick*, that angsty and wonderful teen flick *The Craft*. In grade eight I read *The Crucible* and discovered the witch trials, read everything I could, traveled to Boston on a family vacation and spent hours in the Salem Witch Museum, twice. I took a course in university on American colonial history just to write a paper on the subject. As an eighth grade teacher I made the Renaissance witch hunts a much larger inquiry than the curriculum intended, which led to a character study of Gregory Maguire's Elphaba, a reading of the play *Wicked* and a film study of *The Wizard of Oz*. I'm a big fan of witches I guess is what I'm trying to say. When I pulled on the threads of all those memories, walked back along them, I found that first and formative learning experience about four witches, with four hats, who find four cats. So what I knew about the story was not nearly as important as how I felt about it, because how I felt about it was what cultivated such a passionate response later on. I am a lifelong learner about witches. No doubt.

Now isn't this what we want to inspire with our teaching? Learning experiences that evoke emotion, arouse curiosity, stimulate further learning, cultivate passion for something … anything really—these are what we want to inspire. And when it comes to assessment, I can't say that I have seen any model of testing that could ever accurately measure *that* kind of learning. Our assessment of children is a powerful marker of what we value. When we assess, we are saying: this is what was supposed to be learned, this is what was important about that learning. Show me a rubric, even a so-called progressive, non-numerical rubric that can measure what is actually worth measuring and I will gladly fill in the boxes. But these rubrics do not exist because they cannot. The most important aspects of authentic learning cannot be measured with a pencil and paper in the period before lunch. And when you consider that the kinds of assessment we engage in also say something about what we value in that individual, then the practice becomes even more problematic.

I can see how recent publicity around a move away from traditional assessment could look like a sacrifice of rigour in support of self-esteem. That's what the self-esteem fairy was trying to say, after all. I think what it boils down to is a fear of the unknown, a fear of what is new, what is unfamiliar. It seems to me that the general public tends to fall into the old "it was good enough for me" kind of thinking when it comes to education. Perhaps they think that because they survived it, children these days can too, as a rite of passage. But those of us who care deeply about children and are passionate about learning know that school doesn't have to be something that one *survives*. School can and should be a place of safety and wonder and appreciation and celebration—of inspiration and passion and joy, not of failure and self-doubt. In my teaching practice I have yet to come across an assessment model that can authentically measure what I think is actually important, and the practice of handing out grades that punish some (if not all) becomes even more unnecessary.

***

I started my career at an independent charter school for girls, as part of a small staff of passionate educators who wanted to do the real work of inquiry. We focused on critical thinking and authentic tasks and we had a lot of support and mentorship to encourage us. In my second year at the school I taught grade seven, such a wildly awkward year for many. I can still see Anisa, square-shouldered and tight-braided, thundering down the hallway, arms pumping, braids swaying. Gruff and earnest, she wanted to do well but so many times missed the mark. We were doing innovative things with our teaching but our assessment at the time was very traditional, and Anisa was one of those who did not make the grade. I handed back C after C, and in those heartbreaking exchanges her disappointment was all over her face. Years later I wondered after her, worried about her. Would she forever hope to achieve and always come up short?

One night this winter after a particularly unpleasant shopping excursion with two tired toddlers, we stopped for a treat to grease the wheels for the drive home, and there she was, scooping ice cream at her parents' sweet shop, working part-time to help out while she finished up her third year at university. Engineering. So proud to tell me she was doing well. "I'm so glad I went to that school," she said. "None of my friends in my program knows how to think and I do. I'm so glad I learned how to think."

So good teaching had led Anisa down the right path and we had taught her how to think, but at the same time we handed her reminders of defeat every step of the way. She was resilient, and persevered, and it all turned out okay for her, but I have to ask, What was it all for? Anisa could not tell me the role of Chief Tecumseh in the War of 1812. Not in grade seven and probably not now. And while the role of Chief Tecumseh is certainly worth knowing, was the time and energy I spent assessing her knowledge on that specific topic really time well spent? Seeing her years later encouraged me to ask again, Why? Why do we continue to push students to regurgitate curricular content instead of talking with them about what really matters? Instead, we need to ask, Can you think? Show me. How does this learning change things for you? How will it lead you elsewhere? Where will you go? What will you do?

***

In September 2014 Calgary was hit with an unusual fall storm that damaged and destroyed many of the city's old-growth trees. The morning of the storm we watched through the window of our classroom as a two-hundred-year-old poplar fell to pieces, branch by branch. It's so sad, they said. And it was. We talked about why. Talked about the deep-rooted connections humans have with the living giants among us. We read *The Giving Tree* (Silverstein, 1964) and Suzuki's *Salmon Forest* (Suzuki & Ellis, 2003). We sat on the floor and told our own tree stories to each other, then they went home and brought back the tree stories of their parents and grandparents. Tire swings and top branches. Next it was forest stories—find a forest that speaks to you and tell us its story. They read and researched, collected pictures and information, explored the flora and fauna, the human interactions. They created iMovies about their forest with music and voice-over. They spoke to what was important about the forest and why their forest should be protected. There is no doubt in my mind that this learning was valuable. There is no doubt in my mind that the learning we engaged in has the potential to awaken passions in those children that could inspire curiosity and encourage lifelong learning.

But this is a new school, a new school board, and for the first time in my career I am teaching in a provincial exam year. The end of May finds me living in the struggle that this looming assessment bestows upon me. When I call upon what professional wisdom I have managed to gather, several truths emerge. For example, the idea that children who have been taught through inquiry will perform well on standardized tests because their understanding of curricular outcomes is deep and meaningful. That all children, regardless of socio-economic background, have the capacity to achieve. That if you are good enough and smart enough and differentiate your teaching well enough, then students of all abilities will have access to the learning and will do well. I believe these things in my head and my heart. And yet I feel an anxiety about these tests. I want them to feel prepared, and to achieve this there is still work to do in "filling in the blanks" of curriculum that our inquiries have not yet addressed. My anxiety in the shadow of the ticking clock has led me to Edmonton Public Schools, to the key to the photocopier. I am coaching, I am teaching to the test. It feels wrong, and yet not doing so would feel wrong as well. I will not send them to the slaughter.

Addressing the issue of assessment winners and losers is going to take a shift in thinking, beginning with the understanding that we make meaningful what we choose to assess. As a teacher I can employ a multitude of strategies to work with my students who struggle, but at the end of the day, if I'm giving a grade, there is the potential for those children to continue to build a sense of failure and continue to feel bad about themselves. And when that child is sitting next to a student who has achieved, it exacerbates the problem, making the movement toward inclusive classrooms that continue with traditional assessment an ethical issue. In an inclusive classroom that is working effectively, there is a place for everyone and all students' skills and strengths are valued. This simply cannot be accomplished under the current system of assessment. American activist, poet and farmer Wendell Berry (2013) has said that to know what needs to be done one only has to walk up to the field and ask, *What do you need from me?* As an educator, also in the business of growth and cultivation, if I ask this of any of my students, past, present or future, I'd be willing to bet the answer will never be, "I'll take a C, thanks."

***

This week as I was busily tying up loose ends in Air and Aerodynamics, we made kites from a set of kits I had ordered way back in the fall. They didn't take long to put together and I figured it was good to have a break from the chalk and talk that were taking over like a runaway train. The next morning as I was preparing for the day and planning when we would head outside to fly them, I was overwhelmed with the feeling that it had all been a waste of time. Flying kites wasn't a cost-effective way to teach them airfoil, thrust, drag, wasn't going to hit the curricular objectives I needed to finish up before the weekend. I almost didn't do it. But it was a nice day and I figured it wouldn't take long, so out we went, and on the way out the door I asked them, You know how to fly a kite, right? Crickets. Then a few hands. Seventeen of the twenty sixth-graders in my class had never flown a kite before.

So we flew kites. Until lunch. And it wasn't all that easy at first, but they problem-solved, they helped each other, shared strategies and yelled out tips and encouragement from opposite ends of the field. They pointed out their own and each other's failures and successes. They ran and laughed and tripped and fell and rolled and got back up. They tangled up and sat in the grass together, chatting and untangling. They failed and tried again. They persisted. Running, shouting, laughing, learning, and pretty soon all twenty kites were up, anchored triumphantly by twenty smiling children sprinkled out over the field, each captivated in their own quiet contemplation, holding tightly the tugging lines of twenty airborne kites they had made with their own hands. I resisted the urge to call them all inside so I could point out the scientific properties of the experience, draw diagrams on the white board and make them copy it down in their notebooks, give them a practice test for that section of the PAT (Provincial Achievement Test). I will do that, perhaps, but not today. No test I could give could get at the real learning of that experience. No test could measure, and thus honour, what was really important about what happened out there in the sunshine. So today we will fly kites. I will not make winners and losers out of them today.

CHAPTER THIRTY-SEVEN

It Is All Love

LAUREN SELE

There is a white woman in his kitchen. He can see her turning from counter to stove between the flowers that line their kitchen window. Beside him, his honey-coloured daughter twirls grapes in the air before eating them. It is quiet. Light caught and stretched between day and evening pulls long shadows across his freshly cut lawn. In this abstraction of size and space he sees, traced on the grass, a large and grand image of what his fledgling apple tree might be with time and the kind of luck he's used to. In this moment, and those few like it, he feels the chaos that fuels change, the unstoppable shift that moves one thing to another without thought or question and heeding only the drive to keep on. Squat in this moment of not dark and not light he thinks of time. Of 'one time' and 'that time when.' And of two names (one official, one un-) and the dis/replacement of family. Of plum mangos and the right way to eat an orange. Of his daughter's not and never knowing. He watches her now, grapes eaten, half stumble to the garden in search of the small strawberries he and his wife planted. She passes through the shadows without stopping.

It has been a long day. Six years of post-secondary does not change the way someone hears you talk. Still, he makes enough money and is successful by both the rules of here and by his family's hopes. He traces his life by numbers. Twelve years at home, three there, another few spent waiting, five years close by (American undergraduate degree) and four years here, in Canada. He will be Canadian soon. Marry one and the door opens. He is not a fan of hyphens and is not yet sure he will use one to name himself. Canadian with an accent (can you speak proper English?), Canadian non-white (where is your family from originally?), Canadian grad student (do your credits from back home transfer?). Canadian permanent resident of Liberian descent who loves country music as much as reggae, who loves hockey but refuses to learn to skate, who cooks here with spinach instead of potato greens, lamb instead of goat, and has developed a surprising appetite for bison burgers. A hyphen denotes difference, a desire to be marked and thought of differently. It says it all and yet says nothing. The shifting evening air is getting to him. So much tedious thought. Canadian or not Canadian, he is happy to be here. Happy to have roots, to have the consistency of family around him. He watches his little girl pop something small and red into her mouth when she thinks he isn't watching. His wife likes her to wash it first.

He misses his mother. He sees her in his daughter almost as much as he sees the way his wife moves and talks. It is all love. His mother went to the United States to help take care of his brother's children and now cannot leave. Knowing no English and slipping elegantly into older age she boarded a plane bound for something she knew only through stories and faded family photos. He has found no one here in Canada to mirror exactly his own beginnings, but he will not admit to looking. In front of him, on the wicker coffee table picked up at Canadian Tire and deemed a perfect match for their house and deck, his wife places an open *Maclean's* magazine. Garlicky cooking smells spill from the sliding glass door when she opens it again to go back inside. Pre-dinner reading she has called it. A pre-dinner jolt. He picks it up. He cannot ignore its bold font title. Here, in the twilight, in his backyard garden, in his white/black home, he finds a loose thread. A wrinkle in the space-time continuum. A mediating battleground between here and there and an unwelcome, unloosed trickle of remembrance. "Accused in Liberia, Living in Toronto" the article declares. A description of the *Maclean's* investigation, the accused's name and political/military connections, words like "horrendous atrocities," "alleged massacre," and "twenty-one executed in all fashions." Letters, print, truth and remembering. There is a picture, too. He looks up and notes his daughter has moved from picking strawberries to digging small holes in the dirt beneath the apple tree. He continues to read. She is at that age when she no longer needs to be watched every second of every day. He will be right here anyway if anything really bad is about to happen.

The people described in Canadian print were cutting palm to make oil. Internal borders blurred and made meaningless by civil war, they were harvesting palm from an abandoned plantation. Not theirs really, but neither anyone else's to covet. Concepts of ownership fade in crisis and taking/looting/finding/stealing/using mean the same thing forcing the rise of tomorrow. He imagines the air between the palm nut trees thick and orange. He can taste the richness of the oil in his own mother's cooking. He was still there then but had no idea. No one did. No one, and none by their own fault, could be trusted with news. They prayed for peace and saw the Devil in both sides. Hollow idealism had long since faded but for the few lying, rich men in power. He stares closely at the picture. A man in camouflage atop a large battered truck surveys a line of civilians. Mostly women, a few men. They are being made to move somewhere. Bundles of cloth appear more numerous than faces. There are no discernible children. He holds in his heart the fate of too many stolen children and then lets it go. Too hard to think about. Too far away in the folds of his own mind and too far away from his mud-splattered daughter. He remembers how the weight of a bag of rice felt. How he centered it firmly between his shoulders before he was made to walk. Soldiers need to eat. He remembers it was a small group of rebels who found him and saw purpose in his small, sturdy body. He was in his mother's village in the interior and was helping with the farm. He was alone. He remembers the inevitability of his going with them (as opposed to what?) and the slow march from his village to two others. He remembers the oddly glowing face of a young man who recognized him at the second stop. His face among so many others. He hears the rebel/friend call out to let him ago. He remembers the thud of the rice bag dropping as he backed away. He doesn't remember getting home but he remembers arriving. The panic of his family falling to joy and wailing prayers. He looks up now and calls out to prevent his two-and-a-half-year-old from eating mud, stopping her just before the clump of wet earth meets her tiny, outstretched tongue. Such sweet trouble she is.

He is a good father. He is here now, in Canada, and so is this other man. This man who has killed and he who has not. Twenty-one people taken. And these just in this corroborated story. Truth and Reconciliation. Truth is there are too many people, too many stories that will never be cast in the construction of history. It is an impossible task, but a fact impossible to ignore.

And she knows the impossibility of understanding. From the kitchen she watches him and knows she can only listen. She promises him a New Canadian party with all their friends when the time comes and means it. She knows their daughter will always be loved and he knows his daughter will know only peace. Ripping purple kale she continues to watch. She thinks of the stories he tells at night when his mind is too tired to keep the walls from crumbling and nothing else exists beyond their bed. It has been such a long time for this man she knows. In the long-shadowed twilight she sees his eyes trace the page and remember. She watches the connection between here and there come and go. He knows luck and hard work more intimately than she. She has never stayed hidden save for childhood games. He is here now and she senses the price of his leaving. She can only listen, laugh when he laughs, and serve him white lady food with love.

It is all love.

CHAPTER THIRTY-EIGHT

The Typewriter

KIRSTEN VARNER

I brought an artifact into the classroom
For us to investigate. It is housed in a box
About a foot long, a foot wide and eight inches high.

The students look closely,
Begin to ask what's in it
Not yet, I say
What can the box tell us?
I challenge them to pause, look closely
The conversation takes off, voices added, questions posed

It's old, they say
How do we know?
The colour; the paper is yellowish. Is it paper?
Sort of, but not just paper, it looks like wall paper
There's dust. So there is, in a black molded handle,
Chiseled, letters pressed into its forming
UNDERWOOD, they say
Yes, dust clings in the tapers of the letters

There's a sticker, one says, it's a crest adds another
Boston University
The motto clear: Learning, Virtue, Piety

I know what it is, says a boy, a grin just turning up the corners of his mouth
My Grandfather had one
We have a secret, for a moment it's just ours
Let's open it up
The lid slowly lifted, voices silent, eyes focused, bodies lean forward

A typewriter.

Does it work? They ask
The parts still work, mostly,
The 7 sticks and the ink is dried up
I feel their disappointment; it mirrors mine

This possession that I cherish, that I have never let fulfill its purpose. If I ask what it needs the answer is it needs to speak; to take the words of the author and give them permanence.

I say I should really get it restored
It's a refrain said before and never acted on

I take a damp cloth, clean the strikers and the keys
Can we try it? Of course.

A piece of paper placed on the roller, turned to its proper position.
The excitement returns, anticipation to try a piece of history

The first child approaches and gingerly presses a key; the striker doesn't even make it halfway to the paper. Press harder, you won't break it, this is what it's designed to do. She strikes, firmly. Delight. The moistened ribbon has allowed the ghost of a trace of the letter to imprint on the clean white paper.

Others try
I've made my name
Said with a sense of wonder and pride

Why should this be any different from the typing that is so commonplace in their world?

The function is essentially the same
Strike a key, repeat as needed
The final result, typed words
Ink on paper

But this isn't the same. The connection to what they've created is direct.
My finger on the key, watch the striker squeeze the ink ribbon to the paper, press
the letter into being. My fingers make each letter, each word. The harder I press
the darker the letter; my emotions and emphasis communicated in slight variations of blackness.

Hands using a tool
Hands creating
Hands making thoughts visible

A truth is shared with us from another teacher, a memory from their past. The
"A's" and the ";" are always lighter. Weaker fingers striking those keys. The truth of
this statement rings true with us. Of course the "A's" are lighter, repeated in hushed
voices. Students place fingers on home row. Feeling the difference, experiencing
this truth.

More ghost letters pressed on paper
Names appear frequently, a need
To capture a piece of ourselves
And bits of the culture of the children

#YOLO, I wrote hashtag yolo, one child announces
Another looks, face quizzical
But the typewriter doesn't know hashtag, it thinks
You mean number
Talk of symbols, their concrete forms unchanging
Their meanings fluid
A secret code designed by each new generation to share
Something personal, something of their world

#, now hashtag, still number, once pound
What's pound? one asks
I can't say where it came from; it's before my time
It's enter on a telephone, says one child
Making meaning using the artifacts of their own time
Others nod; this fits into their world

There is something about these artifacts from an earlier time
Inspiring such wonder and curiosity
The manual nature of them
The physical nature of them

Gears and strikers, moving pieces fulfilling function
A process watched and interpreted by the naked eye

In a world where everything happens in a magical instant of electrons and invisible reactions there is something about this typewriter. Something observable, something tangible, something real.

CHAPTER THIRTY-NINE

Curriculum Artifact

Guided Reading Table

JACKIE SEIDEL

People will do anything for their children to help them in math and reading scores. I made a fortune just servicing that market. I love the terror in a mother's heart when she sees her child fall behind in reading. I made a fortune from that.

—KEVIN O'LEARY
(*Dragon's Den*, Series 6, Episode 19, March 14, 2012
http://www.cbc.ca/dragonsden/pitches/ukloo)

From an advertisement for Guided Reading Tables:

Gain your students' full attention with our Classic Guided Reading Table! Perfect for teacher directed activities and small group guided reading. This table will provide a unique learning environment as your students will be riveted to the lesson being taught and will learn valuable listening and eye-contact skills. Kidney shaped table … features a scratch resistant melamine surface and attractive black vinyl t-molding. … Rounded edges for added safety. (Wintergreen, 2015)

Not long ago, while looking for a project on a crowdfunding website, I came across a post by a teacher from the United States (or maybe Australia, or maybe it was the UK). She was asking strangers from around the world to donate several hundred dollars so that she could purchase a Guided Reading Table for her classroom. She extolled the table's virtues, telling would-be donors that it would improve her students' reading abilities and that she was unable to deliver a strong literacy program without it.

During my years as a classroom teacher, I—like many others, including the crowdfunding teacher—felt anxious about how best to approach reading and writing in my classroom. In the late 1990s I took a leave from my teaching position and studied for an MA in Language and Literacy Education at the University of British Columbia. I decided to learn everything I could about contemporary research in the fields of reading and literacy. Learning to read educational research with a discerning and critical eye was life changing. During my studies, I often longed for a time machine to return to my past classrooms for a do-over. But one thing that was never talked about, in all the course work, in the research literature, or in the work I did for my thesis, was classroom furniture, and especially not classroom furniture to improve the implementation of one reading methodology: Guided Reading (which I also had not yet heard of). In 1999, I went to the University of Alberta to start my PhD. I took courses and taught undergraduate courses in Language Arts curriculum, teaching and learning. Classroom furniture was not mentioned and again, neither was Guided Reading.

In 2003–2004, I took a position for one year as a Lecturer in Literacy Education at a university on the other side of the country. It was here that I first encountered the term Guided Reading, which was brought up by some teachers in a course I was teaching. My first response was anxiety. Was there a new reading theory and method I didn't know about? Had all my studying brought me still to a place of ignorance? Was I falling behind in my knowledge of the field? I was invited to a school to lead a professional development session about 'literacy.' We met in a room where the staff proudly showed me the newly purchased, leveled, Guided Reading books upon which they had spent their entire school budget for materials. I asked to see their school library—where were the other books? "We don't have a school library," they responded. During our session, we looked at beautiful children's literature: picture books, novels, nonfiction, graphic books. Some teachers became distraught and angry. They said: "Why don't we have these books in our schools?" They wanted to know whether schools in other provinces had them. They worried about all the money they had just spent on leveled books with promises that it would radically increase their reading test scores—had they been had? Anxiety all around. This was the beginning of an understanding that came full circle when I heard the echo of the crowdfunding teacher desperately pleading for a reading table to improve reading scores in her classroom.

The phone rang in my office at the university. It was a school superintendent. She had heard I was not teaching the "Guided Reading method" in my undergraduate Language Arts courses and was angry that I wasn't properly preparing new teachers for the classroom. We had a brief conversation. I explained to her that the course was about implementing the entire Language Arts curriculum; a curriculum that did not mention Guided Reading, and even if it did, or we could interpret that it did, it was just a minuscule part of what teachers were actually expected to do with what is called the "Language Arts." I said the university's purpose is to teach thinking, not fads or methods. She was furious. Their goal was to get their literacy levels up. I wasn't helping. That was my job, she said. She complained to my administration.

I moved back west across the continent, and was hired to teach grade three. The first thing I noticed when I walked into my classroom, even before the mouldy carpets, or the barred window that looked out on another rusty portable trailer wall, was a huge, hideous curved table that resembled a toilet seat and seemed to fill half the classroom. I didn't know what it was but I wanted it out. It seemed utterly useless. I walked down to the principal's office and asked where I could put the table and whether there was a more suitable one that I could use. KABOOM. That was a very expensive, brand-new Guided Reading Table and I was supposed to use it for implementing a leveled-books reading program with all the readers they had spent so much money on. By now I had enough experience to know it was time to quietly nod and go my own way. I shoved the rounded part of the table into the corner of the room, put some plants on one side, and a computer station with three chairs for children to gather around the other corner. It looked great. Welcoming.

There were shelves of Guided Reading books in that classroom, and sadly not much else for the children to read. I sorted through them and put the most hideous away in a cupboard. The rest I gave to a group of children on the first day, along with a package of round, random-coloured stickers, which I asked them to stick over the levels on the books. They looked at me with fear and disbelief. So I sat with them and together we unleveled the books. They were already so strongly inducted into the Guided Reading culture, it took them awhile to stop asking what level of book they should read. Eventually they understood that they were free to choose what they wanted or needed to read. The principal had commented one day that a particular child was a dull person, not very bright, a weak reader. A short while later, I walked past that child lying on the (mouldy) floor reading *The Magician's Nephew* by C. S. Lewis. For a moment, I almost fell for the principal's assessment, but then I stopped and sat and asked how the book was: "Great!" the child exclaimed, and proceeded to tell me all about the story and offered to read me the awesome paragraph she was in the middle of. What guidance or surveillance was required here, other than to say, "I loved that book too!" and "If you're interested, when you finish that book I have some other suggestions for you."

In a way, I have come to love Guided Reading Tables. They teach something about ourselves and this institution and what we have become. They tell us something about what we (some of us) think reading is. They tell us something about what we think teaching and learning are. They are a warning of how easily schools and teachers are fooled into buying something to ease our panic and make us feel like everything is under control if we just follow the procedures. I recall now that the teacher who was begging for money to buy the table that she needed to get her classroom literacy levels up gave one reason she needed the table: So that she could *see* everyone at once. Because guided reading, with its checklists and little plastic baggies for the leveled books raises the spectre of surveillance of children, teachers, classrooms and schools to a completely new 'level.' At once, we might be propelled by fear to purchase something to alleviate that fear and to fill our lack. This is how capitalism works. Someone makes a fortune from that.

But there is no end to the panics that can be manufactured and schools are the biggest potential marketplace of all. There is no end to the amount of clutter that can build up in schools, to fill the insatiable terror-hole created by the call to improve children's literacy or math scores for the good of the economy. It is a self-serving cycle that perhaps might only be broken by the insights provided by studying and thinking for oneself or together with others. Because then the table begins to reveal itself as the wasteful clutter it is, amongst so much other clutter, hideous against the mould, the leaking roofs, the windowless classrooms, the hunger in so many children's bellies. That's what actually might create terror in our hearts and what people like Kevin O'Leary don't want us to think about. For then, we might start to think about justice and love. About the world. About using what we already have. About what is already good enough.

In 1912 Maria Montessori (2009) wrote about children's desks. She was worried about how hard they were, that they separated children from each other and the world, and even that a spinal brace was being invented to help children sit straighter for longer periods of time. She was concerned that science was being (mis)used to convince educators that this was The Way. She described this in contrast to her own vision for children, which was a radical kind of freedom for children and teachers together to pursue the path that was calling to them, and that was the spirit of science, of inquiring together into the world where we find ourselves together. I think of Maria, more than one hundred years ago pondering the furniture in classrooms, pointing to how ridiculous it was, how damaging to the children, to both bodies and spirits—and I wonder how it is today that we find ourselves in this place with expensive, trademarked tables sold to teachers and schools for the express purpose of using expensive, trademarked reading materials (not books) for the express purpose of practicing detailed surveillance over children in the name of standardization. Maria's concern echoes across a century as children and teachers become hostages to so-called scientific programs designed to make them zombies.

The number of programs or products that can be sold to schools to save them from themselves, to alleviate the manufactured fears about preparing children for the future is infinite. It is the nature of capitalism to both create and capitalize on such fears. Learning to breathe and slow down enough to recognize that the things that matter, and that is most things in schools, life and relationships, that cannot be bought, sold or trademarked, is the most difficult work. The Guided Reading Table might stand as monumental reminder of this fact. But then again, maybe not. Perhaps we are utterly lost. I had bookmarked that original crowd-funding plea for a Table, but it has disappeared. No matter. A quick search revealed another one on a different crowdfunding site. A kindergarten teacher begging for a "real" Guided Reading Table to enhance her use of their "donation of an incredible Guided Reading Library." Not only is the table going to help her students who are in the "highest poverty" category improve their literacy skills, but she is also going to be able to see all the students at once, and it will stop the arguments and disruptions happening presently at their too small table. The enthusiasm of a true believer almost convinces me. Everything's going to be fine. It just costs three hundred dollars. I'm tempted to pledge her some money. Or perhaps I should suggest she take the children outside to play in nature. Or feed them. Or perhaps I might invent some furniture to improve reading scores. I could make a fortune from that.

Postscript:

My eye is caught by an article in *Business Insider* (Moss, 2014): "Now You Can Buy a Bulletproof Blanket Specifically Made for Kids to Use During School Shootings." The article displays photos of small children wearing thick blankets strapped to their backs like backpacks, or hunched under the blankets by their desks, or a teacher taking them out of a large, plastic bin in the classroom and handing them to a line of children. The company's advertising is cited above one photo: "When seconds count, Bodyguard blanket can provide a quick, simple solution for maximum protection against a school intruder." The only thing that comes to mind is to cite David Jardine's oft-repeated refrain: "Well, there you go then." Indeed. Fortunes will be made.

CHAPTER FORTY

New Stories AND Roles

ELISA RAPISARDA

New stories and roles are possible because I am that narrative and I also am not that narrative. I am that narrative because such stories compose my sense of self. Yet if the self were only that narrative there would be no possibility of abandoning that story and obtaining a new one.
—DAVID LOY (2010, P. 38)

Dear Beginning Teacher,

It may be hard to realize this at first, you may need some experiences to relate to, but one day you will question what your role is as a teacher. When you first start teaching, you will think you know your role. It may even be a narrative you've inherited without knowing it or without having questioned its origins. You may not have been awake to it and so you may not have noticed it is your narrative. You may think your role will be to engage, teach, reach and possibly even save the ones entrusted to you—a daunting task, surrounded by fear within your own heart and the hearts of the parents of the children you teach. You will fear failing and may have times when you feel that you are. Your role is those things, but it is also not those things.

You will begin to wonder what your role is because it will feel like everything and everyone may question you or maybe because something will feel amiss. You will even find you question yourself. You may begin to feel a bit helpless amidst the expectations, deadlines and constant defense of what you do within the four walls of your classroom. You may become overwhelmed at first, and eventually you will be ready, always with a defense. This is not necessarily a harmful experience. It will benefit you to think about your teaching and why you have made pedagogical decisions. Practice and experience stating these reasons eloquently will serve you well. If you feel inadequate at first, keep trying. Being eloquent and professional is what our profession needs.

Always remember that new stories are possible because *you are* and *you are not* that narrative. There is freedom in realizing a different narrative. Your identity will change if you choose it to or choose to seek these changes out. There are many new narratives that can be obtained. Instead of viewing everything you do as a need to fix the children entrusted to you and get them to behave in a specific way, you can choose to enjoy them, just as they are, with all that they bring. Delight in the child who questions everything, even without a hand up; he brings wonder. Relish in the child who runs in the classroom to be first to reach that picture book you just read; he brings the joy of new things. Embrace the child who blows the leaves of a still-life drawing around; she brings perspective and lightness. It is not that these behaviours will not seem to disrupt your plan of an effective classroom, but a different narrative will create space for these children and will create a sense of lightness, where you can smile.

When the parents of these children, ask you—with all the fear present in their hearts and written out on their faces—will my child be *okay*? You will have to be ready to share a story with them. What story will you choose? It is my advice that you choose the one that matters most. You may be able to conform a child to behave a specific way, but you may not be able to easily restore the wonder, joy, excitement and new perspective that was once there, especially if you were not awake to see it there in the first place. Especially if you are busy living out a narrative.

Whenever you need to, find the freedom of abandoning a story to obtain a new one.

CHAPTER FORTY-ONE

Too Young FOR AN Identity Crisis

KYRIA PIRES

When I was eleven, I started making up for myself a very thought-out identity crisis. Most pre-teen, teen girls experience your standard "do I do what I want or what my friends want?" identity crisis. Mine was not your standard crisis. It was the type of crisis you go through when you leave everything you have ever known behind and attempt to decide who you are in a place that doesn't even speak the same language you do. I haven't talked to very many immigrants about this, but I know this crisis, this inner conflict of holding on to a place that once was while staying true to your new place exists. Or so it did exist for me from eleven to twenty-two years of age.

Such a numbers kid I was that I honestly thought that math, with its certainty, could deliver me from this identity crisis: until twenty-two, I would technically have lived most of my life in Brazil so it only stood to reason that I would technically think, act and feel mostly like a Brazilian. My confidence in my math skills was shattered whenever I would visit my homeland and be introduced to others by my own extended family as a "Canadian." Their label hurt me not because I was ashamed of being Canadian but because their label automatically denied me of the very experience of being Brazilian. How to explain to them I was here and there at the same time? How to explain that my heart could be 100 percent in two places?

I suffered from a sickness, not being able to see how wonderful it might be not to be one thing or another. To be in between. This is a sickness many of us in the West suffer from. If we are this nationality, religion, we cannot be this *other* thing also. We hold on to our identities as though seeing and hearing the other side might kill us. This lack of listening to the *other*, it "deafens, fundamentalizes, and literalizes"(Jardine, 2008a, p. 13). So it did with me.

This black-and-white, no room for gray, dualistic perception of who I should be, worked for me. Or it did—until I was twenty-three and wasn't mostly or less of anything. The numbers 12 and 11 didn't add up to 23 really. You cannot measure who you are with numbers. A teacher is not 90 percent traditional and 10 percent inquiry oriented. A teacher adapts and goes in between, she plans her lessons by listening to her students.

It was Thomas King in his own questioning of identity (King, 2003, p. 36) that reminded me of my little numbers experiment. I thought, too, about my current identity question as a teacher. I call it a question instead of a crisis because the crisis comes from having to choose between extremes. When you don't have that, it's not a crisis—it's just a question of where you are going that day or where you want to go in the future.

I stand in my classroom every day and I do not yet know completely who I am as a teacher. I am in between that story I learned as I went to school, that of my students' parents and the one I am striving for my students. That is okay. It is not a crisis. Besides, I'm too young to have another identity crisis.

I'll fit myself between
The twinkles in their eyes
The questions and the answers
Prejudice and acceptance

I'll fit myself between
The sergeant and the private
The student and the teacher
Open and shut doors

I'll fit myself between
Their laughter and their tears
Their chatter and their ears
Their quest and their uncertainty

I'll fit myself between
Having it all together and losing it altogether ...

CHAPTER FORTY-TWO

From Darkness TO Light

Observations From Inside
the Linoleum Cavern

KATE SCHUTZ

Meditation [has] the power to reveal and heal.

—THICH NHAT HAHN (1975, P. 60)

And so, these days, he can articulate. He has spent weeks now, alone with himself. Away from me and our life and all the distractions within it. In this space, he has acknowledged his thoughts and feelings as being there. They exist. He exists. He is alive. But his head is spinning. Everything is a barrier—the potential, the possibility. There is so much to overcome, to fail at, to have to do. So much that *even though it seems good now* could be really bad later, really bad. Or worse! Unknown (with a capital U, yes!), that which cannot be named. Unknown could be really big and horrible and out of his control—you just never know what it can turn itself into. If he allows himself to think too much about it he gets smaller and smaller and is paralyzed. And that isn't a nice place to be. (I thought meditation was supposed to be relaxing?) He can make Unknown disappear. Don't think anymore. Stop noticing. Stop inquiring. Stop listening. Stop feeling so much. Stop being still. Turn the lights out on those thoughts.

(But monsters grow in the darkness, you know.)

"If you want to know your own mind, there is only one way: to observe and recognize everything about it" (Hahn, 1975, p. 37).

I had a friend in high school whom I met during a spare. For weeks, he crouched on the floor, completely immobile, with his knees squeezed to his chest. He would wrap his forearms across his head, nestling himself deeper and deeper into the small space between his kneecaps the way a gopher digs himself into his burrow. He sat like this every day. I don't think he ever went to class or to the bathroom or home or anywhere. And no one ever talked to him or really ever looked at him. But in that spare, it was just him and me and the echoing linoleum cavern that was our school hallway. For weeks I sat opposite him and he never looked up once. Eventually, over time, the width of the hallway grew smaller and smaller, squeezing us together like the trash compactor in *Star Wars*, until one day I found myself staring at the top of his head and clasping his forearms. His hurt and loneliness had finally become part of me and I couldn't bear the suffering.

"The suffering of others is our own suffering, and the happiness of others is our own happiness" (Hahn, 1975, p. 49).

Enough already! Better to flick on the light and reach under the bed and yank that monster out by its tail or big ears or whatever you can clutch in your fist. Don't let it wiggle away, reach deeply and purposefully and once you've got him, don't let go. Squeeze tightly and pull. Heave until you are face-to-face, nose-to-nose, eyebrow to furrowed eyebrow and look that monster in the face and say "YOU! You are here!"

And then—you have seen it, and named it and you know you can begin.

CHAPTER FORTY-THREE

Hypocrite

JODI LATREMOUILLE

I know what you need, dear …
You need to be fully present with students, expand your sense of time.
(Who is that kid knocking at my door?
Don't they know I'm busy writing dead-lines?)
Good nutrition is essential. Practice moderation and the enjoyment of really great food—no regrets, no excuses.
(And sneak chocolate bars after they go to bed)
And only step on the scale first thing in the morning.
(And delay the next meal,
this gnawing faint weakness is called willpower—
oh, didn't you know?)
You should try meditation. Time is not running out. Enjoy the moment.
(With knots in my stomach and shortness of breath)
Read. Re-read. Study. Learning cannot/should not be commodified. Sit with it.
(And hear the knock on the door—is it my old friend?
Yes! It's Amazon Books! Come in, have some tea!
There's only one here—I ordered three last week, what is taking so long?)

You are enough. Yes, you are. No, your work is not perfect. Indeed, it is so imperfect I don't even know where to begin. No, you don't need to stand against the ruler. Keep studying, keep writing.

(And I think, if only I had been taller—what then?
Could I have looked down upon the fumbling, struggling mess,
breathing cleaner air?)

Your daughters are beautiful—not models, not movie stars, not even a little bit. But beautiful curly-haired tornadoes nonetheless. You don't need model children. You need real children.

(Some days I can smile at myself, a sidelong, "not bad" kind of smile.
Other days, I avert my eyes and wonder what it would have been like
in the days before looking-glasses.)

You don't need to be perfect, no.
Good girl.
　　　In the real world …
You are such a good artist!
How can I help you?

　　　　　　　　　　　　　　　　　This is for your own good.

I am so sorry.

　　　　　　　　　　(Our professional obligation is to care.
　　　　　　　　　　Cure? Yes, care, that's what I said.
　　　　　　　　　　It says here on page 32 in the manual.
　　　　　　　　　　You need to cure and be careful.
　　　　　　　　　　Yes, care, that's what I said.
　　　　　　　　　　Isn't anybody listening?)

I know what you need! You need …
To care for yourself—first! A-ha!
No, really. Try it.
The world will not stop.
I promise. I know.

　　　　　　　　　　　　(… you go first! And report back to me)

CHAPTER FORTY-FOUR

Two Young Fish

DEIRDRE BAILEY

There are these two young fish swimming along, and they happen to meet an older fish swimming the other way, who nods at them and says, "Morning, boys, how's the water?" And the two young fish swim on for a bit, and then eventually one of them looks over at the other and goes, "What the hell is water?"

—DAVID FOSTER WALLACE (2005, N.P.)

Humanity has evolved to seek meaning, to find beauty that stirs the soul and attempt to connect with it. We were born to experience, to understand from experience, to gain knowledge directly through the senses and the gut. But our senses have dulled. We have transformed beauty from a place to an object, confused it with pretty or attractive, mistaken it for happiness and assumed it can be possessed. "We suffer from being focused on 'the wrong things' and from being without much focus" (Sewall, 2012, p. 266) and slip easily into diversion and distraction; our default settings.

> And the so-called real world will not discourage [us] from operating on [our] default settings, because the so-called real world of men and money and power hums merrily along in a pool of fear and anger and frustration and craving and worship of self. (Wallace, 2005, n.p.)

It is an anesthetized existence. One in which more is better, and skepticism is safety, and power is success. It is a world in which we criticize rodeos for cruelty while gnawing on a McDonald's hamburger, or condemn the oil sands for endangering ducks while fueling our SUVs. It is an existence in which questions become infuriating because their hollowness lays bare an appalling absence of wonder in youth who only want to know how to minimize effort, maximize comfort and win a prize at the end.

The Lorax says he speaks for the trees and we watch as nobody listens and we say to ourselves that WE will speak for OUR trees but nobody *really* looks at the trees and nobody listens. Nobody notices that they already speak of solitude and fortitude and persistence, and that if we could only cultivate the ability to *see* them as they are, we would not find ourselves always so desperate to speak. And we might even find peace in their quiet confidence.

> In their highest boughs the world rustles, their roots rest in infinity; but they do not lose themselves there, they struggle with all the force of their lives for one thing only: to fulfill themselves according to their own laws, to build up their own form, to represent themselves. ... And every young farm boy knows that the hardest and noblest wood has the narrowest rings, that high on the mountains and in continuing danger the most indestructible, the strongest, the ideal trees grow. (Hesse, 1984, n.p.)

I don't want to teach plants, poetry or politics. I want to teach perception and awareness and sensitivity and vulnerability. I want to teach youth to deliberately exercise control over how and what they think and help them focus their attention on what matters. I want to teach trees and roots and *water*. Beauty is not a possession or an attribute. It is a perspective. How we look at things or choose to construct meaning can create beauty in the space around us. It is not a simple task, but we owe it to humanity to dig deep, take root, be still and grow hope:

> ... while reminding ourselves over and over:
> *This is water.*

CHAPTER FORTY-FIVE

Whisking Away THE Table

TOWANI DUCHSCHER

The man in the shimmering black cape whirls around the stage
causing my eyes to dart
here
     and there
         and everywhere.
His assistant, long legs, sequined dress, and mounds of make-up,
steps carefully up on the platform
and lies down on the red satin draped table.
The crowd watches as the magician whirls his cape back,
flourishes his hands,
and in one quick movement
whisks away the table.
I gasp and hold my breath as I watch her float in mid-air.
What holds her up?

CHAPTER FORTY-SIX

Spontaneous Learning

PAUL LE MARQUAND

Room-temperature diamonds are not forever; at 298 K (25 °C), graphite is eternal by comparison. In grade 9 science, I often use diamond and graphite to help introduce allotropes (Gk., *allo* = other, *tropos* = manner). Both are elemental forms of carbon; however, they differ in their spatial connectivity. Graphite is two-dimensional carbon; its multiple honeycomb-like layers can slide over one another, making it great for 2HB pencils. As an aside, at this point I do clarify the misconception regarding pencil "lead" by showing students the gray dot of graphite in my right hand made by an errant, airborne pencil. As discussed in grade 8 science, diamond's 3D structure results in its being the hardest known material; meaning that, in a scratching contest against another substance, diamond always comes out unscathed. And, similar to new releases in movie theatres, 3D carbon is much more expensive and rarer than carbon in 2D.

Yet, a chemist can definitively say that at room temperature the conversion of diamond to graphite is spontaneous. In thermochemistry, spontaneity describes whether a process with certain characteristics and at a certain temperature will proceed or not; it provides no guidance as to timeframe. A spontaneous reaction will certainly occur; it just may take a while. Gibbs Free Energy (ΔG) can be thought of as an indication of spontaneity; if the value of ΔG is negative, zero, or positive, then the conversion is spontaneous, in equilibrium, or non-spontaneous, respectively. For example, equation 1 shows that the spontaneous breakdown of diamond to graphite has a ΔG value of -3 kilojoules.

$$C \text{ (s, diamond)} \rightarrow C \text{ (s, graphite)} \quad \Delta G = -3 \text{ kJ} \quad (1)$$

Learning can be thought of as a confluence of processes of layering and peeling apart, of entangling and untangling. Depending on the student and subject matter, studies can be very quick or scholarly. Gibbs Free Energy and its relationship to enthalpy (ΔH), temperature (T) and entropy (ΔS), as outlined in equation 2, may be able to provide some practical insights as to how we can make sure our school communities are places of spontaneous learning, where ΔG is negative.

$$\Delta G = \Delta H - T\Delta S \tag{2}$$

According to equations 3 and 4, a process will certainly be spontaneous if, at a constant temperature, ΔH and ΔS have negative and positive values, respectively.

$$\Delta G < 0 \tag{3}$$
$$\Delta H - T\Delta S < 0 \tag{4}$$

Enthalpy is a measure of how much heat a process requires or releases. If scientists designed a faucet, the knobs would say hot and less hot; by convention, cold does not exist. A theoretical piece of matter without any heat or motion is defined as being at absolute zero (0 K). When exploring this concept of heat with grade seven students, I also use a relatable example involving a refrigerator door; its role is to keep heat out, not cold in.

A space for spontaneous learning with a negative ΔH value would be exothermic, referring to its release of heat to its surroundings. Said a different way, an observer would sense the process as being warm. This exothermic state could be manifested in a classroom in a variety of ways: a warm smile, a warm welcome, a warm embrace of both opportunities and challenges. A teacher's lesson plans and interpretation of curriculum would not be dispassionate or impersonal, but relevant to the dynamics of students' lived experiences. Schools would be sources of energy for the entire community of learners.

Entropy describes whether a process results in an increased or decreased level of disorder in a system. I recruit grade eight students to kinesthetically model water molecules as they transition through the solid, liquid and gaseous states. The students begin in a rigid arrangement holding hands in one corner of the room and, by the time that they have undergone melting and evaporation, they are moving quickly and independently in every direction. Referencing an industrialized model of schools has aided some students in their comprehension of this topic. A school can be viewed as a highly ordered space: students are grouped by age, seated in a matrix, shuffled between classes according to a table of fixed times, and assessed on a particular day using a standardized test.

A spontaneous learning environment requires an increase in disorder. It is important to clarify that the Greek letter delta denotes change. A classroom with a positive entropy value would not be complete anarchy, void of any structure or boundaries. It could be a loosening of the constraints on a student's learning and a gradual transfer of responsibility; or it might be manifested as an increase in options, an expansion of the safe pasture where students can explore.

A final thermochemical encouragement towards incremental changes in a learning space's enthalpy and entropy may lie in the fact that ΔH and ΔS are both state functions. All that matters to a state function is where you started and stopped; the exact intermediate steps have no bearing on the function's overall value. One can imagine getting on the only elevator in a building at the third floor. You select the fifth floor but the carriage is already heading down to the first floor. An outside observer would be unaware of your slight detour. The concept of a state function provides for flexibility and differentiation, as each member of the school community can have their own path. It allows for times when a teacher needs additional support from colleagues (increase in enthalpy) or uniform compliance (decrease in entropy) from students, especially with respect to their safety; small perturbations are natural. The goal is to make changes such that the overall trend is towards a welcoming, dynamic environment where learning is spontaneous and pencil graphite is plentiful.

CHAPTER FORTY-SEVEN

"I Love THE Terror IN A Mother's Heart"

DAVID W. JARDINE

The Introduction to *Pedagogy Left in Peace* (Jardine, 2012) sketches out the threat-mechanism that causes us to entrench into the tried and true in order to protect ourselves and our kin. "Time Is [Not] Always Running Out" (Jardine, 2013b) makes links between industrial assembly, efficiency, and the sways of the market economy, and how such mechanisms create, rely on and maintain a low-level panic in order to sustain themselves. It traces, then, how this "cult of efficiency" (Callahan, 1964) took over the imagination and practices of education and led to the rendering of the living disciplines of knowledge into things akin to industrial objects to be efficiently assembled. This promise of efficiency then dovetailed with the never-fully-fulfilled promise of market logic—once efficiency movements in industry reach a certain threshold in their satiation of market demands, market demands themselves became the topic of psychological manipulation to increase demand (see, e.g., Leach, 1994). In both of these texts, there were only hints at the issue of the deliberate manipulation of fear and dissatisfaction that might inform educational practices. I always tended to pull back for fear of exaggeration and distortion. I have also always warned new teachers that they are easy prey for the predatory practices of publishing companies and their promises to relieve their anxieties.

So, in this light, I now offer this, from Kevin O'Leary. It is cited from the Canadian Broadcasting Company's series *Dragon's Den*. O'Leary has more recently been seen on the American TV show *Shark Tank*. He is affiliated with The Learning Company, a software company currently owned by Houghton Mifflin Harcourt, one of North America's largest providers of various packaged educational products and "learn to read" series such as *Carmen Sandiego* and *Reader Rabbit*:

> I'm all for children, but I want to make a buck. I *am* "Carmen Sandiego." I *am* "Reader Rabbit." People will do anything for their children to help them in math and reading scores. I made a fortune just servicing that market. I love the terror in a mother's heart when she sees her child fall behind in reading. I made a fortune from that. (O'Leary, 2012)

Just to close this loop, this market logic does not work properly when one simply takes advantage of such terror and satisfies it. Such terror must be *cultivated* and *maintained* in just the right measure. Market economies are premised on the creation of dissatisfaction and the promise and semblance of just enough satisfaction to allow dissatisfaction to re-emerge once the promise is forgotten. The hidden complicities of those who love and foster terror and then magically appear just in time to alleviate it—*this* is a story as old as the hills.

Reading and understanding *that* story allow me to begin stepping away from its allure. It allows me to interrupt the panic-manipulation and to return to the lovely, difficult work of learning to read with children.

CHAPTER FORTY-EIGHT

Dear Adam's Teacher

LISA TAYLOR

Dear Adam's teacher,

Hello. My name is Lisa Taylor and I am Adam's camping companion, ski partner, late-night texting buddy and most important his auntie.

I understand that you are Adam's science teacher. You are very lucky to have this role and to get to spend so much time with him. He is a curious boy and especially loves the subject of science.

I'm not sure how much you really know about Adam but I wanted to share a few things about him. He is brilliant. He can start a mean campfire and has this thing about organizing his room just so. He doesn't like reading but loves being read to. He can make my four-year-old son laugh hysterically and has a confidence with tools that I wouldn't go near. He has a strong desire to learn and an even stronger desire to fit in.

I've recently learned that you want Adam to take an exam to determine what he does or does not know in terms of the Science 8 curriculum. As a fellow educator I understand your intentions, your need to know where your students are, your responsibility to the assessment process and your commitment to the curriculum. I have also tested my students for the same reasons you want to test Adam. I challenge you to consider an alternative. I ask that you question the traditional system and ask yourself what it is that you are really looking for and what really matters with the results. Does it matter what Adam scores on the exam? Will it make a difference for him in your class or in his life?

Over the years Adam and I have had many conversations about school and about teachers. And with every conversation I draw the same conclusion—Adam loves so much of what school is about. He loves that he gets to hang out with his buddies and talk about what they did on the weekend, he loves that he gets to go to the gym and play dodge ball, he loves joking around with his teachers, he loves his new locker and he loves being introduced to new topics. He doesn't complain about school or his teachers too much and is filled with such joy and positivity that I find refreshing coming from a grade eight boy with learning challenges.

I worry that this amazing attitude towards school is slowly coming to an end. I worry that the education system of which you and I are both part is going to methodically and predictably take this love of school and learning away from him. I worry that teachers won't see Adam for the curious kid that he is and see him as another coded kid that they have to figure out how to deal with. I worry that he is going to be placed in special classes for kids "like" him and taken out of lovely science classes such as yours. I worry that he is going to feel forced to memorize facts for exams and be pressured to produce work for no reason other than for a grade to be determined. And all this for the sake of knowing what letter or number to put beside his name come report cards.

Adam was the first little one in our family to go to kindergarten and I have been in awe of his successes over the past eight years. He has accomplished a great deal, all with a positive attitude and loads of perseverance. I can still remember watching his little hands manipulate the alphabet cards lining up the letters A to Z perfectly. And how he used my fingers as digits to add 7 plus 8 when he ran out of his own. I don't remember what age it was that he did those things but I do know it wasn't at the age in which the developmental milestones books told my sister it was supposed to be. He didn't care that the doctors or his mom couldn't check off the list of things he was supposed to do at three, four or five years old. Just like he doesn't care now about scoring a high mark on an exam. And neither should we. It's not about what Adam knows or doesn't know; it's about his journey as a human being and his love of learning.

Why can't he sit in on a science class as a curious little boy who wants to be there just to listen to what is being taught? Not to score a certain grade, or recall the water cycle or memorize the periodic table but to be part of the conversation, to be part of the magic that happens in a science class. Why do we have expectations and predicted outcomes for every student before they even walk through our doors? Why can't we let students and my nephew enjoy school for the wonder that it is? These are some very complicated questions not intended for you to answer but for you and me to ponder as teachers.

Adam is different. So are you and so am I. We are all different. We have our strengths and our challenges. Unfortunately for Adam, the things that challenge him the most are much of what traditional education is made up of. He can't read well, he has a hard time memorizing things, he has a difficult time making complex connections between topics and he becomes exhausted quickly when he asks his brain to process too much, too fast. We know all that. How do we make sure that those obstacles do not limit Adam, do not send him to special classes and do not disadvantage him so much that he stops caring about school and learning?

I hope my words inspire you to think differently about the great responsibility that we teachers take on. I hope that maybe you can see how important it is for Adam and all kids to be given the opportunity to love everything about school and be measured in other ways besides scores on tests and assignments. Adam is so much more than what any test score will tell you.

Please allow Adam to demonstrate his understanding a different way. Please don't have a preconceived idea of what he is supposed to learn or produce in your class. And know that the things that matter the most, such as Adam's joy, curiosity, perseverance and self-confidence, are all unmeasurable.

Thank you for the amazing work you do with students every day. I think as teachers we have the most important and challenging job of all.

Kind Regards,
Adam's Aunt and a fellow educator

CHAPTER FORTY-NINE

Remembrances OF THE Land AND Rocks IN My Pocket

LESLEY TAIT

The music of the land rose up in all its many textures, each tree, each cliff, each place he'd passed, until finally the song of home added its voice to the others. His cave called out from the blanketing shrubs and pillows of moss at its mouth, and Chiro followed the familiar sound back into the sheltering earth.

—ARI BERK (BERK & LONG, 2012, N.P.)

The hands of my children are continually picking up rocks and stones. Their fingers grip tight to their latest treasure. Each groove and bump is felt as their small fingertips run over the surface. Soon their hand is turned over and an open palm allows their eyes to examine each facet of its being. These are not necessarily the prettiest rocks or the biggest, but simply stones that somehow meet their unknown needs at that particular moment in time.

After this thorough examination, these same hands unceremoniously shove these stones into pants pockets, coat pockets and when all other options are full, their mother's pockets. These stones then find their way into all aspects of our home. They become bath toys, decorations for a Christmas centrepiece, pets for various stuffed animals and toppings for delicious mud pies.

I have watched my children lament over the loneliness of a solitary stone, create entire stone families, and stop mid-sentence to address the needs of a distant rock calling out to them. To them, these stones are precious. They have the ability to feel, be lonely, cold and afraid. They can also be comforted and feel love.

It is easy to dismiss these activities and attachments as childish; to view these understandings as make-believe or simply the games of children. It is more difficult to see them for what they are: deep and true understandings of the world and our land. Rocks are grounding. They provide us with a weight and gravitas and pull us back to the earth in a way that does not first surround us with a protective layer. Rocks are foundational and markers of meaning. They seek to remind us of our long-forgotten relationship with the land.

This is how my children travel through the world; attentive, wisely aware and hands at the ready, in search of a stone needing saving in their pocket.

CHAPTER FIFTY

Fish Bones IN THE Trees

ERIN QUINN

The sole work of La Loba *is the collecting of bones. She collects and preserves especially that which is in danger of being lost to the world. Her cave is filled with the bones of all manner of desert creatures: the deer, the rattlesnake, the crow. But her specialty is wolves.*

She creeps and crawls and sifts through the montañas, *mountains, and* arroyos, *dry riverbeds, looking for wolf bones, and when she has assembled an entire skeleton, when the last bone is in place and the beautiful white sculpture of the creature is laid out before her, she sits by the fire and thinks about what song she will sing.*

And when she is sure, she stands over the criatura, *raises her arms over it, and sings out. That is when the rib bones and leg bones of the wolf begin to flesh out and the creature becomes furred.* La Loba *sings some more, and more of the creature comes into being; its tail curls upward, shaggy, and strong. And* La Loba *sings more and the wolf creature begins to breathe.*

And still La Loba *sings so deeply that the floor of the desert shakes, and as she sings, the wolf opens its eyes, leaps up, and runs away down the canyon.*

—CLARISSA PINKOLA ESTÉS, FROM HER BOOK *WOMEN WHO RUN WITH THE WOLVES*
(1992, PP. 23–24)

It's a bright, warm morning in mid-May. Our toes brush the dewy grass as we descend into the green space next to the school. We stoop to collect twigs and leaves. Pockets bulge with pinecones. One student ducks into a grove of spruce, and yells out in surprise. We come to gather near her. She points to the skeleton of a fish. We wonder why it is there, in the middle of the trees, kilometers away from any river or lake. One student guesses that a bird must have caught it in Fish Creek, then brought it here for its supper. Maybe she was feeding her babies, a boy supposes.

We keep wandering. Our eyes on the ground, we try to find the most beautiful specimens that nature gifted us. We examine every smooth stone, and every fallen branch. One girl cups her hands together to scoop up soft amber tamarack needles left over from the season before. Three students sit on the hill, their sticks and stones in piles beside them, making chains of dandelions that have burst forth in brilliant yellow a few weeks before it's wise to. The threat of frost is not yet gone.

It's quiet, but we can hear a robin singing and the wind gently ruffling the poplar leaves. Bursts of young voices punctuate nature's song. I don't rush them, but soon they begin to collect near me, showing me their collections, the unique shapes of the sticks, the hues of the pebbles. We return to our classroom with our treasures and lay them out together to create our design. Each student is involved in this part. Everyone's voice counts. We listen to each other. We admire our work as it gets reassembled vertically on the door.

The challenge is a door-decorating contest. What's the point of this? Why would we spend our time doing something as inane as putting paper up on a door? Here's the thing, though: what's the point of *anything* we do in school? What's the point of quadratic equations, biomes, or onomatopoeia? If you treat a thing right, then it becomes something that matters. If you look for those things "in danger of being lost to the world," then you find the point.

Because we are looking, we find our fish bones, between the trees. We sing over our fish skeleton. We sing to breathe life into this walk in the woods, to this decoration on our door. We sing to ignore the pressures of programs of studies and final projects. We sing over the things that matter. As we keep singing, in spite of it all, our fish skeleton gains scales, and then gills, and splashes off into the waves.

CHAPTER FIFTY-ONE

Let's Take A Journey

KIRSTEN VARNER

We are going on a journey,
all of us, together.

I choose the space.
A place to meet,
to begin.

Here we gather, all of us.
together, in this space
sitting in a circle
peer out, gaze up
try to take in the vastness
begin to wonder.

I will leave you here for a while,
to while in wonder and dream.

I forge on ahead
scout the trails
plan, map out possibilities
What wonders, hazards, secrets
each path offers
Don't worry, I won't dig up all the treasures,
I will leave them for you.

I find places to stop, to gather again
Space to breathe, to ponder
to take in the view
to share what has been and what's to come.

When I'm ready I'll return to you
Ready to listen
to where you need to go
Ready to hear
which path you are set to tackle
Ready to know
what catches hold of you, lights a flame
questions building pressure in your chest
answers you long for
what are you searching for

We are ready now.
To start our journey, all of us, together.
We surge forth into the wilds,
disappearing into whispering trees.

CHAPTER FIFTY-TWO

Old Dog, Same Trick

DAVID W. JARDINE

Your cause of sorrow
Must not be measured by his worth, for then
It hath no end.
    —ROSS TO SIWARD, ON THE DEATH OF SIWARD'S SON. *MACBETH*, ACT V, SCENE VIII

Give sorrow words: the grief that does not speak
Whispers the o'er-fraught heart and bids it break.
    —MALCOLM TO MACDUFF. *MACBETH*, ACT IV, SCENE III

"The individual case … is never simply a case; it is not exhausted by being a particular example of a universal law or concept" (Gadamer, 1989, p. 39). There is no such "thing" as sorrow or grief. It is always *this* lamenting in *this* arc of telling, of seasons, of breath and faces. To paraphrase John Caputo (1993), sorrow always involves proper names, grieving is always one's own and, one way or another, in one shape or another, "from it no one can be exempt" (Gadamer, 1989, p. 356).

That we might commiserate in such matters is not made possible by each of us deflecting upwards into some governing concept or essence or law or theme under which our sorrows fall. My sorrow does not find much voice or relief in such falling. It is not *given* words but is taken away and rendered and handed back as bones.

"The rule does not comprehend it" (Gadamer, 1989, p. 39).

We don't experience our affinity via this abstracting route. Commiseration cannot be sought in experiencing ourselves as examples or instances. Affinity is, instead, a lateral pass, one of kinship, kindness, love. In these matters, I am always, for good or ill, *someone*, full of gesture and just this word and withholding and waiting and perhaps embrace. And just this error of having waited too long full of good intent. All this.

I find myself nearly apologizing to some of the people who've read this. This work is hard to bear and, if it works (and it doesn't always work, and its working is in the hands of those to whom it is addressed), it's hard to put down. And I'll admit that there is a resounding joy to it precisely because of this. "Free spaces" (Gadamer, 1992, p. 59) and some relief, some lifting and lightening, some setting it down by taking it up and setting it down in words.

So yesterday, November 3, 2014. Father and grown daughter outside the Bragg Creek vet's place, big and old Great Pyrenees on a leash, matted and woolly and friendly and black and white. Big splayed paws a good six inches across. Well trod and often.

Inside to buy dog food, and, I'd say by her age and carriage, a woman and wife and mother, a bit in tears as she and the doctor emerge from a side room.

Yep. Got it.

It's time, it seems. And that semblance swirls up and around in the air.

Made sure I stopped on the way back to the truck to tell the old thing that he's a good dog. A little unspoken thanks. You need to thank your teachers, but the best thanks is turning away and practicing the teaching.

The language of this intimacy is a rough ride. Every pull towards generalities feels like a betrayal and yet I must give sorrow words. I can "identify" with that spot these neighbors seem to be in, but that word is too easy to use, too flip. Part of it is the coming due of the silent bargain some of us have made with these domestics. I remember a black-humored version laughed over years ago with friends:

"Don't worry. When the time comes, I will kill you."

Hah! Yes. I will. I promise.

I can identify with the spot they are in precisely because of *how* we are identical. Our cases are incommensurate and *that* is how we are the same. *That* is how each new case is an act of revival and rejuvenation, not just repetition. That is how our kinship remains alive, there, unspoken, in that parking lot. Our kinship is not identity under a rule but is had in and through the incommensurate and stubborn grace of particularity. We lean towards. What we hear beckons. We are properly stilled and summoned. This child, this patient, this turn of phrase in a text, this upwell of warm air coming up off the wood for winter, that old Fido full of specific fidelities and keeps of memory, makes me stop over it and wait for what is to come.

Thus our cases, each intimate, need names and faces and occasions to be what they are. Sit. Stay.

Ivy. That was my dog's name. Ivy, right there all over again, up and run in that chance morning meeting of pets and coos and matted feet and leash pulled taut in the air of coming grief. Ivy's flesh being only half torn to bits by an inefficient cougar that didn't finish the job. The weight of her in my arms, tipping back in blood and glazed look and the sizzle-panic nickel-spittle rush for what turns out to be useless help.

My being drawn to this morning event is thus a lateral pass. It is not a passage through some shared "identity," but a passage into the passable kinship of the flesh, the eyes that see ghosts shimmering around and nearing from all directions, the big long nose arced up and sniffing something in the air. Beheld in my arms. My bones start tearing, but hush now. There is a secret pleasure here, too, to be near this happenstance, this teaching, this moment, and to write in order to stay near and draw others near.

Say it, then. Almost jealousy. That they have such luck to have such proximity to such a great teacher.

Good boy.

I remember after Ivy was half-killed and we had to put her down. That's such a phrase. It summons gravity and the falling of flesh to the earth. But it also says that we had to put her down, because if we didn't put her down we couldn't bear the weight of it.

And those post-traumatic reveries, still close and fraught and suddening, still imagining her running towards me down off the green hill, and having to say, again:

"No, Ivy. Go."

Good girl.

CHAPTER FIFTY-THREE

Thoughts ON Being Neither Finished NOR Unfinished

MEGAN LIDDELL

Dear New Teacher,

As you turn out your classroom lights today, you may smile a little about some good moments of your day. That brief smile is complicated, so often followed by the heavy weight of discouragement that all teachers feel from time to time, moment to moment, and year to year. My best advice? Embrace that feeling. That feeling, that weight, that discouragement, is a part of teaching. It warrants a moment of recognition; as David Jardine has called it, a moment of "Ah. There it is." Where is that overwhelming feeling coming from? The panic that accompanies the lump in your throat when you open another e-mail from an upset parent, or the quickening in your pulse when you look at the pages of Program of Study outcomes and worry that you haven't covered enough, and that time is running out? Who is scripting the voice in your head that is whispering that you're not cut out for this? Reminding you of your every misstep, keeping you up at night with guilt over the kids you just didn't get to again today. That little voice has so many examples to choose from on a daily basis. There are so many ways to go wrong, and to disappoint yourself, and everyone else, as a teacher.

Many of the complaints will revolve around not getting to everything, not remembering everything, or failing to stay 'on the ball.' It will seem that colleagues, mentors and veterans have this mastered, but 'getting to everything' is actually not what they have mastered, and you don't have to either. Take a deep breath. Then take another one. To continue on with teaching is to learn to *reframe unfinished-ness*. This is possibly a harder task than getting to everything in the first place, but a more important one.

David Loy (2010) tells us in his work *The World Is Made of Stories* that:

> the most interesting narratives pursue something that is unattainable in the way sought. In the process of questing, however, the one who quests is transformed. By foreclosing any closure, no-thing-ness transcends whatever situation one finds oneself in. I may be so caught up in stories and roles that I am unaware of my no-thing-ness, yet 'it' is never bound. Like a prisoner whose cell gate has never been locked, I may not notice this freedom but insofar as I am 'it' there is never anything to attain, only something to realize and actualize. (pp. 40–41)

Looking back ten years into my career, I wish I had spent fewer sleepless nights worrying about 'getting to it all' and staying 'on top of things,' making lists and letting checking things off become the most important thing. I wish I had spent more time learning to accept the *unfinished-ness* of teaching. Practicing deep breaths when I missed something, and focusing more on my *next* step than on my missteps. I wish the voice in my head had learned to tell me that what I did with kids in *each moment* mattered as much as the whole collection of moments.

In *The World Is Made of Stories*, Loy also reminds us that "our stories are never finished and therefore never unfinished. If reality itself is always incomplete, each moment becomes complete in itself, lacking nothing" (p. 40).

Don't let that voice tell you platitudes like 'You are good enough' or 'Forget about any mistakes you made.' These aren't the message of reframing unfinished-ness. Rather, such vague comforts only reinforce the myth of finished-ness; another alternative to constantly feeling unfinished being to convince ourselves that we are finished. You aren't good enough, and you won't be. Pursuing that 'end' is such misdirected thought and energy.

Immerse yourself in meaningful, rich and deep work with students and you will forget about finishing it. I wish I had met Wendell Berry earlier in my career and taught the voice in my head to ask questions that matter instead. The questions that Wendell Berry asks in his interview with Bill Moyers in 2013: "What is the right thing to do?" and "What is this work asking of me?" These questions are at the heart of reframing, embracing and loving the unfinished-ness of our work.

Teacher, you are never finished, but you are also never unfinished. What matters most is what you do with the very next moment in front of you.

CHAPTER FIFTY-FOUR

There Is Only This Farm

SCOTT HASSETT

Our damages, to watersheds and ecosystems will have to be corrected one farm, one forest, one acre at a time.

—WENDELL BERRY (2005, P. 62)

Great problems call for many small solutions.

—WENDELL BERRY (2005, P. 65)

There is only this farm, only this place. This truth strikes me, catches me in my tracks and forces me to reconsider; reconsider what I can accomplish, more important what I have the right to accomplish. "Arrogance cannot be cured by greater arrogance" (Berry, 2005, p. 65), a reminder that despite my best intentions, my deepening roots of understanding, my desire to act in concert with others, my influence is, and must always be, limited.

Only here and now, what is immediate and close. How can this be, how can this place be enough? The darkness seems so overwhelming, the land is dying, children starve for food, for love, for authenticity, and I need to fix it, feel an obligation to somehow make it better. "And here is where we turn our back from our ambitions to consult" (Berry, 2005, p. 65).

This farm, this place, it seems so small, the temperature rises and conflicts rage; don't I have a responsibility to "fix" it, to start a revolution? Evil prevails as I sit by in my small corner of the world. So much I have learned, so much I have come to realize, so easy to see the fixes to the problems. Yet I begin to see how my own understanding towards that which I do not truly know only seems to work, my own judgment of oversimplification becoming its own arrogant answer. Wendell Berry concedes that amidst global crisis there are no global solutions. We have no superheroes to save us from the overwhelming villains that haunt us.

I listen to stories, theories of revolution. Revolution of schools, of teaching, defeating "traditional" learning and all its efficient flaws as we strive towards "authenticity" and "personalization." These revolutions bring to mind those that have come before. Better ways to be, replacing those who take with those who need. Like the fairy tales of my youth these stories always seem to promise happily-ever-after. Whispers in these stories remind me we have been here before, the people have risen up before to care for each other, to look after those most taken advantage of, to protect and share more equitably, yet somehow like those fairy tales I realize I have heard this story before. Slowly I begin to realize that there are no grand solutions; regardless of the intention or the importance of the ideas, if the revolution fails to address each farm and the spaces in between, they will simply become one more monster, ultimately another failed chance to change the world.

Still, something nags at the back of consciousness, a line from an old song; "our conscience keeps us quiet while the wicked love to speak" (Goo Goo Dolls, 1995). Those full of arrogance speak without hesitation, oblivious to the inherent incompleteness of all knowledge. Those who see this truth, stumble over it. How can we speak when we can't explain what is unexplainable? So often what is most needed to be said is left hanging, fearful of its own incompleteness, aware of its own inability to live up to the myth of "truth." How then to balance humility with the need to be heard, not just because of my own ambition but because I believe in what I believe? I've seen how quickly the land can be conquered, how easily the beauty of each aspect is lost, forgotten or defeated. If not me then who, if not now then when? How then to remain rooted, and yet still stretch outward? To make a humble, yet brazen, call for a farm-by-farm revolution.

Only this farm, only this place, how humbling, how freeing, no grand ideas and ways of being that only "seem" to make sense. In this place, only here and now, it's not my job, nor my destiny to free the world or inspire a generation. Not my path to solve what plagues education, my responsibility simply to care for what has been entrusted to me, find what it needs and cultivate what can be. A humbling proposition, wipe away the grandeur and all that is left is reality.

Within this stark realization, hope, assurance, a breath of truth. Responsibility for the world lifted, my attention shifts to this time and this place. A redefinition of what is possible, here I can work despite the demons, here I have power and a voice, here I am able. Within this comes realization, as theory shifts to practice, the depth of work left to be done becomes clear. The tangible touch of reality unearths the true challenge. Work that needs not to be thought about or talked about, but actually completed becomes clear. Slowly I begin to see how far I have to go, how much remains to be done, and the devastatingly beautiful realization that no one can take it in my stead.

This farm, this place, so rich, so complicated. The more I spend on the here and now the more its complexity is revealed to me. I could spend a lifetime and never truly know this place in its entirety. Maybe this is why my eyes always turn outward, so much easier to apply quick fixes to things I do not actually know, throw my static knowledge towards distant issues. Why is it so much harder to simply stop and listen, to accept that solutions are not created but negotiated? Be an example; if I tend this place, truly listen and care for it and those who live within it, I will care for myself.

So much can and needs to be done, but a focus on this time and place allows it to become possible. Moments of wonder collect and nourish, but somehow shadows creep and I fight to keep them at bay. How often my focus shifts to the plant that doesn't grow at my demand or the seeds that never took root. As I shift my focus to this place, the intimacy of that which I am responsible for intensifies. My mistakes magnified, my failings are real and tangible, complete with names and faces. So quick to dismiss that which does work as accident, that which does not as fault, still under the spell that I can somehow control. How to hold myself more gently accountable, this farm requires me to be present, and honest, but also forgiving: of it, and of myself. With my guidance there is hope, flawed, imperfect and incomplete hope that miracles can grow. Not those beyond what is believable, but those that make one believe.

CHAPTER FIFTY-FIVE

How TO Love Black Snow

DAVID W. JARDINE

(This is the Introduction to Michael Derby's [2015] Place, Being, Resonance: A Critical Ecohermeneutic Approach to Education. *Michael visited our class and has contributed a chapter to this text on bees.)*

> Despite the likely alien and awkward feel of the concepts involved, we might, when hearing a sutra, experience a quite innocent sense of wonder—a brief moment of almost childlike, delightful surprise, perhaps colored by a subtle tone of promise and potential. In line with the teachings set out in this book, we might say that just such a brief clearing within simple, unprepared wonder is what constitutes the awakening of faith in the Great Vehicle.
>
> From the "Translators' Introduction" to *Ornament of the Great Vehicle Sutras: Maitreya's* Mahayanasutralamkara (Doctor, 2014, p. vii)

> Now little riverbed stones impress upon my bare feet the aggregate intelligence of form and fit, particular trees stand tall in my memory as pedagogically significant, the cheap yellow paint on my pencil peels and reveals *flesh*—what kind of mushrooms are these? From somewhere deep within the inquiry, beneath the words—*how is it possible!*—a world approaches. (Derby 2015, p. 2)

FROM CHAPTER ONE, "THIS IS THE MYSTERY: MEANING"

This book is worth every moment of while it takes to read it. It must be read as carefully as mushrooms that always just might be poisonous even if delicious, just might be nourishing even if acrid. We are in a fix—pedagogically, ecologically, in body and mind and otherwise—and it's going to take some doing to even start undoing this fix.

The object of concern in this beautiful book is grave and imminent—the tear of flesh that is surely coming in these ecologically sorrowful times. Michael Derby's book is rife with soaring, awakening insight into the often ignored, often trivialized and Romanticized, nature of our ecological intimacy, our Earthly Being beyond the confines of the all too human. And it couples these insights with detailed and careful thought to the pedagogy of these matters and to long and tangled histories of human images and thinking in which we have "b[ou]nd ourselves without a rope" (Loy, 2010, p. vii).

Read this book slowly and repeatedly. That is what it needs and deserves. If you read it too fast, the pull of the gravity and imminence of our circumstances will only increase. Read slowly, the pull starts to lessen and we can then slowly start to see where we are, what has happened to us and our kin, what we have done, what we might now do.

Hurry will only lead to panic that is distracting and of no use. It will only tighten the knots and the tangle and the confusion.

Here, right off the bat is one great gift of this book. We hurry.

And that last sentence can be read too fast. We hurry, and when our circumstances become dire, we react by accelerating, with little or no understanding of how our hurry is profoundly complicit in increasing our panic, thus increasing our hurry, and so on.

It is no accident that Buddhists characterize the deepest human afflictions as caught up in a Wheel.

The spell of this ever-accelerating wheeling must be broken. Great and increasingly loud and monstrous hallucinations about how we might Save The Earth (capitalized, and then in all caps, and then bolded, and then in a larger letters, and on and on) must stop. This just increases the spellbinding.

In its stead, awakening, brief clearings, little riverbed stones and particular trees.

This book has been of great use and great remind to me in understanding a school I visited last week, listening to and watching French Immersion Grade One children couple together found words and post them for all to see—and then up goes this accidental couplet, *neige/noir*, "black snow," and how we all gasped a bit at the beckoning incomprehensibility of it: the feel of a world approaching, of aggregate intelligence, of language living instead of dead, and of the warm presence of us huddled together over this classroom happenstance. So momentary, but just because of this, the true weal of words is felt approaching and whooshing overhead. We duck and giggle. In brief.

Neige noir. I must remember this.

This isn't a big deal, this. It's a small one. One among many pleasures in this book is that, read the right way, it is full of such clear and clearing messages about commonplace and everyday events inside and outside of commonplace and everyday classrooms with commonplace and everyday children and adults and the territories in which they might meet their more-than-human kin. It is about how we might make schools not just *livable* and *sustainable* but *beautiful* and *wise*. It is not just *about* poetry (Chapter Three) or *about* metaphor (Chapter Four) but demands that "here, where it seems impossible that one life even matters" (Wallace, 1987, p. 111), here, we seek the feel of mycelial pulls, "right now, in the midst of things, *this* and *this*" (p. 111).

This book asks me to stop over things, to stoop, to think. "With *this* bird" (see Chapter Four). I am so relieved to say that this book is *not* about "environmental education" as some sort of subject area (usually a sub-division of Science Education or Outdoor Education or both) among others inside or outside of schools. This literal minded image of environmental education simply abandons the rest of our human inheritance and of the lives of teachers and students to countless ecological disasters, one worksheet after the other.

Instead, this: *All of our thinking and being and imagining is ecological.* All knowledge entrusted to teachers and students in schools comes with place and inhabitation and faces and tales—*fields* of wonder that call for the sort of thinking proper to such fields and their cultivation and care. This is an ancient Aristotelian reminder of *mensuratio ad rem*: thinking which finds its proper measure, not in the methods of human approach, but rather in the thing being thought:

> Thinking is not a means to gain knowledge. Thinking cuts furrows in the soil of Being. About 1875, Nietzsche once wrote (Grossoktav WW XI, 20): "Our thinking should have a vigorous fragrance, like a wheatfield on a summer's night." How many of us today still have the senses for that fragrance? (Heidegger, 1971, p. 70)

From the beginning of Chapter Two:

> Occasionally, we may happen upon the fruiting bodies of this living, subterranean entanglement (if we live, or make time to go, or are taken to the places where fungi still bloom, and if we pay attention) and only then do we become aware of the vibrant webwork beneath us and, perhaps, if our earthly connection has not been severed or schooled out of us, we are reminded of the interdependent ethos of a "humus filled" existence. (Derby 2015, p. 18)

We, too, are fruiting bodies, as is Pythagoras and Andromeda and Coyote, and place value, and this is no more and no less a metaphor than it is of fungi. Coyote always arrives with earthly connections and subterranean entanglements. And when you place something in a place, that place itself is not just an empty, abstract spot, but has a value (Latin *valere*, two meanings of which are "be strong, be well" [Online Etymology Dictionary]) that affects how to think about what happens to what has been placed there. Change the strength and well-being of the place and things in that place change. My work could not have become what it did had I not lived in these Foothills. Place value.

Simple! Mathematics and its Roman and Arabic numeric roots are forms of ecological awareness, of locales and ancestors and relations and imagining. As a

Grade Six student once told me, of course Roman numerals have no place value, because Rome was an Empire, and every place it went was Rome—"the vibrant webwork beneath us."

"The way we treat a thing can sometimes change its nature" (Hyde, 1983, p. iii) and we mustn't simply go outside (although we must, we must) and abandon everything left inside the school walls. This is the tough, exhilarating work that this book asks readers to practice right in the midst of the circumstances we face. Here. Grade One. If it can come to be treated the right way, for its fragrances. If we don't treat it that way, our sense for this fragrance becomes uncultivated, unpracticed, dimmed and distant. Its loss of fragrance and our nose for it rise and fall in concert.

Thus, this book lays out a bit of a rescue mission, to learn to read even little Grade One word searches as eco-poetic, eco-pedagogical gestures, to become studied and still enough to stop panicking and let ourselves remember how both right-angled triangles and the curves of vines around a tree *both* become *more* radiant in each other's presence. Hans-Georg Gadamer (2007a) calls this, in an indirect way, an experience of beauty. Each reads the other out into the open, and releases it from its literal self-absorption and self-containedness. In each other's presence, each becomes exquisite and irreplaceable in the fullness of things and their ways. Treated properly, each is radiant, lighting up the dependently co-arising place of its residing, its strength and well-being, its place value.

"We should apply this to *every* phenomenon" (Tsong-kha-pa, 2005, p. 182), our "selves" included.

Mycoremediation (Chapter Seven). Inoculation (Chapters Five and Six). Home-making and re-indigenization (Chapter Eight)—perhaps overall we are dealing with the ability to read properly, with a honed and practiced sense of place and proper proportion, with enough studied memory and experience so that the "resonant ecology of things" (Chapter Nine) can be sensed ringing in the air. We must allow ourselves the hard labor of this repeated and perennial task of recovery, of waking up, again, in search of brief clearings.

Frankly, there is great joy to be had here, but it has got an ecological sting: "Everything is teaching you. Isn't this so? Can you just get up and walk away so easily now?" (Chah, n.d., p. 5).

There are two intertwining paths in this book, one more immediately pleasing than the other. More than any other book in recent memory (I might put Don Domanski's *Bite Down Little Whisper* [2013] alongside here), this book feels and writes and speaks up out of the lift that comes when we step aside from our heavy inheritance and undo its cloak and instead wander, wilder, with stones underfoot and the duty of noticing. It is equally easy to recoil, as it is to rejoice in the deep experience of our conspiracy with trees and other terranean and subterranean entanglements. Coming to still enough to experience for myself such dependency is, as Michael shows in great detail, deliciously, properly and repeatedly humiliating. With practice, you get used to it. "It is somewhat difficult to establish, but once you are used to it, it will be like meeting an old acquaintance" (Kongtrul, 2002, p. 67). In such meetings, our hearts become undone.

This book thus speaks about acts of true teaching and learning in ways that lift and open the heart despite its sorrows, but not in order to turn away to some vaguely stupid Ecological Romance or equally distracting Ecological Panic. No, this lift allows *those very sorrows* to be sung in words and harmonies with ravens and stones and trees, and not just suffered in silence and isolation.

Neige noir and our huddling over it.

"Oh sorrow" (Seidel, 2014, p. 112).

"Hush, child" (Latremouille, 2014, p. 30). Do not panic.

Deep ecological stillness and experience—persistent, repeated, generous, patient, persevering—are vital to beginning to undo our fix, but they are not sufficient. There is another trail in this book that gives heart and courage. It stares dead-on, articulately, and in great detail, into the inheritances of thinking and imagining that have helped get us into this fix. How have schools become so often so deadly and boring and afraid? How has literacy lost its ear for orality? How have the wise ghosts of the land underfoot become lost from memory? How has beauty fled, and why, and what happens if we raise our kids in a world without ears, without ghosts, without beauty? This is the second path, which is at once the same path. *We need to study* in ways that win back our living from its entanglements in unearthly fantasies and fears. Undoing ourselves from the fix we have inherited is going to take some doing. *Our study of our circumstances is going to have to be as complex and as difficult and as entailed as those circumstances themselves.*

There is no way around this and its great ironies. We humans, having disgraced and desecrated the more than human world (and, to our shame, the human one as well), have an all too human task facing us. We must seek wisdom. We must think clearly and without fear and consequent animal panics. As per hermeneutic insight, seeing the world and our fix only in light of and as an outcome of its imminent and grave impingement on us blocks us from seeing *it* as it is, as it stands there, in its own repose, "over and above our wanting and doing" (Gadamer, 1989, p. xxviii). It takes wisdom to escape our selves and the world that then appears only in light of those worried selves and our projections and fears and repressions. We must break our reflection in the water. We must come to, not in order to turn away from the spell, but towards it, now, finally, a bit awoken and more alert.

"You can't get anywhere without reading a yak's load of books" (Tsong-kha-pa, 2004, p. 219). One must cultivate "an attentive ear for the language in which the thinking experiences of many generations have been sedimented, long before we begin to attempt our own thinking" (Gadamer, 1992, p. 18). Part of the work here in this book is unraveling how our current ecological concern is, at least in part, a function of how so many of these generations have cocooned themselves (and therefore us, our language, our inheritances, our schools, our teaching and learning) and long-since lost an Earthly measure of things. And so many of these generations have demanded of those they met that they, too, must lose such measure and its language, its culture, its places. These circumstances are complicated, historically, culturally, philosophically, linguistically, spiritually. They involve colonialism, gender, dreams of heaven and progress and monstrous hopes for mastery over the world, and on and on and on. They include institutional codifications and market economies and media distractions and the "you're either for us or against us" logic of much political wind. We can step away, momentarily, from this tough work, as I often must, seeking the relief of ravens and wood to split and tomato seedlings on the sill. But simply stepping away leaves our path still blocked.

This is why this book leans heavily into the phenomenological and hermeneutic traditions of inquiry—Edmund Husserl, Martin Heidegger (see especially Chapter Five), and my old love, Hans-Georg Gadamer (see especially Chapter Six). I've taught a graduate course in the University of Calgary's Faculty of Education on Gadamer's *Truth and Method* over twenty-five times, and it has proven to be true, over and over again, a hermeneutic adage: "[the world] compels over and over, and the better one knows it, the *more* compelling it is. This is not a matter of mastering an area of study" (Gadamer, 2007, p. 115). This tradition, at its best and most vital, lends its attention to the life world, the world as lived, the living world. This tradition—part of the very Eurocentric orbit that has caused so much of our fix—seeks the break of the spell, seeks the Trickster who knows the trick, seeks waking up, it seeks beauty and repose, it seeks to understand "what happens to us over and above our wanting and doing" (Gadamer, 1989, p. xxviii)—all out from constructivist cocoons and somnambulant projects and delusions.

Here is where this book becomes slightly magnificent, because the author does not wish to simply swallow whole this tradition of phenomenological and hermeneutic philosophy because it, too and of course, contains sedimented and hardened elements of precisely the unearthliness that has gotten us into the fix we are in in the first place. What the author makes crystal clear is the need for what he brilliantly calls "ecohermeneutic inoculation." From the first pages of Chapter Five:

> Ecohermeneutic inoculation in this respect is a deliquescent move—at once critical and remedial—that compels a tradition to reveal what it knows, what it has yet to teach, and where it needs to reconnect in order to remain in resonance with the world and our lives as they are now lived. In this sense, an ecohermeneutic imagination is ... concerned with ... "salvaging" and revitalizing these philosophic substrates to bring them to bear on ecological pedagogy in a more-than-human world. (Derby 2015, p. 61)

I do adore the fact that I had to look up the word "deliquescent." This is one of the leisures (Latin *schola*) of study. Unidentified words, like unidentified mushrooms, come to be experienced ecstatically, as a trail with beckonings along it. And, as with mushrooms, getting the etymology wrong can make us lose our way: "from Latin *deliquescere* 'to melt away,' from *de-* ... + *liquescere* 'to melt,' from *liquere* 'to be liquid'" (Online Etymology Dictionary). This is why we learn to spell. Because if we don't, the spell gets lost, the threads of ancestral memory get cut, and we no longer have any aid in finding our way.

We become lost, and, because of our loss, we eat mushrooms that are deadly.

It is an ecological disaster.

Yes. Wait. Here. Got it! Deliquescence. Hermeneutics "makes the object and all its possibilities fluid" (Gadamer, 1989, p. 367) so that we can experience its living arising and living place in our lived experience and that of our dependents:

> All this has as its aim not simply philosophical erudition and the like. The aim of such meditations and work is the cultivation of the intimacy and immediacy of the experience of everyday life, here, as this next child draws breath over a text, here, where reading aloud and learning to pronounce can too often be treated as simply ordinary and commonplace. Not only is "wherever you are ... a place of practice" (Tsong-kha-pa, 2004, p. 191). Tsong-kha-pa also insists (and this is a feature that distinguishes the Gelug tradition from other Buddhist lineages and makes ripe its affinity to hermeneutics) the purpose and object of study is *precisely* the deepening of practice itself. After all, "why would you determine one thing by means of study and reflection, and then, when you go to practice, practice something else?" (2000, p. 52). And this is why Gadamer insists that hermeneutics, with all its philosophical erudition and study, is "a practical philosophy" (2007a) with both theoretical and practical tasks (2007b). All those complex philosophical and historical twists and turns that typify his work are meant, in the end, to make us more susceptible to the beautiful abundance of things as we walk around in the world. (Jardine, 2015b, p. 246)

"Texts are instructions for [the] practice" (Tsong-kha-pa, 2000, p. 52) of precisely paying more intimate and proper attention to the resounding. Don't worry. Study, properly practiced, will not ruin the *aesthesis* of ecological reveries, only their limited and limiting naiveties.

Study this book. It can help you become more alert and less afraid. It can provide the courage to face our circumstances full face, and crack the facade that seems so grave and imminent and that beckons us to panic and retreat or to fall prey to useless, however understandable, ecological hysterics.

Come revel, then, and feel the amp of the sun increasing. I end this introduction with a sense of very strange relief. My own work is now being outlived, as Michael ventures into many places that I have not been and many I have trouble going to without too much ache. My work belongs to a different time and place even though I'm in conspiracy with Michael's words, and better for his help.

This book, too, won't last forever. But it is, I believe, what is needed now.

Bragg Creek, Alberta, March 2–12, 2015.

CHAPTER FIFTY-SIX

Bee & Nothingness

MICHAEL W. DERBY

Jem was scowling. It was probably a part of the stage he was going through, and I wished he would hurry up and get through it. He was certainly never cruel to animals, but I had never known his charity to embrace the insect world.

—HARPER LEE (1982, P. 238)

I. INTRODUCTION

My exact age and some of the finer details of these encounters remain hazy from years of vigilantly not-knowing the internal relation buzzing between events spanning half a lifetime. Trembling little hands bury something in mother's garden in bad faith. It is not that it would be impolite to discuss such things at the dinner table or in the classroom; it is that such things *must not* be spoken. At first this requires only a red plastic beach shovel; then, perchance, some Tonka trucks, a pellet gun, the Bible, television and eventually the crucible of schoolyard indifference. After that it gets a little easier. Other people help you not-know. But, and this is truly one of the awe-inspiring geometries of existence, these things have an inexplicable tendency to recur in our lives until they are addressed. Not-knowing thus requires steadfast effort, both individually and as a culture. Despite easing back and clearing a space for some of these memories to resonate within the privacy of my own inner world, the cultural space and means to make sense of (to even *allow* for) serious reflection on such encounters remain liminal, and for the most part, unwelcomed.

When asked, as one often is in educational programs, to reflect on an important teacher in one's life, I have started to respond with: a bee. A particular bee (at
least, initially), not bees in general, not bees as a symbol for hard-working perseverance or in some other metaphorical sense; a particular bee I encountered as a
child who gifted me with a sense of nothingness, even as I killed and mutilated her.
Mind you, it took almost thirty years to recognize the teaching and the teacher.
After all, one takes certain calculated risks in speaking of the profound existential
teachings of insects: incredulity, professional disdain, accusations of succumbing to
a primitive sentimentality. And yet, and yet.

Two years ago, I was giving a presentation at the annual International Conference on Imagination and Education, having recently finished my first round
of grad school. Kieran Egan (1997, 2002), the celebrated scholar and conference
organizer, was there, educational philosopher and keynote speaker David Jardine
(1998a, 1998b, 2012) was there, my entire grad school committee was there, and
the room was otherwise packed with colleagues, visiting scholars and in-service
teachers. It was not going well. The presentation, which I had haughtily entitled
From Ecoliteracy to Ecofluency, was intended to highlight the significance of oral
kinds of understanding on the emergence of ecological consciousness (Abram,
1997; Judson, 2010), but my reliance on specialized terms and neologisms was falling flat. I abruptly abandoned my carefully prepared notes and stood in awkward
silence at the front of the room, frantically searching my mind for some way to
revitalize the content—to breathe life back into all this ecological theorizing. *Tell
them about Buber and the horse.*

Without proem, I burst into an anecdotal account of how the existential philosopher Martin Buber, when he was a boy of eleven years, stole into his grandpar-
ent's barn in order to pet a horse.

> [I] felt the life beneath my hand, it was as though the element of vitality itself bordered
> on my skin, something that was not I, was certainly not akin to me, palpably the other, not
> just another, really the Other itself; and yet it let me approach, confided itself to me, placed
> itself elementally in the relation of *Thou* and *Thou* with me. (Buber, 1967, p. 38)

These encounters of profound connection with "more-than-human" others, Buber
would later admit, were fundamental in the development of his relational philosophy,
which emphasizes the significance of such elemental moments of *Thou* and *Thou*,
as well as the potential to reach towards God through mystical experiences of the
Eternal Thou (Blenkinsop, 2005, p. 287). Buber even claims, reflecting again on a
childhood encounter, that he first discovered himself as *I*—that is, an *I* in relation
with others—when he happened one day on a piece of mica lying beside the highway.

> And suddenly as I raised my eyes from it, I realized that while I looked I had not been
> conscious of 'object' and 'subject'; in my looking the mica and 'I' had been one; in looking
> I had tasted unity. ... I looked at it again, the unity did not return. But there it burned in

me as though to create. I closed my eyes, I gathered my strength, I bound myself with my object, I raised the mica into the kingdom of the existing. And there ... I first was I. (Buber, 1964, p. 140)

The room was showing signs of life. People could emotionally engage with a story about a child and a horse, and clearly Buber was describing an experience that was at least partially shared, but there was still a lot of philosophical *Thou-Thou*-ing and God-talk. What did any of this have to do with ecological education? A room of eager eyes awaited synthesis and clarity. And now all I can think about is that bee and my standing over it. My trembling hands and the need *never* to speak of this. And all the bees since, droning and circling back along the tessellating fringe of my bad faith. Demanding to be addressed.

Look, I plead, half to myself, we are not going to magically shift into some ecstatic new mode of ecological consciousness, there is no green god *ex machina* to whisk in and save us; there is only our relation with the world and how we enact it; how we, as adults and as educators, respond to children as they encounter and make sense of particular elemental moments with otherness. And, in the end, how we respond to a sense of loss commensurate with extinction at our hands. This is what "ecological consciousness" means; this is what education is for. (A bee waggles into the darkness of the garage. I understand now, I *see* nothingness. The bee and my standing over her in the garden with dirt-encrusted hands and a red plastic beach shovel: I have done this and I am what I do. So I close my eyes, gather my strength, and raise her into the kingdom of the existing. And there ... I first was I.)

The room stirs with unease. This is not the hope-laden sustainability-thinking that most are accustomed to hearing; and yet, there is new life. Now I lean in, with something cupped between my hands; I tell them, I have never told these stories to anyone before, not even my mother, but—a room of eager eyes awaits—one of my most important teachers was a bee.

II. ANGUISH

First, what is meant by anguish? The existentialists say at once that man is anguish. What that means is this: the man who involves himself and who realizes that he is not only the person he chooses to be, but also a lawmaker who is, at the same time, choosing all mankind as well as himself, can not help escape the feeling of his total and deep responsibility.
—JEAN-PAUL SARTRE (2004, P. 347)

In the first story I am a child; a young boy of no more than three or four years adrift in the luminous timebend of childhood summer days and idle play. My father's shop was by no means forbidden, but it was replete with power tools, razor-sharp metal teeth and flammables, and in retrospect, I was likely not supposed to be in there by myself. The lure of the old motor oil bench had tempted me before. It was marvelously filthy and beneath the elongated oil tray there were two shelves with a diverse array of spray paints, lubricants and aerosols. I recall something deeply satisfying about the cause-and-effect mechanics of aerosol cans, especially as I had been warned repeatedly not to touch them. And just as I happen to reach for the bright red can of Raid, a bee waggles into the darkness of the garage.

At first it was just a game of tag. I chased behind it expelling micro shots into the air, anticipating its movements and clouding its flight path with a fugitive cloud of insecticide. It was not long before the poison began to inflict its nervous system and I watched with delight as the bee lost altitude, zipping drunkenly in an erratic pattern and landing dazed on the concrete floor. I read later that the compounds used in Raid were originally synthesized from chrysanthemum flowers and that bees exposed to these chemicals are often paralyzed before they die. The bee was probably still technically alive when I started to quash it. I recall crouching on my haunches, back to the garage door and—is it possible?—humming pleasantly to myself as I crushed its body with a greasy-handled ball-peen hammer, alternating between the flat and the round sides for effect. I killed the bee like I was catching a bus.

The nothingness dawned in a moment of unnerving stillness. I recall a distinct shift in light, but the physics make no sense. The hammer—now a dirty and deplorable instrument—falls from my hand and I look quickly over my left shoulder to double-check I am not being watched. Sartre: "For every man, everything happens as if all mankind had its eyes fixed on him and were guiding itself by what he does" (2004, p. 348). What have I done? *No.* Now I am not catching a bus, now I am hovering behind myself hunched over something. I peer over my right shoulder at what I am hiding, but there is nothing. Now I am standing in mother's garden with a red plastic beach shovel and a vertiginous sense of anguish. It is not my fault, I tell myself, this is what we do, it is simply human nature. Now I take flight and *never* speak of this.

III. FORLORNNESS

When we speak of forlornness ... we mean only that God does not exist and that we have to face all the consequences of this. ... That is the very starting point of existentialism. Indeed, everything is permissible if God does not exist, and as a result man is forlorn, because neither within him nor without does he find anything to cling to. He can't start making excuses for himself.
—JEAN-PAUL SARTRE (2004, P. 349)

The second story takes place many years later. I am a fourteen-year-old adolescent learning what it means to be a man in a working-class family. My uncle has hired me on as a labourer for the summer to help him roof the perilous gradient of an old church in the small prairie town of Grenfell. Working grunt labour ten hours a day is significantly cutting into my imaginative daydreaming and idle play, and my uncle is unimpressed with my lack of knowledge regarding the different saws, screws and hammers (too much book learning, he figures). Mercifully, my uncle and auntie have a small cabin on Crooked Lake in the ancient and preternatural Qu'Appelle Valley, and we spend most evenings and weekends there, hiking the foothills looking for old Indian arrowheads and swimming in the algae-green waters.

One afternoon, I am sitting on the deck by myself enjoying a well-earned moment of daydreaming when some invisible gravity pulls me to my feet and draws my attention to the sweeping expanse of the lake. While going for lengthy swims was not unusual, I recall feeling unusually *compelled*, and without much thought I jump off the dock and begin to swim and swim and swim. Just as my arms begin to critically weaken the impetus eases, and out there, in the vastness of the lake, well beyond where I should be by myself, I encounter a bee struggling hopelessly to break free from the surface tension of the water. The impulse to quash it beneath the waves briefly crosses my mind, but instead, for no reflexive reason, I cup my hands beneath it and raise it up. The instant the bee is free it ascends rapidly over my left shoulder and I look back into the piercing gaze of the sun as it merges into mere light. There, I come into direct contact with the *Eternal Thou* and momentarily let go of my bad faith; at once, a bee waggles into the darkness of the garage. Now I hover behind myself as a child, hunched over something and peer over my right shoulder to see what I have done. It is not my fault, I tell myself, this is what we do, it is simply human nature. *No.* I see her. As I swim back towards the shore I realize: we are condemned to be as we choose. Sartre: "If existence really does precede essence, there is no explaining things away by reference to a fixed and given human nature. In other words, there is no determinism, man is free, man is freedom. ... So, in the bright realm of values, we have no excuse behind us, nor justification before us. We are alone, with no excuses" (2004, pp. 349–350).

IV. DESPAIR

As for despair, the term has a very simple meaning. It means that we shall confine ourselves to reckoning only with what depends upon our will, or on the ensemble of probabilities which make our action possible. ... Actually, things will be as man will have decided they are to be. Does that mean that I should abandon myself to quietism? No.
—JEAN-PAUL SARTRE (2004, PP. 353–354)

In the final story, I am a young man of twenty-seven years aspiring, with some reluctance and trepidation, to become a teacher. Years of environmental activism, writing poetry and a brief pilgrimage to the Himalayas have left me poverty-stricken. I am impelled to live in my hometown of Courtenay (the tradi-tional territories of the K'ómoks nation) with my parents—who are in the midst of daily quarreling over marital tensions—while completing my practicum at a nearby secondary school. My "mentor teacher" is a piece of work who boasts that he uses teaching as his own personal soapbox and advises me just to lie to students if I do not know the answers to their questions. I feel fraudulent and shamefaced; I avoid mirrors at all costs. I do not even want to be a teacher, I just do not know what else to do. How do I reconcile the sense that all of existence is … radiant—that *everything* is lived together—and the banal absurdities of every-day life? Mostly, I am just tired of working in mills and having to directly bear witness to extinction at my hands. I thought being a teacher might be a way out; I thought the education system might provide a means not only to *conscientize* students politically (Fanon, 2008; Freire, 2006), but also to bring us all back to life as it is lived together and, perchance, to raise the world into the kingdom of the existing. But obviously it is not. So I turn to self-medicating on the weekends and a desperate quietism on school days.

One Saturday afternoon, as I prepare a lesson plan for Social Studies 10 on "responsible government," a scientist comes on the CBC to discuss the alarming collapse of honeybee colonies over the last decade. While a multitude of possible explanations has been put forth, the two leading theories as to the primary agent point to either an infestation of mites or a new agricultural technique whereby seeds are coated with neonicotinoid insecticides, or "neonics." Unsurprisingly, the insecticide companies (notably Bayer Crop Science and Syngenta) and *some* scientists insist on a mite epidemic, while some *other* scientists point to the neonic residue found on many of the dead bees and the perniciously systemic nature of these insecticides. With corn, for example, the built-in neonic coating is not only meant to protect the seed but also the entire plant as it matures. Ideally, this means that the pesticide is buried with the seed and pollinators are never exposed. In reality, the equipment used to sow corn fields invariably kicks up much dust and as the neonic-coated seed moves through the hopper (the seed is sprinkled with a talcum powder to help it move smoothly), it expels a fugitive cloud of insecticide into the air. More concerning yet is evidence that suggests there may be neonic residue within the corn pollen itself, so that whenever the plants are in bloom they expel a micro-shot of bee-killing poison into the air and water. The scientist on the CBC claims this is a problem, mostly because "one-third of the food humans eat is reliant upon pollinators and bee pollination is estimated to affect two hundred billion dollars worth of crops annually."

I turn the radio off and stop trying to make William Lyon MacKenzie seem hip and rebellious for a moment. The nothingness dawns in a moment of unnerv-ing stillness. *No*. The problem lies elsewhere, buzzing on the fringe of our cultural bad faith. On some level—*never* spoken but of vital import—the whole seemingly tendentious debate over mites versus pesticides is nothing more than subterfuge and spectacle to lend license to our collective not-knowing. The real problem lies in the kind of hubristic thinking that follows from systemically distorted relations with bees and which seeks to rationalize only in terms of human concerns and capital losses. This kind of thinking requires a learned and methodically sustained severance between human and Earth, child and bee (Evernden, 1993). It requires a pedagogy coated in neonics from the beginning to ensure the child has a built-in pest management strategy as she matures. Now I am hovering behind myself, peering over my right shoulder at the history lesson plan I am preparing and feeling paralyzed.

I need to do something. I need to remember why this work is important despite the wretched ensemble of probabilities looming on the horizon. Without proem, I head downtown and waggle into a local tattoo shop for no reflexive reason. What do I want? And now all I can think about is that bee and my standing over it; that bee struggling hopelessly to break free from the surface tension of the water. And becoming mere light. I tell the tattoo artist I will take two bees on each side of my chest, each adorned with the eye of the Sun on its thorax. Why? And even then, I cannot bring myself to recognize the teachings and the teachers. I tell people: I just like bees.

V. EPILOGUE

The phenomenology of experience is particularly relevant in situations where there is evidence that certain experiences are shared but also ignored by ideological emphases in the culture. Attending to their phenomenology is one way to begin to take them seriously; and begin to reflect on the politics of their marginalization.

—Jan Zwicky (2003, p. 109)

It is late June on the Sunshine Coast (the traditional territories of the Shíshálh nation) and it is, as the news headlines so innocently put it, "unseasonably" hot and dry. Apparently a heat wave is wreaking havoc across Western Europe and California is being ravaged by "historic" drought conditions once again, but you would never know it by the smooth breathing of everyday life here.

In the evenings, after the heat breaks, I go jogging along a remote stretch of highway running through Halfmoon Bay to a nearby lake for an eventide swim. Tonight, my right knee begins to tweak a little on the way back, so I walk meditatively along the shoulder instead, praying to the god of knees for quick reprieve. Then, amongst the cigarette butts and plastic jetsam bespattering the highway's marginalia, I see her. I stop and pick up her little fuzzy lifeless body, then, a few steps later, another and another and another. The highway is literally littered with dead bees. I look quickly over my left shoulder to make sure I am not being watched. As I gather up a handful of dead bees, a vertiginous sense of anguish arrives with unnerving stillness. *What have we done?* Immediately, my bad faith begins to exonerate: What are we to do? Stop driving cars! Embrace insects! Take responsibility for … *everything*! I close my eyes, gather my strength, and bind myself with the bees; I lower myself into the kingdom of the existing. I despair. And yet, there is new life, and much work to do.

CHAPTER FIFTY-SEVEN

Turning In/wards

JODI LATREMOUILLE

My hometown province is in a crisis
B.C. Teachers' Strike continues, unchecked
And they said parents hate teachers and teachers use kids
To gain in this game for more money and leisure hours
But if leisure is scholarly, and money is time
Then yes, that's exactly what our kids need

And they fear monger, "kids are sitting at home rotting
In their own stupidity"! Yes, we bought it—stupidity
Because if kids can't be educated in the regular way
If schools don't keep running at this frenzied pace
Revolving doors shoving the kids into place
spinning out workers into the knowledge economy

It's chaos, I tell you, and besides, who pays the bills?
Well, Apple is waiting to fund all those frills!

But public education is an all-holy virtue
And besides, taxpayers pay good money
For you to keep their kids out of everyone's hair
And our workshops and coffee shops, job fairs and public squares
It would be chaos, I tell you, all those kids up in our faces
Asking questions and wanting to know about all these places

And they're paying B.C. parents $40 a day
To keep their kids out of … trouble
You give me 12 kids and an internet connection,
A library pass and carte blanche to explore
I'll show you trouble and so much more
In some circles, it's called "play," but what's it for?

Listen, I'll take your meager $40 a day
I'll show you music and live theatre and nature
I'll show you kids that can compute and pontificate and calculate
Kids that can learn and love, no need to be taught how
But public education is an all-holy virtue
And besides, who would I be accountable to?

And here in Alberta, my daughter tried out kindergarten
I hoped against hope that it would be a good decision
I hoped she'd burst out, "Mom, guess what I learned today!"
But the bus ride, tests, yellow cards and level readers
Standing in line for food, attention, the right to speak, and water
Had me asking: where was my bubbly, curious, shiny 5-year-old daughter?

So we packed it all in and opted for learning … life learning.
Known to most as homeschooling, or home education
The choices in products and textbooks have me reeling
For even here at home, the lifetime guarantee is appealing.
Wendell Berry calls up from under the mountain of profit,
Yes, you could this, or that, or the other, but is it the "right thing to do?" (Berry, 2013)

And yet, it is implied, that turning my back on the entire show
Is a cop-out, disloyal, an affront to everything I know
Stay and fight for the others, the masses of victims
They don't have two educated parents, they grew up in the system
Who do I think I am to retreat from the fray with my children in tow?
And don't I want my child to be a good, productive citizen?

And what would the world come to if everyone turned schooling in?
Turned it in …

For time to bake cookies, to call it "Life Skills"?
For playing with Legos *and* math memorization drills?
For trips to the museum with no pre-set agenda?
Entrepreneurship to "cover" Math and English curricula?
For camping and hiking, climbing trees, drawing deer tracks?
For learning in joy, not for prizes and plaques?

What would the world come to, indeed?
And so on the verge of yet another new teaching adventure:
Teaching "Pragmatics of Teaching," U of C, Education.
Will they call me a fraud, a blight on our nation?
Will they call me a hypocrite, coward, elite?
Wonder how my kids will toughen up, be socialized, compete?

And so, what do I tell those pre-service teachers
Those young ones, so new, their bright eyes shining?
Do I tell them of stakeholders, the conflicts, the whining?
Do I tell them of strikes, colour-coding, and IPP's?
Or do I tell them of face-painting, laughter,
volunteering, and trees?

Do I tell them it's useless to try to resist,
To toe the line and fall in with the rest?
Or do I echo Pat Clifford, who said it best ...
"It must be possible, for you see, it exists!"
The whole world awaits,
so get ready to play!

CHAPTER FIFTY-EIGHT

Radiant Beings

KARI SIRUP

It is only in the fabric of actually working through a topic and opening up its particular possibilities and free spaces that a sense of this interpretability of the world and ourselves arrives.
—DAVID W. JARDINE (2012, P. 220)

I often say that as a teacher I feel like more of an artist than when I was in art school. What I mean to say is that curriculum serves as a sort of medium; something that we manipulate to create experiences in the classroom. Children, in turn, offer up new suggestions and understandings based on said experiences. It's a conversation. What a wonderfully creative space to live in; one that enables me to see things in new light year after year. The juxtaposition of ideas and concepts always results in something unexpected, new or unnoticed, and there are a million possibilities for how the year might unfold. There is something so interesting in placing two ideas side by side. They speak to each other and cause us to view them differently as a result of their comparison.

Our work then as teachers is to allow light into spaces that never see light. We wait patiently to notice; for things to gather. We "set right anew" (Jardine, 2012, p. 2), open up and make room for the life world to enliven our classrooms. This is what I love most about teaching; wandering and wondering alongside children, awaiting what the world might reveal.

CHAPTER FIFTY-NINE

Additional Thoughts ON THE Terror IN A Mother's Heart

An Allegorical/Pedagogical Speculation on the Economies of Knowledge

DAVID W. JARDINE

This speculation has its origins in a passage from George Grant's *English-Speaking Justice* (1998, p. 1):

> [Immanuel] Kant's dictum "the mind makes the object" were the words of blessing spoken at the wedding of knowing and production, and should be remembered when we contemplate what is common throughout the world.

For those of us in education, this provides a hint of the legacy relationships among constructivism, the methodologies of the natural sciences, and capitalist/market economies of production and consumption. It also codifies beginning links between knowledge and power which will, by the end of the nineteenth century, give rise to Nietzsche's (1975) terrifying insight into how what is fundamental in human ways is not *what* is posited as a foundation, but the willful act of positing itself which, in such willing, takes productive and consumptive command over that which is known and eats it up into its own power-orbit. Thus portends an ecological disaster where the material well being of the world is only fulfilled in its submission to the will of human production and consumption. That constructivism has, to varying degrees, fallen for this logic hook, line and sinker and insinuated it into education as an indicator of students' liberation and empowerment, is worthy of pause.

Thus I offer a brief series of naive allegorical speculations.

Rene Descartes's work (circa 1640/1901), a full one hundred fifty years before Immanuel Kant's *Critique of Pure Reason* (1797/1964), was, in contrast, more mercantile in its understanding of knowledge. The criteria of clarity and distinctness guided the accumulation and hoarding of the wealth of knowledge. Anything clear and distinct was gathered under the hard-won clarity of the "I am." This is thus akin to the colonial gesture of dragging booty back home and storing wealth under the crown (of consciousness). Knowledge is thus imagined as accumulative—"amassing verified knowledge" (Gadamer, 1989, p. xxi). In schools, one aspires, under this image, to hold on to what one has accumulated at least long enough for it to cash out its exchange value for marks and grades that then are exchangeable for future prospects.

On the contrary, Immanuel Kant's work laid out the conditions for the *production* of such wealth. In schools, we have not only the accumulation of knowledge and the trading of such accumulation for the marks of success, achievement and advancement. We also toy, now, with ideas of knowledge production, of students not simply "accumulating facts" but understanding how to produce knowledge, whether methodically through natural science means or through the imaginativeness and reasoned arguments of the social sciences, art, history and philosophy. Students are deemed "active learners" and the like once Immanuel Kant's work passes through the developmental filters of Jean Piaget's "constructivism."

However, the production of knowledge in the natural sciences (see Kant's nod to Newtonian science and Euclidean geometry) can be laid out in ways that are standardizable, survey-able, manageable, and issued from a central authority. This is Kant's nod to Cartesianism, that "it must be possible for the 'I think' to accompany all my representations" (Kant, 1797/1964, p. 152), but this clear "I think" finds its warrant through the categories of pure reason which, in their transcendental functioning, describe *how* I think about any possible object, and therefore provide the means of *constructing objectivity* according to rules in line with which *any* "I" must, necessarily and universally (*a priori*) think. Knowledge thus becomes dovetailed with a universal and necessary *method of thinking* not uncoincidental with "the concepts and categories of established science" (Inhelder, 1969, p. 23) (these concepts, categories and methodologies thus become those fields of genetic epistemological exploration in Jean Piaget's work; see Jardine, 2005).

It is only thus, as universal and necessary, that credence is given to forms of knowledge production in the institution of schooling—only to the extent that students' productions are *themselves* standardized, survey-able, manageable. It is thus not just *the fact of production* but *the standardization of production* that provides knowledge its warrant (and provides Piagetian theory with its teleological end of development). Of course, this loops back to Kant's work, because the categories for the production of knowledge found in his *Critique* were precisely those of Aristotelian logic, and the *a priori* structures that underwrote his work on space and time were those of Newtonian physics and Euclidean geometry.

What happens then is a great clustering of attention in education, where issues of how to assess student learning begin to overrun issues of what is being learned such that if universal and necessary assessment is not possible then learning is not viable. Thus an old adage of Martin Heidegger's (1972, p. 63) that the matters we are considering become transformed into matters of method (this, too, being an allegory for the efficiency movement's insinuation into schooling, such that what is to be learned is trumped by how efficiently it can be assembled and tested). Thus, too, the deep suspicion that comes with hermeneutic explorations of education wherein "the hermeneutic phenomenon is basically not a problem of method at all" (Gadamer, 1989, p. xi).

Clearly another trail here is one that moves from knowledge as a product produced in a market economy up through Marx's work on the alienation of those workers who produce knowledge from the means of that production, thus positioning students as having to trade in their productions for markers of 'success' which are themselves linked in a market economy most strongly to consumption rather than production. Part of the resistance to introducing knowledge as production to students is that it begins to hand over the means of production to precisely those who are meant to be subservient to the institutional regimes of power of schooling itself (see Smith, 2009). Another part of the resistance that comes from students is that they very often understand far better than their teachers that even if the means of producing knowledge is handed over to them, in the long run of school, they are eventually handed over to Provincial Examinations which require accumulation and trade, not capitalist production.

The trail through the marriage of knowledge and production up through the alienation and "deskilling" (Braverman, 1998) of the worker from the means of production gains a new face in the work of F. W. Taylor in the early twentieth century. Here the productive assembly of industrially produced objects finds its literal and allegorical kin in how schools become organized. Production loses its participatory and creative edge and becomes equated with obedience and submission to the already-laid-out rules of producing and rubrics of assessment.

And, once the manipulations of desire are figured in (Leach, 1994), "lifelong learning" unwittingly becomes attached to the necessary almost-true-but-never-quite promises of consumerism.

We are left, then, writhing with an insatiable beast that is suppressed under the current accelerations and panics of schools and classrooms and the life they are portending. To reiterate, *this* is a story as old as the hills. It is possible, not necessary, and we are not stuck with it.

Reading and understanding *this* story allow me to begin stepping away from its allure. Luckily, there are long lineages of work in education bent on breaking this spell. They seem "radical" on the face of it, and they are: (Latin, *radix*) rooted instead of caught in the glimmery surface skittering of attention.

CHAPTER SIXTY

Josh

SCOTT HASSETT

though sometimes it is necessary
to reteach a thing its loveliness

—GALWAY KINNELL (2002, N.P.)

There is no sacred and unsacred places, there's only sacred and desecrated places
—WENDELL BERRY (2013, N.P.)

I've been thinking a lot about Josh

Josh was broken,
I don't know if I can say that
But I don't know what else to say

Josh was broken
Broken by chemicals rewiring his brain before he could raise a cry of defense
Broken by chaos, anger, hate and neglect,
Broken by a system designed to reject him
Broken in mind, body, and soul
I used to think that he was broken and couldn't be fixed

Josh is lovely
Not in the ordinary way
Not even in any unordinary way
But Josh is alive, a part of the human condition

His polished, clever wit, contrasted by his outbreaks of senseless hatred
An unquestioned love and loyalty to a family despite the betrayals
A gentle touch hidden beneath the chaos
Maybe fixing was never the point

When I think of Josh I get sad. Sad because we failed him; his school, his community, his living ancestors. Sad because beauty hidden is always tragic, and sad because of what he revealed about the system. The exception proving the emptiness of the rules.

His ghost would haunt staff meetings, our need to find control, to fit the square peg in the round hole would hijack the agenda and exhaust the most caring of teachers. I still remember one particular meeting where, after an especially difficult week that involved multiple physical restraints, thrown tacks, and sexually explicit comments directed towards staff members, one teacher asked, "Who's advocating for us?" and another asked, "Why do we put up with it? Why is he allowed to come to school?" Memories striking in what they revealed, I still wish I had said more, had asked, "Who's advocating for Josh?" had pointed out that if not us, then who would reteach this boy his loveliness, yet the current so strong I chose not to sail against it?

Why did these people who had chosen to dedicate their lives to helping children so quickly abandon the one in the most need. So quickly the majority created an enemy out of the marginalized, a decision easily justified and consolidated through the lack of dissenting voice.

Some of it was defensive. Josh spewed anger and hate, his language striking and painful, cut deep, pushed away those who might help him. Yet it was through Josh that I truly lived the realization we so often speak: "It has nothing to do with you."

It was the day before Christmas break, and my class was having a potluck and doing art. Josh's class had a substitute. Josh did not do well with substitutes, so Josh spent the day with me. My wife and kids came to visit and I watched (a little anxiously) as Josh crouched down, hugged my son, and told him, "Your Dad is AWESOME!!!" (the memory of which is one of the great gifts Josh gave me). Yet, within hours he was flicking paint at me and calling me a *!$# head. What could I possibly have done to create such a change? Was it my personality? Something I said? Arrogant questions revealed in their absurdity.

There was something deeper that pushed teachers to the brink. Something much more systematic than individual imperfections, or unkind hearts, something rooted. Perhaps a need to control, an ideal of what it meant to be human, civilized. A preconceived definition of what it looks like to teach, a power hierarchy Josh had no intention of participating in.

Our inability to find the right strategy, the right approach, the right consequence or reward left us feeling powerless. The concept that Josh couldn't be fixed left no other option than to reject him, to dehumanize. Did it stem from an inner need to know that "everything will be okay," that every problem has a solution, shields against the realities of an imperfect world. Like disease, war or tragedy, Josh offered no quick fix, so we chose to reject and justify, to box him up and label him the exception. Without Josh, education can still be about control and efficiency, it can still rely on the transfer of the answers and fixing of problems. Without Josh, problems can still be fixed, answers justified and everything can still be okay. If we reject Josh, then his story can't give insight into the human condition, can't scream at the flaws, the false logic, the ungrounded goals and aspirations. If we reject Josh, the institution remains unblemished, unbroken.

Who then asks why the "thing" has more worth than the life
The idea more important than its reality
The machine so well polished that even when it doesn't work
It carries no guilt, no blame

The system is broken
So is Josh
I know whose side I'm on

CHAPTER SIXTY-ONE

Curriculum Theorizing

JACKIE SEIDEL

Undergraduate Course:
Language Arts Methodologies.
37 students.
Ages 17 to 50.
Backgrounds: Diverse.

Student approaches after class:
"Every time
you say the word
Curriculum
I feel like I'm going to throw up."

Me too, I tell her.
Me too.

Interview WITH THE Gym Hall Water Fountain

IAN WALSH

Ian Walsh: Thanks for taking the time; I know you have a long day ahead of you.

Gym Hall Water Fountain: I sure do, the Gym class is into a pretty serious dodge ball tournament right now so I am running 'fast and cold,' as they say.

IW: I know you don't get a lot of attention; you are often assumed to be around somewhere or lumped in with the bathrooms. Does that bother you?

GHWF: It is true, but we are not show-off types; we like to do our job and stay quiet. No loud flushes, no automation, just a nicely arcing stream of what you need when you need it.

IW: Besides providing water on demand, what does your day consist of?

GHWF: My location is great, I see every student every day from this spot. Some of them drink from me for seven years almost every day. Really busy during gym classes, obviously, so I see a lot of large group usages, "1, 2, 3 next …" kind of stuff. After recess is pretty predictable too. My stream is known to be the coldest in the school so, you know, I get line-ups. Occasional budging, which is just awful to watch from my perspective. I get so embarrassed for you. Cold-winter-day-recess can also be fun, lot of kids getting really slow drinks and taking the long way. Some are actually talented little sneakers.

I love the chatter, the chatter is just fantastic. It can be about the games in the gym, life on the playground, life in general. I know romance, sadness and boredom. I see it all and hear even more.

IW: Boredom?

GHWF: Lot of my usage is from wanderers, either escaping to me or sent there for respite. They will come and just let the water run sometimes; if they are angry they block it, make a mess. I don't question them, if it seems like what they need. I've taken plenty of kicks too. I win most of those tussles.

IW: Do you even actually strike back?

GHWF: No, I don't 'strike back.' I am a water fountain.

IW: Okay, wrong question. Do you ever get angry?

GHWF: All I am saying is I don't feel picked on. I can give more than water. I can be an escape, refreshment or a target. No problem. In fact lots of kids have told me things. Whispered to me about everything from love to revenge. They confess and plot, complain and sing. I am a very good listener.

IW: What is something that has been said to you?

GHWF: Protected under child–water fountain privilege. But think of the things you have said to a fountain and they are similar.

IW: I'm a fountain talker?

GHWF: Most people are. If not talking—thinking or reflecting for that moment. We often turn to a water fountain to calm down, take a break. To a kid it can be enough for a fresh start.

IW: What do you think about the water bottle craze?

GHWF: Well, it hasn't made me obsolete because they use me to fill them all the time. I guess I am just lucky about my basin design. Deep enough for those bottles to fit. Lot of colleagues being replaced by those duel faucet rigs. Times are a changing. That being said my Grand Pappy was a bucket and ladle!

IW: Really?

GHWF: No.

GHWF: The water bottles are also a part of another problem I have. The less people drink from me (only fill) the more they see me as a drain than a drink. Huge increases in foreign substances being poured down me. Coffee, juice, smoothies, cappafrappa-chinos, even Ichiban. It can affect how clean the fountain needs to be. If you actually drink from it, you want it cleaner than if you just think of it as a tap.

IW: Okay, so not unaffected by water bottles, but what about water coolers?

GHWF: Water wise, I think they are unnecessary, I heard that when they finally got around to cleaning the one around here it had ants in it! No ants on me. Plus the water our city provides is just beautiful. As for getting the scuttlebutt, I know water coolers are known as the go-to place for hot conversation, but water fountains are the exact same, but for the young. I admire the teachers that allow a reasonable level of conversation during a watering. Especially after a hot fall recess when the soccer cavemen and grade oners meet. It is true nature. It could be narrated.

Kindness, impatience, hustle, want, need, greed and satiation.

IW: Do you think the students ever consider how important it is that you bring them water?

GHWF: You would panic if you had to think about how important water is every time you drank it. Besides, I need them as much as they need me.

IW: Do you get along with the other fountains?

GHWF: There are other fountains?

IW: Ahem. What is it about *your* contribution to this school that sets you apart?

GHWF: Okay, on a good gym day with any combination of active recess and intramurals you are going to get most kids in this school drinking from me. Over two, three days, all of them. I am a part of them. Physically inside them. At any given time a huge percentage of the school has Gym Hall Fountain water in them.

As a community they have me in common, if nothing else. My height, button pressure, stream, arc, drainage. I am something that goes from too high to too short while we know each other, but at one time we were the perfect fit. I have made them sick with the germs that linger and made them stronger with the ones they fight. I've had winners gulp in victory and the defeated sip between sobs. Junior high kids come back and scoff at me, 'so cute' they say. But we know each other, we really do.

IW: Water fountain wise, you have given me a lot to think about, thank you Gym Hall Fountain. Any last words?

GHWF: Stay thirsty, my friends.

CHAPTER SIXTY-THREE

Beyond THE Outfield Fence

JUDSON INNES

An old friend of nearly forty years started the story with, "Hey Jud, do you remember the time at J. P. Dallos Field when Mr. Lupul … ?"

Instantly I knew what he was referring to. It was the story of a seemingly simple act, one human recognizing the humanity in another. A story that unfolded over just a brief wisp of time, but fleeting as it was, it had been seared into both of our memories and carefully tucked way. Though we had not spoken of it on that day thirty years ago, or on any of the days that followed, as my friend continued the story the long-dormant images of that day flashed through my mind.

One of the great things about growing up in a small town is that some of the friends you make in preschool become friends for life. Perhaps some of that value lies in the lifetime of shared stories. Often these stories change based on which friend is telling the tale. Some details are left out, some are added, often the points of emphasis change, and of course the key actors rise and fall depending on the current speaker. In this case, though, the story of Mr. Lupul, my friend and I remembered it in strikingly similar ways, despite being only eleven years old when we witnessed the events play out.

It was Seafair weekend, a special celebration in our small town. Though, to be fair, our Seafair was probably not unlike those of most other small towns on the coast, highlighted as it was by lumberjack competitions, arts and crafts exhibits, food stands, a parade on Saturday morning, fireworks after dark on Saturday night, and in our case an aerial performance on Sunday afternoon by the Canadian Air Force Snowbird Squadron, which was based at the time in nearby Comox.

For us, though, the real highlight of the weekend was always the baseball tournament played at J. P. Dallos Field. The field was at the geographical heart of our part of town, and often served as the social hub for my friends and me on summer weekends when baseball games were under way. Of all these tournaments "Seafair" was the biggest one of the year, with top-caliber women's and men's teams traveling from around the province to play.

So we rode our bikes, Doug and I, up to the field on Saturday morning and stationed ourselves along the chain-link fence behind the outfield and began watching the first game of the day. Behind us, to the north, beyond the outfield fence was a perfectly manicured soccer field that also served as an approach for people coming to the park or just passing through. The east side of the field was guarded by soaring Douglas fir trees, while directly to the west, about a kilometer off and down a gentle slope, lay the glassy waters of the Salish Sea.

Early on this particular morning the bleachers along the first and third base-lines were already nearly full, though the outfield fence at the moment had only a smattering of people leaning on it watching the game. Directly to our right was a fenced-off area, probably not more than a thousand square feet of green grass, housing another Seafair tradition: the beer garden. As you might suspect, the beer garden filled gradually as the day progressed, an assortment of lumberjacks, fishermen, miners from nearby Texada Island, even a few local members of a notorious biker gang trickling in. A rough-and-ready bunch for sure, not unexpected in a resource town. By mid-afternoon the beer garden was at full roar. To us, though, it was barely noticed, merely a sideshow; we were there to watch baseball.

Though we didn't see him at the time, also in the outfield, leaning against the fence watching baseball on that calm morning, was Mr. Lupul. He had situated himself somewhere to our left, at a safe distance from the beer garden. At the time I knew nothing of him beyond the fact that I had seen him at the park before, a small, unassuming man, probably in his mid-fifties. I would learn more of him later that day.

So, the day flowed along, morning becoming afternoon, and we enjoyed the sights and sounds as one game ended and another began; our attention on the action interrupted by trips to the concession stand and other typical kid rambles. Sometime in the afternoon there was a faint ripple among the people standing, by now shoulder to shoulder, along the outfield fence. Like the others, I turned toward the soccer field that stretched behind the beer garden to see what had garnered the attention of the crowd. Alone on this field and heading in our general direction, in fits and starts, was a sad, bedraggled soul. Obviously highly intoxicated, which was clear to me even then, he staggered and fell, rose again, took a few unsteady steps and once more crashed to the green turf.

Gradually, painfully, he made his way toward the park. When I look back now, I suppose I would best describe this man as worn out, the product of a hard night clearly, and probably a hard life. He was rail thin, his hair was long and matted, and deep lines marked his face. His clothes were tattered and torn, his T-shirt punctuated by the vomit trailing down the front.

Eventually, exhausted I suppose, unable to take another step, this frail, vulnerable person went down once more and did not rise. Excruciating to recall, the beer garden crowd howled and cried, taunted and denigrated from the moment they spotted him roiling across the field, and continuing until he collapsed virtually at their feet. The crowd along the outfield fence watched, muted, yet did not move. Maybe some wanted to help, had notions of helping, would have helped if given more time, I cannot say for sure, but only one stepped forward.

Step forward he did. I remember Mr. Lupul walking stone-faced in front of his friends and neighbors lined along the outfield fence, continuing past the taunting beer garden crowd toward this suffering person. He leaned down and gently helped the prostrate man up off the ground, wrapping one arm around his back and placing one of the man's arms around his own neck. Once up they paused only long enough, before moving off, for Mr. Lupul to turn to the crowd and ask but one question: "What the hell is wrong with you people?"

Linked side by side as they were, they began moving toward the shade provided by the giant firs along the park's eastern edge. The crowd by now had ceased taunting and stood silent and chastened. Embarrassed, one hopes, and exposed, all present looked on as this devalued man was helped up.

Slowly, they made their way to the protection offered by those great unquestioning firs, shielded from the sun—it was a hot day—and the onlookers. In short order two ambulance attendants, typically on hand for these events, arrived and took the man into their care. Mr. Lupul walked back out of the park, down the long grassy field from where the man had first appeared.

For my friend and me, this was a formative moment in our lives. A scene that remained perfectly preserved in our minds for thirty years, though neither of us had ever given it words. I last saw Mr. Lupul a few summers ago when I was visiting. He was alone at the top of Old Westview Road just past the place where the pavement turns to gravel, picking blackberries along the side of the dusty road. I was passing through on my bike: we recognized each other, we both said hello.

CHAPTER SIXTY-FOUR

American Dippers AND Alberta Winter Strawberries

DAVID W. JARDINE

I

In the seventh month the Fire-star declines,
In the ninth month winter garments are handed out.
The eleventh month comes with the blustering wind;
The twelfth month, with the shivering cold.
Without cloak or serge
How are we to see the year out?
from "In the Seventh Month," compiled in the Shih Ching, twelfth to seventh century
BC, China
—LUI & LO (1990, P. 9)

The American Dipper is a small black bird, halfway in size between a Robin and a Sparrow, L-shaped with stubby upright tail and head balanced high. These Dippers are common all year long along the Elbow River that winds out of the Rocky Mountains and through Calgary, Alberta. Walked this past winter, in −40 degree winds, along the Elbow and its swirls of ice fog over rare still patches of open water, most of the river steeply hurrying east.

Dippers. Swim underwater upstream about ten feet at a go, feeding on water-carried food. Then standing there dipping up and down while waiting for the next dive. Or rush to low water-surface flights full of a distinctive twittery warble. Like the muskrat in the steaming cold beaver pond nearby, remaining here as I leave. Remaining here, −40, what little left of low-riding sun setting.

Leaving, under the darkening air-blue arch of what I hope is a gathering Chinook, caught in bitter cold that breaks your bones.

The twelfth month comes with the chopping of ice—clanging stroke after stroke

The first month comes—we bring ice to the cold-house for storage;
The second month comes—we rise early
And make offering of garlic and lamb.
In the ninth month comes the severe frost. (p. 11)

Home, eating freshly bought fresh strawberries. Delicious red juicydrip taste. Then suddenly grotesquely beautiful. Suddenly out of place. How can these be *here*? And as these strawberries begin to taste unbecoming of this place and this cold, I end up feeling out of place as well. Eating these strawberries betrays something of those Dippers and that ice and my living here.

II

In the seventh month the Fire-star declines,
In the ninth month winter garments are handed out.
Spring days bring us the sun's warmth,
And the orioles sing. (p. 9)

I recall growing up in southern Ontario, in what was then a small village crouched between Hamilton and Toronto, just at the west end of Lake Ontario—full of black-orange orioles, singing, and their droopnests branchended on silver maples or Royal Oaks, named like the red-and-white dairy trucks that delivered milk and cheese and butter and eggs.

Undeniable ecological memory, stored too deep, it seems, to switch. Earthy flesh memory born(e) in the body of the child I was raised. We carry memories of where we were born, and the triggers of such memories are themselves bodily:

In the seventh month the shrikes cry (p. 10)

And in such a cry is borne part of my self crying back for the remembering of a seventh month, when strawberries arrived and arose out of our waiting and whiling (Jardine, 2008b; Ross, 2004).

So "bioregions" are not simply places with objectively nameable characteristics. They infest our blood and bones and become odd, unexpected templates of how we carry ourselves, what we remember of the Earth, and how light and delicate are our footsteps in all the places we walk.

Burlington was, in the 1950s, a market garden area—small twenty- to sixty-acre farms bursting full and an area with many canning factories and wooden fruit-basket factories (up in Freeman, a once-named crossroad near the rail lines that has since disappeared). Back when such things mattered, Burlington was right at the hinge between the north/south rail route up from the fruit-growing areas of Lincoln County (Vineland, Jordan Harbour, east to Niagara-on-the-Lake) and the east/west rail routes to Toronto, Kingston, and on to Montreal, or west to London and Sarnia or down to Windsor and Detroit. Swimming, 1957, Lake Ontario, off the redbrick Legion Hall parking lot south of Water Street, just after the Aylmer Factory had burped out the leftover bilge of tomato canning, and how this hot-scented red-scummed flotation that made the water flapthick muffled and fly surface buzzy melding into the Polio Scares and the summers of no swimming at all.

I remember, growing up in Burlington—then a small village of four thousand, long since overgrown into the anyplace bedroom of nearby city condensations—having to *wait* for strawberries.

> *In the fourth month, the small grass sprouts*
> *In the fifth month the cicadas sing.*
> *In the eighth month we harvest the field,*
> *In the tenth month the leaves begin to fall* (p. 10)

Their appearance once meant something deeper and more difficult than their obvious bright pleasure-presence to the tongue: about place, about seasonality, about expectation, about era, about arrival, about remembering, about reliance, about resignation and hope and little-kid pleasures, about time and its cyclicalities. Strawberries once belonged *somewhere*. They thus arrived not as objects but as bright and brief heralds. As heralds, they were always young, always new and fresh, always delicate and timely, always soon to take leave, leaving grief again at their passing.

III

> *In the sixth month we eat wild plums and grapes,*
> *In the seventh month we cook sunflower and lentils.*
> *In the eighth month we strip leaves of their dates,*
> *In the tenth month we bring home the harvested rice,*
> *We make it into spring wine*
> *For the nourishment of the old.*
> *In the seventh month, we eat melons.* (p. 11)

Pulling strawberries into continuous presence, into continuous, indiscriminate availability is, in its own way, a sort of objectivism. These Alberta winter strawberries are only in the most odd of senses here in my hands, even though, clearly, *here they are*. Something about eating them is potentially dangerously distracting. They are no longer exactly Earth produce even though, of course, they are just that. But they are commodities lifted off the Earth and floating above it, taking me with them. As they begin to float up into detached, oil-soaked commodification, I, too, begin to float, detached, unEarthly.

Such odd, objective strawberries, ripped out of the Earthy contexts of their arrival—no Earth to smell, no resignation to waiting fulfilled, no sunny warmth—can, however, also be alerting. This subtle disruption of a sense of seasonality (one that my own son was just barely raised up into) that transports and oils and technologies have brought us: odd pleasures, since, in the grip of cabin fevers, these strawberries have also saved my life. And yet, my pleasure …

I love them even though they are covered with oil this time of year. My love of them now, indiscriminately, is part of the "trouble in the Middle East." My pleasure is a reason for the war, just like the rainbow-stain gasoline that drove me out West to the edge of the Elbow River to see those Dippers in the first place.

IV

I cannot stop remembering a tomato tossed out against the backyard fence in late Ontario fall and yielding, of itself, without me, beyond desire and necessity, a great green clump of bushes four feet across, with that unmistakable near-acrid smell of fat and furry vines. This Dipper-place is a harsh place, which will yield potatoes and peas and not much else.

Another walk, moose cow, great Alert Being, chest deep in snow near the river. An odd coalescing point, a great gathering in what must be a large habitat. This moose body as a place of great intensity and great need. Seeing her munching on those small fir tree tips seems near-ludicrous and courageous and near-impossible all at once. How large must the territory of tree tips be for there to be such a being?

And me, in winter, here, sucking strawberries.

I am living in a place that a hunter should live or someone with animals to slaughter and offer and eat:

> *In the tenth month we clean the threshing ground*
> *With a pair of goblets we hold a village feast.*
> *Let's slaughter sheep and lamb.* (p. 11)

Out in the greenhouse, sheltered in part from the place, tomatoes. Great Alert Beings, here and yet not here.

An ecological grieving for that deeply imprinted place where I was raised and a joy over the potatoes burping up out of tilled soils, and the young Gray Jay just now flirting with the feeder.

Ecological grieving for the waiting that is no longer necessary.

V

In the fifth month the locust stirs its legs,
In the sixth month the grasshopper vibrates its wings.
In the seventh month, out in the fields;
In the eighth month, about the doors.
In the tenth month the crickets
Get under our beds. (p. 10)

Winter has cracked, or at least blinked. I, too, am a Great Alert Being, surprised to find that some of that alertness, as well as some grieving, is carried here, to Alberta, from the place I grew up.

It took me years to even begin to actually experience this place and its beauties. Too much of my thinking, too much of my experience is placeless. And yet here, summer, finally, heartbreaking blue against the yellow green of pines.

Hale-Bopp's nightly bristle, Mars between Leo's arms, Orion already set, the great hunter that I am not.

And "*Liu-huo* ('cascading fire')" (p. 8), Antares, Great Red Giant in Scorpius, soon to rise.

Time to tend the tomatoes. Because, in the seventh month, the cascading fire of the Scorpion descends and winter begins its miraculous return.

CHAPTER SIXTY-FIVE

Advice TO A New Teacher

KIRSTEN VARNER

You are beginning a tale with many twists and turns. At times it will be overwhelming. There will be days when you feel that you can't possibly keep up, with the work, with the expectations, with the needs of these students placed in your care. There will be days when you feel that you have failed; to get to it all, to get through it all, to get to them all. Keep strong. Do what you can do; it is all that you can do. This is a journey that takes courage. Courage to take a risk, and when you fall, the courage to stand back up and continue on this path.

There will be other days. Days when you get swept up in the excitement of a class beginning a new adventure together. Working to discover new truths, create connections, to make sense of it all. It is exhilarating, it is what you have been waiting for, it is why you do this work in the first place. Take refuge in these moments. Be present in them and let them fill you.

Your journey continues. There will be moments of joy, doubt, success and failure. Each one will show you something, if you let it.

You will be told many versions of the story of what education is and what your role as a teacher should be within it. Alasdair MacIntyre says, "I can only answer the question 'What am I to do?' if I can answer the question 'Of what story or stories do I find myself a part?'" (as cited in Loy, 2010, p. 21).

Acknowledge the stories you are a part of: narratives of standardized curriculum, accountability, report cards and timetables; narratives of inquiry, community and meaning making. Take from them what you need and set the rest aside. Trust yourself to find the stories that really matter to you. Turn to your students, honour the stories they tell you and that you create together. Listen to the disciplines, rich fields of knowledge waiting to be explored, stories that will unfold before you in their own time. Choose the stories that feel most important and play your part to do them justice.

Be aware of the culture we are in, and recognize its influence on you. When we view the world through a single perspective it comes with a kind of ignorance, to it being the right way, "the way things are." "Primarily, ignorance is the result of being trapped in cultural and parochial understandings and accepting them as universal truth" (Smith, 2014, p. 40). If you surround yourself with the dominant cultural stories of efficiency and sprinting towards progress, you will get caught in the rush. The work that flows from this mind-set will take on its character: hurried, fragmented, anxious. Be open to other interpretations; as you collect other perspectives you will see the possible. Gather around you stories of place, of ancestors, of mindfulness, and the work that flows from it will take on its character: whiling, interconnected, meaningful.

"Although I play different roles in different narratives, a few become my habitual stance in the world and end up providing self-identity" (Loy, 2010, p. 23). The choice is yours. What stories will you tell? What characters will you play? Find a place for yourself within the tale that feels right for you. As Wendell Berry stated (Berry & Moyers, 2013): "We have to ask what's the right thing to do, and go ahead and do it, and take no thought for the morrow."

CHAPTER SIXTY-SIX

Girls, Go Close THE Doors!

NEELAM MAL

"Telling our story" is how we make sense of the world and ourselves.
—DAVID LOY (2010, P. 27)

My family, extended and immediate, is filled with amazing cooks. In particular, my parents and sister have incredible talents and palates and can throw together a culinary masterpiece out of leftover odds and ends in the fridge. (My brother and I are the late bloomers in this respect.) Growing up, at least four times a week, we ate Indian food. Punjabi Indian food typically starts with the same base. Fry onions, garlic and ginger. Let it brown and get fragrant, add salt and spices, then tomatoes. Add your vegetable, lentil or meat of choice. Simmer. Enjoy. Our white friends loved to come over for dinner when we were having Indian food. My mom always makes Indian food for potlucks—usually chicken. Always a hit.

The part that no one saw was the meal preparation. Before *any* cooking got started, we had a ritual. My mom or dad would yell at us, "Girls, go close the doors!" Our job was to run around to every room in the house to make sure closet and bedroom doors were closed. Dresser drawers had to be closed. Jackets hung up in the closet with the doors closed. Blankets or sweaters lying around on the couch … put them away, close the door. This wasn't Mom and Dad's ploy to get us to tidy up the house. This was a basic requirement so that we didn't smell like Indian (food) when we went out in the world. The aromatic scent of "thurka," the foundation of all our food, the aroma of our daily lives, on anything but our plates was social suicide. My dad had sat on the C-Train listening to other people talk about the "disgusting smell" that permeated the clothing of less vigilant Indians. My family's collective fear was to be the ones other people talked about. We learned early on which pieces of being Indian to share and which to keep behind closed doors.

It was okay to bring food to a potluck, maybe even leftovers for lunch. To let the thurka introduce us was a crime we were not going to commit.

Before I cook, I yell, "Girls, go close the doors!"

CHAPTER SIXTY-SEVEN

So Many Voices

SCOTT HASSETT

So many voices, so much noise. So many theories, ideologies and priorities, a cacophony of how to's and why not's. Noise so thick that even the reasoned voice, the sound advice is lost in the background, overwhelmed by questions and evolving assumptions. I fight to break through, to hear what matters, to find footing in an avalanche. How can I untangle the chains that bind from the roots that ground, wipe away all the noise and hear the whispers through a tainted filter? Flailing to reorient in the midst of chaos.

I need a breath, space to think, to recognize what really matters.

With a deep breath I plunge outward past the illusions, the false logic and the assumptions shined up as truth.

And from afar only wisdom remains, not truth or lies, not answers or even questions, only wisdom, wisdom and humility. Each moment offering infinite complexity, lineages and ties. That which binds, and connects runs under, between and beyond, and demands of me more than I could ever hope to offer. What then to do, how then to proceed without a map, or a net, knowledge becomes an empty basket in the face of a world far beyond my capacity. Only wisdom seems to offer any help, an elusive promise that there may be a way to proceed, that all is not lost, that I stand a chance against the monsters, demons and angels that dance around me.

"We have to ask what the right thing to do is and do it, and take no thought for the morrow" (Berry, 2013).

The paradox of each moment is found somewhere between its utter irrelevance and ultimate importance. Each moment so minuscule in the face of an unmapped universe. Tiny against the scale of our oceans filling up one drop at a time, and mountains growing from the sea. My influence lost in the shadow of societies' wars against each other, the Earth and themselves. Yet despite these global, universal forces the simplest truth remains; this moment is all there is, and how I act within it is all that really matters.

Action rooted in planning the future is akin to caring for that which does not exist. The future is simply an abstraction, a collection of possible outcomes entangled. Outcomes with roots as much in fantasy as reality, what is as much as what we want it to be. How can the actions of the present find root if they grow from land which does not yet exist? No, the future cannot dictate the past, and yet action without foresight is arrogant and self-indulgent. To do what is right in a given moment is not what is best in the moment, but instead best for that moment. Instant gratification (while at times joyous and necessary) lacks the substance necessary to feed the soul, and so what is right for a moment must somehow remain detached from an imaginary future, but yet act in service of it. Desire and fear are both edges of a sword that cut ourselves from the present. There is only this time, only this place, yet never just here, never just now. How to proceed, a delicate balance that can only be held by wisdom.

Slowly images begin to take shape, the order of chaos only readable through the lens of humility. Images appear not as they are, but how they are in relation to each other. There is no way to be wise, no well-worn path to enlightenment. The closer it seems to be in my grasp, the quicker it seems to slip through my fingers. As soon as I think I know how to proceed, what the "right" thing to do is, I stumble on a new truth and the path becomes impassable.

Yet just as the waters are the muddiest, a new perspective reveals truth. Balance, always balance, wisdom unattached to a moment spirals towards monstrosity. So quickly even the most beautiful ideas seem to fall towards the edges where they become stagnant, lost in their own self-righteousness.

Hermes on my shoulder, never seems quite satisfied.

"Yeah but …"

"Just about …"

"Not quite …"

"Ummmm, maybe …"

A frustrating barrier to knowing, every discovery a new way to be wrong.

And so the question remains: What is this wisdom? My feeble naïveté leaves me lost, a gullible child flailing to recognize the charlatan from the healer, the wicked from the wise.

A pause, time for thought, meditation of the average mind, slowly simple truths revealed. The shape of wisdom begins to become distinct from the infinity of knowledge. It carries a depth, a connected soul, it is not explainable, measurable, or knowable, and hence nontransferable, except for those times when it is. It is a sense of direction cultivated through time, through community, through practice. It gains its strength from its communal nature, the gathering of perspectives, not as competing warriors battling for the victor's flag of supremacy, but as shared souls whose stories gain meaning in the context of each other. The wisdom of ancestors near and far: Gandhi, Mandela and Malala, Berry, Greene, and Fredrick Taylor alike.

Wisdom traditions, cultures and ideas beyond my small scope of existence. Individuality, autonomy, self, separateness, defining features of a culture, and my soul withers. The very lens by which I see the world is tainted by a life lived in dirty water, polluted by the myths of disconnection. Arbitrary lines between myself and others, myself and nature, myself and the spirit of life, and somewhere beyond these lines the river of wisdom flows. A nurturing drink that connects and replenishes. There is no me and you, only us, and we must drink this water together.

Wisdom is a feeling, but not exactly. A type of knowledge, except that it's not. Somewhere in between. Yes it's felt, but so much more structured than an immediate response. Yes it's known, but so much more alive than any type of understanding.

And so I move forward, realizing that wisdom, like any organic life, needs to become rooted in fertile soil. Under the right conditions these roots may cultivate healthy growth, nourishing branches that stretch towards eternity, with roots grounded in the present. The organic nature of roots is contrasted with the concrete poles of knowledge that simply prop up what is already there. Roots need to grow, to diversify, to search new fertile ground. They break through the cement, crack the foundation of what is "supposed to be." Strong roots act in concert with their environment, shaping and being shaped, an intricate part of the living world.

And yet roots may find themselves in infertile ground. Ground that drains without empathy, that asks for your soul without compassion, and gives only that which can be counted and traded. Poison not in the logic of its argument, or the promise of riches at the end of the rainbow, but in the gods it serves, making even the most honest of us fuel for the machine. Poisoned minds, poisoned rivers, poisoned definition of what is natural and what is somehow not. And so as I search to plant my feet in the ground, I must always ask, What spirit does this ground serve, what fruit does it hope to bear? So easily led astray by demons of that which shines, glimmers and feeds my most selfish of inclinations.

Ego
The need to change the world
All in the name of what is good
Reaching beyond
Writing the stories of others
In glory of my own

Eyes turned upward lose sight of the ground beneath them
Stop
Breathe
Humility the toughest pill to swallow

"It takes practice to become practiced in such practices" (David Jardine's advice to us in class).

What little I understand begins to take shape, and I remember that life is practical, and will take practice. There's a reason its people speak of a heart of wisdom, not a mind of wisdom. Wisdom lives not in the rational understanding of things but in lived experience. True wisdom runs not from neuron to neuron, but through each and every cell of my body; cultivated through practice it infuses itself into the very DNA of who I am. It is not simply what I have learned, but who I become. It is itself a living, breathing thing, living symbiotically in me, asking simply for practice in order to nourish.

And yet despite of all the time, the meditation, I seem only to dance around the core of the truth. To touch on the margins of defining wisdom, I have yet even to start to answer "the question." Within the emptiness, the unfulfilled part of me sees the irony, that the agonizing unanswerable nature of the question is what gives it meaning, is what defines it, a necessity of its promise.

> It is not easy to speak about wisdom without insinuating that one knows what it is. Any such insinuation is itself simply foolish if not highly dangerous. (Smith, 2014, p. 32)

And yet that fact alone does not excuse the absence of its exploration. That no answer exists does not preclude that there is nothing worth answering. All too often the fear of not doing everything leads us to do nothing. It is the indefinable nature of wisdom that demands something more than an answer must be sought and so I continue my quest. Aware that the very notion of an "answer" falls into the myth of autonomy. I must remain open to all voices, each acting as a vision of what might be. An awareness of the dangers in believing a story instead of believing it possible. And so my hopeless journey continues, success redefined, no pot of gold, simply the rainbow.

CHAPTER SIXTY-EIGHT

An Ode TO Xmas Present

DAVID W. JARDINE

Please don't let me fear anything I cannot explain. I can't believe I'll never believe in anything again.

—ELVIS COSTELLO (1991)

To begin, consider David Pope's (2015) cartoon published at 7:09AM, January 7, 2015 (https://twitter.com/davpope/status/552844593046097920/photo/1). A slightly pudgy, balding man lying in a pool of blood, his pencil, bent glasses and a piece of paper with a sketch on it beside him. Standing over him, a hooded figure with an AK47, still smoking, saying:

"He drew first."

It is always rather disturbing to discover that something that I have felt or believed or been resigned to or took to be true is a fabrication that has no necessity to it at all. There is a terrible vertigo that comes in finding that believing it to be permanent or beyond question or fixed is just the outcome of causes and conditions that have fallen from memory and view. Such occluding amnesia is, it seems, a perennial part of the human condition. It makes my intimate and heartfelt experiences *seem* immediate and obvious and "simply the way things are." A life of semblance has its own comforts, of course. Such "moon-sickness" (Gadamer, 1989, p. 25) makes it hard to see straight after recent events, and not let the inherited-and-forgotten immediacies of media flurries turn to whiteouts and skidding off the road. Nice Canadian metaphors, eh? There is nothing necessary about freedom of speech, just as there is nothing necessary about real or feigned religious effrontery. Such things only persist in the persistence of one or another kind of "attention and devotion" (Berry, 1986, p. 33). Even studious claims of "false flag operations" (Barrett, 2015) are fabrications of fabrications. I mention this last thread following on conversations with a friend wherein we spoke of what happens when every single event in the world becomes full of a monotonously same hiddenness. When I got to this point in writing, I knew that if I looked, there would be false flag commentaries. Of course. It's simply the way things are. It's like Santa Claus, who is always just out of view and because you've never seen him, that proves that he exists. The CIA as the new monotheism behind every event, and all-new arguments from design take center stage in off-stage suspicions.

Yet please, I plead, don't get me wrong. It is my lovely friend lying there in that cartoon, and our love itself lying bled out with glasses bent and askew.

When vertigo strikes, possibilities become endless and the bleeding cannot be stopped.

Hans-Georg Gadamer (1989, p. xxii) nailed something of this phenomenon with great precision and a wicked sting: "the naive self-esteem of the present moment." To find that the world is nothing but Santa Clauses all the way down, and to feel again and again that terrible ear popping of growing up that came with finding out the truths about this taken-to-be-saint, and the whole worlds of experience that had to be left behind in such finding—such is the lot of interpretation. Once glimpsed, nothing can stop this cascading collapse, not even the ground on which that body slumps.

But it is essential that this be properly counterbalanced, because the naive self-esteem of the present moment is only *initially* replaced with a vague humiliation at having been so sleepy and at the hot bile that comes up the esophagus. This pivot point is profoundly important, because if one gets stuck there, what can follow is a life of cynicism, paranoia, and complaint and the life goal of breaking everyone else's bubble in an act of skillful woe. There is, right at this pivot, a "hitherto concealed experience" (Gadamer, 1989, p. 100)—a way of engaging this vertigo world of dependent arising—whose bristling radiance far outshines what was lost in the shifting. In fact, I'd venture that what is gained is an understanding that there is, in fact, something "true" of the thunder and lightning of reindeer, and the saintliness of the gift, and the Northern Hemispheric brainstem draw of passing the stopping of the sun's sinking and feeling its *tropos*, its "turning," that goes far beyond the surface story. There is something true in the arrival of the child that outruns every attempt to give it a proper name. Even your eye's ability to dance over these words belies fundamentalism of any sort, whether Christian, Islamic or hidden or overt American ops in the name of freedom and terror. Fuck that. And this isn't either for or against Christianity, Islam or America. It is against false and delusional *believing* that turns the agony of our living into a hardened enemy and turns our believing into something whose hardening we don't have to face. It functions like a hidden wound, festering precisely because of its unutterable hiddenness. Unutterable because of liberal openness to "difference" and "diversity." Self-cancelling, because we must be open to that which despises openness, tolerant of that which is intolerant. And no, not just "Islam" at its worst (or Christianity at its historical nadir—I'll leave it to you to decide when that might have been). The CIA, too, protecting market-economics at all costs under the guise of protecting "democracy" at all costs. Droning hits of civilians. Beheadings. Tea Parties? Take your pick.

Robert Bly said it somewhere: if you want to survive this world, study. But not the bland study of piling one piece after another of "amassed verified knowledge" (Gadamer, 1989, p. xxi) on top of a pile whose weight simply weighs us down and confirms our cynicism and gives us grey gravity. No. The studying that provides some relief to the weight of the world is studying one's living itself, studying that very movement of vertigo that comes in the collapsing of the world and the arrival of the child. We build it up to let it go. The goal is not gravity but lightness, even in the face of a fellow writer killed for writing, killed for the very giggled child-heralding that is writing's goal, pushed up against the senilities, seriousness and naive self-esteem of the present circumstances. Trickster poof and prod and dance, pivoting on that sidewalk even in the moment of being shot, of falling.

Like this: to herald that a child is born is something that will take a lifetime and more to fully understand. Because that child will awaken in our loving arms and see Ferguson, Missouri, hear of Michael Brown, see cartoonists being offensive and being shot for it, see claims of hidden hands at work in the world, and evidence upon evidence of muttered common breaths co-inspiring ("Hush, a child is born, I hear"), and look us in the eye and say "*what?*" What *is* this? What the *hell* is going on? That, I'm afraid to say (because saying so lays out a "terrible trial" [Berry & Moyers, 2013] of being patient in an erupting emergency that follows in the wake of such giving), is the Magi's gift no matter how or whether we answer these questions.

And I get it, this contradiction between the eruption of the child and the call to grow up and give up the naïveté of believing.

Freedom of speech is a fabrication, the protection of which is a decision, not a God-given or God-forbidden right. Decide.

Guess what God, the CIA, the faculty I'm leaving, the flags, false or otherwise, the scurrying, the distraction, the fear mongered and felt? Guess what, Xmas? Guess what, Gadamer or fat Buddha squat? I don't *believe* in any of you.

Instead, I write. *That* is how I love you all.

Je suis Charlie, but guess what? I don't *believe* that either.

Happy Xmas, then.

CHAPTER SIXTY-NINE

Dear Cohort

IAN WALSH

Do you remember when we first met, way the hell up in Tuscany? It may have seemed like my mother signed me up for my master's and I was there against my will. Maybe I was. That was when I did things because I was supposed to, not because they were the right things to do. My motivation for starting was not in line with my motivation for continuing. I continued because of you, because of Jackie and David. And Wendell, and David Smith and Loy and Thomas King. Maxine and Joseph Campbell, Thich Nhat Hanh, Gadamer and all the others.

This journey has led me to rethink my thinking. To take that extra breath and consider what is important, what is the right thing to do. It is not easy to change, to make adjustments to lifelong styles and attitudes. To read your writing, listen to your words, nod and know that there is, even on the darkest day, a small group of people doing the right thing. Thank you.

One of the many examples of the content becoming a part of my process is that I will never hear or use the word 'believe' in the same way. David's *An Ode to Xmas Present* (Jardine, 2015a; and in this book) changed that. The change is not complete, maybe never will be. It is a work in progress, to stop believing.

My final piece for this cohort is a short poem, with a lifetime of footnotes and citations:

What will I do if I don't believe? I will study.[1]
What will I do if I don't believe? I will read.[2]
What will I do if I don't believe? I will write.[3]
What will I do if I don't believe? I will breathe.[4]

NOTES

1. "The aim of interpretation, it could be said, is not just another interpretation, but human freedom." David Smith (1999, p. 29) speaks of the freedom that comes with being the reader, the student. Instead of focusing on what the author is trying to say, I feel more comfortable figuring out what message I am receiving, how it relates to me—now, then and later. I swing into other viewpoints, accept ideas without agreeing and understand that all interpretation is open to evolution. I don't believe. "You have to study the text as it is presented, whether it's a page or a field," Wendell Berry says. "You don't graduate from it" (Berry, 2014, n.p.). Wendell helps. Look on a completed task and say, "And now?" The task becomes incomplete and stays that way. Our real work is not about completing a checklist; it is about being involved in work that takes a lifetime, more.

2. Gadamer (1989) makes sense to me when he tells me that my reading of the world is possible, not necessary. Stories are always becoming what they are. Sometimes I marvel at the amount of content I have not read, how it waits for me. It doesn't need me either, but comes to life when I hold it. What will it lead me to? Will it linger with me hours, days, years later. Will it be the same when read a second, third, thirtieth time? Packaging reading into a box with levels, instructions, black and white destroys what reading is truly for. I learned to read to hear the stories, to learn about people, places, things. Reading is not a task; it is possibility, a beginning. I will never let a student feel that they can be 'done' learning to read. There is no level Z.

3. "The writing had allowed, indeed demanded, of the writer to slow down, to concentrate and focus, to remember, and to be still enough to allow for a certain purification of soul so that what might be written might also escape the tentacled entrapments of pure self-interest" (Smith, 2012, p. xii). I am on this journey, to remove the 'I' while continuing to write about what is important to me, because it is important. When I hear of beliefs and the grief they bring, I aim to write and make truth out of the lies. Once written the work becomes itself and has no recourse through explanation or clarification.

4. "Breathing in, I know of I am of the nature to die. Breathing out, I know I cannot escape dying. Breathing out, only my actions come with me" (Nhat Hanh, 2008, p. 117). I take 23,000 breaths per day, very few with thoughtfulness, appreciation, clarity. Start with one, build from there. Stuff, ego, pride, power, money, status—bullshit. If I am remembered at all, it will be for what I have done. Start acting in ways that will be remembered. Kindness, patience, reliability. Jackie's voice in my head, telling me to breathe. Multiple moments every day when one breath can make the difference between a smile and a suspension. One breath that can build love or build hate, make room for a second chance. Breathe.

CHAPTER SEVENTY

An Address

JUDSON INNES

All I have ever really known about my paternal grandfather is that he was a quiet man. On occasion, in my youth, I would make inquiries about the man, tall and angular, of whom an aged black-and-white photo hung in the hallway of my childhood home. After a long pause, and some searching, sometimes a fragment of a story or an atomized historical fact would be offered, but always quickly followed by "He was a quiet man." Invariably these shards, pieces of stories, slipped through my fingers, eluding my attempts to turn them into a unified whole.

Last week, late on Monday night, I stood in the lobby of my condo complex and examined the small package, no more than a few hundred grams in weight that had been placed in my mailbox. At a quick glance I saw it was from my aunt in Kamloops, and surmised she had remembered my birthday, as she always does. Still in the lobby, I tore open the yellow manila envelope and examined its contents, a weathered and worn paperback book. On the cover was a picture of the Stanley Cup, of hockey fame, with the title, in bright bold red letters, *Hockey Dynasty: The Fascinating History of the Toronto Maple Leaf Hockey Club*. In the top right corner of the book was the price, $1.25, and the printing date, February 1970.

Now why would she send me this? I thought: a curious gift indeed. I reached back in the torn envelope and searched for the card that I knew had to be inside. Finding it, I carefully unfolded the card and read the handwritten note. It read, in part, "I'm enclosing this pocket book that my Dad, your Grandfather, bought many years ago. It was printed in 1970, so Dad must have purchased it just a few months before he died. I like the fact that he signed it. I hope you find this interesting, a little bit of your family history."

Having read the note I turned back to the book. On the inside of the cover, my grandfather had signed the book in neat handwriting:

Robert H. Innes
5870 Mowat Avenue
Powell River, BC

Needless to say, I was thrilled to see my grandfather's handwriting and intrigued to understand why he had included his street address: I had never seen that before. I opened the book further and leafed through the pages, receiving one more surprise when an old newspaper clipping fell out of somewhere near the middle of the book. Perhaps it had been used as a bookmark. I picked up the dried and delicate old newspaper clipping off the floor and carefully unfolded it. It was from page six of the *Powell River News*, November 8, 1956. On it was a picture of my own father, my gandfather's son, and underneath it a short description of the high school basketball game my Dad's team would be playing against Vancouver High School later that week.

Slowly, late at night, down there in the lobby of my condo complex, over the following days, and as I write this now, I have begun to understand, to mould together the pieces of my grandfather, a man I have always longed to have known. He first came to Canada from Scotland at age five, landing with his family in Truro, Nova Scotia. As a young man he went west, eventually boarding a train headed for the farmland around Edmonton. During the Depression, now married to my grandmother Mary Innes (nee Tataryn; now ninety-eight and still living in Powell River) and with a young family, he saw his farm fail and he was displaced once again. Forced to hit the road, for a number of years they traveled from town to town following the work, before finally settling in Powell River in 1948, when my grandfather took a job in the town's thriving pulp and paper mill.

Which brings me back to the address on the inside of the book, 5870 Mowat Avenue; a small, two-story, well-built house on a gentle slope a few hundred feet above the shores of the glacially carved Powell Lake. A house my grandfather built himself, and as I now understand, must have taken immense pride in. Through my childhood I made weekly visits to the house to see my grandmother, never considering its origins or the man, by then absent, who had chosen so well after so many years on the move. Yet the house has long had a hold over me, forever drawing me in. Just this year, over the holidays, though it has long passed from my grandmother's hands, I found myself on Mowat Avenue in front of the old house, just checking to see how it was doing.

When my grandfather died, suddenly, in the spring of 1970, his two sons took his ashes down the gentle hillside and to their boat, which waited, moored at the small wooden dock on Mowat Bay, just a few minutes from my grandfather's hillside home. They traveled twenty miles up the lake, past the First Narrows and into the lake's east channel, a narrow, V-shaped, flooded valley, enveloped by towering peaks, before arriving at Rainbow Falls.

Here, occasionally, on warm summer days, glacial water from the mountains above trickles and flows down the granite rock facing of the falls and when the angle of the sun is just so and one is the right distance from the shore, a rainbow will appear. Hovering over the water, the kaleidoscope of colours shimmers and roils, animating the landscape, as do the ashes of my grandfather, which were spread on this spot where the colours sometimes appear. It was his favourite place on Earth.

A few hundred metres from Rainbow Falls, still in the east channel of the lake, is a small island populated primarily by giant Douglas firs and lush, bright green salal, which surrounds the thick bases of the towering rain forest sentinels. On one edge of the island is the most recent incarnation of our family cabin, first built in 1958 and having undergone several metamorphoses in the intervening years. On pleasant summer days I can stand on the deck of the cabin and look across the water to contemplate my grandfather in the fractured light, alive and reflected off Rainbow Falls. I suppose I will understand him a little better now, and truthfully perhaps myself too.

CHAPTER SEVENTY-ONE

Becoming Uncongealed

DAVID W. JARDINE

It is somewhat difficult to establish, but once you are used to it, it will be like meeting an old acquaintance.

—JAMGON KONGTRUL (2002, P. 67)

It's like making a path through the forest. At first it's rough going, with a lot of obstructions, but returning to it again and again, we clear the way. After a while the ground becomes firm and smooth from being walked on repeatedly. Then we have a good path for walking in the forest.

—AJAHN CHAH (2005, P. 83)

In the work of interpretation, what begins to emerge is an experience of, shall we say, trace-lines in the world, lines that have been hidden or obscured by day-to-day practicalities, distractions and duties. In our class, we can read a phrase from David Loy's book (2010) and now, after all the rough going we've been through, all the difficult reading and reflection and writing, some phrases start to sound familiar, some images draw us in, some passages start to ask to be underlined. And what becomes clear is that re-reading it makes different things emerge precisely because of what has occurred in the meantime. It does not stand still as something I have already experienced, but comes back as a sort of new summons. I ask for page numbers when others are reading partly because I don't want this or that to be simply lost. I want to be able to go back to it, to get used to it, to live with it and remember it and see what happens. What would become of me if this were true and I lived my life accordingly?

That is what it means to read, because then the reading isn't simply "What does this author mean?" but "What would happen if it were true?" What would I be asked to do, to practice; how would my cadence shift in the world? "Texts are instructions for practice" (Tsong-kha-pa, 2000, p. 52). This is why hermeneutics talks so much about the phenomenon of "claim" (Gadamer, 1989, p. 126) and "address" (p. 299). Reading, with practice, becomes a way of not simply sussing out the author's claims, but dealing with what happens to me if that claim claims me and puts into question what I previously have lulled my life over and felt in sleepy awareness. Reading, study, become forms of becoming uncongealed—doubly, both myself and the object of study are released from torpidity in the act of interpretation. "Against fixity" can be interpreted as "makes the object and all its possibilities fluid" (Gadamer, 1989, p. 367), and not only this. It draws me into an understanding of *myself* as precisely composed, not of a fixed identity, but of precisely such ongoing fluidity—not "licentiousness" but rather something quite different.

Through the concerted and repeated practice of interpretive work we gradually, and sometimes suddenly, find ourselves:

> Living in the belly of a paradox wherein a genuine life together is made possible only in the context of an *ongoing conversation* which never ends and which must be sustained for life together to go on at all. The openness that it requires is not a vague licentiousness, but a risky, deliberate engagement of the full conflict and ambiguity by which new horizons of mutual understanding are achieved. (Smith, 1999, p. 133, emphasis in text)

This is something like the emerging experience of belonging in the long and ongoing struggle of being human and making our way in the world. It thus also highlights the error of some forms of thought and action, which work against or defile or marginalize or desecrate this insight for fear of it (see Jardine, 2012). Such animal-panic retractions are understandable and situationally forgivable. But they are not true to what is our lot and, I suggest, our deeply human responsibility.

Some of these things we read even start to sound like old acquaintances the meeting of which provides a combination of comfort and thrill. I recall years ago waiting for someone in a terribly busy and crowded intersection of Bloor and Yonge streets in Toronto and glimpsing how the passing faces just passed by, and then, suddenly, the meeting of an acquaintance, how they emerged up out of the rush and roil, and the relief that comes, the wake up. Recognition. Like this:

> We do not understand what recognition is in its profoundest nature if we only regard it as knowing something again that we know already—i.e., what is familiar is recognized again. The joy of recognition is rather the joy of knowing *more* than is already familiar. In recognition what we know emerges, as if illuminated, from all the contingent and variable circumstances that condition it. (Gadamer, 1989, p. 114)

Even if this passage from Gadamer is a little murky, I want to be able to linger near what it says and let it into the building of the path. "The question is not so much 'What do I learn from stories [citations, study, listening]?' but 'What stories do I want to live?'" (Loy, 2010, p. 25). All the complexity of ecological thought, of Buddhist thought, of hermeneutics, resolve down to this little sacred thrill of experiencing the dependent co-arising of the world and the arising and passing away of myself right in the middle of it all. Of it *all*.

The more we study in this way, the more we are able to feel the pull of the fabrics of the world. And the more this happens, the more we are able to enter into that fabrication, in Latin, *textus*. Two things. We become agents in the stories we have inherited, tellers and re-tellers and, at the same time, we don't just fall into these stories but become conscious of them *as* stories. If we lose sight of this dependently co-arising fabric (action), we begin to believe that it is not a fabrication but "just the way things are" (reification—making into a permanent and intractable given, an object). "Mental tendencies congeal and we bind ourselves without a rope" (Loy, 2010, p. vii). The "outer" parallel with this "inner" tendency to congeal is called reification.

Becoming uncongealed, therefore, is not just an issue of a sort of meditative inner life, but of unbinding the world as well and letting ourselves fall in love again with its ongoing flow of arising and falling. Parallel here is all the Buddhist talk of not "grasping" when we feel the vertigo of such movement, but settling, composing ourselves, and, for me, composing, writing this, not as a way of stopping this flow but of inviting readers into an experience of it and its ways. Hermeneutic writing is not, therefore, deliberately "poetic" or "obscure," but is, rather, an instance of an old Aristotelian principle, that the investigation and articulation of something need to find its proper character and measure in the thing being investigated and articulated (*mensuratio ad rem*).

Our tendency to pull away from this insight and work is understandable. We tend to see the world *through* our stories and don't tend to see those stories as stories that could be told otherwise, stories that are told by others in a manner different from the way we tell them, and so on. As teachers, we are always right at the cusp of this phenomenon, because we have taken on as our profession the waiting on and attending to arriving voices that will have something to say about the stories we have taken for granted, the lessons we've taken as the ones needing to be taught. "Meaning is improvised together" (Loy, 2010, p. 27), and no matter how hard we try, we can't outrun this circumstance with plans and procedures. Whatever I do, what I do will be read back to me other-wise. And the legacies of hermeneutics, Buddhism and ecology say to us as clear as a bell that *this is not an error that needs to be fixed* but rather a circumstance that we must learn to live with well and must help our students learn to live with, this making of a life in this world with all its ancestries, all its shared and contested inheritances, all the terribleness and all the beauty. All of it. This is where our best commiseration lies, in this great irony of scholarship as an ongoing practice of composure.

So, again, *textus* does not refer only literally to "texts" but also to the fabric of the world:

> The understanding and interpretation of texts ... obviously belongs to human experience of the world in general. The hermeneutic phenomenon is basically not a problem of method at all. It is not concerned with a method of understanding by means of which texts are subjected to ... investigation like all other objects of experience. It is not concerned with amassing verified knowledge, yet it is concerned with knowledge and with truth. In understanding ... not only are texts understood, but insights are acquired and truths known. But what kind of knowledge and what kind of truth? (Gadamer, 1989, p. xxi)

The sort of knowledge being hinted at here is at the root of what we are exploring and it is, in a strange way, a very simple matter: "Oh, yes, right, I've heard that before, I recognize that bloodline, that phrase, that name" and then, in such recognition, I get drawn into taking those paths, studying more. Through study, through reading and remembering texts, I increasingly experience (Ger. *Erfahrung*, hiding the root verb *Fahren*, "to journey") the movement of lines of influence and life, of images and ideas, stories told and re-told, and of ancestors (Ger. *Vorfahren*, literally, "before-journeyers") forgotten but then rising up now as acquaintances. There is a hidden fabric to this world I'm in and that my students are in, my loves are in, my breath is in, a fabric that is often obscured through the day-to-day work of getting by. This fabric is real, and its threads run right through me. And the more I can articulate this run-through, the more that others will notice that there is a path with a chance to take it, and the more they notice, the clearer is my own path.

This is why Chogyam Trungpa (2013, pp. 56–57) said, regarding the path we are on, that "as practitioners carry on their journey, they are preparing the road. Practitioners are not only journeyers, but they are also road builders." This sounds grand, but it is very small and simple and immediate.

I just found out, for example, that the phrase "one fell swoop" (Jardine, 2014c) is from *Macbeth*—finding this out does not congeal and amass and simply add one more piece of information to some pile, but rather is more like a door opening out into *even more*, like a side-path glimpsed along the way, one that I could follow, one that has traces of others having been there before, acquaintances met and unmet. I brought that phrase forward into awareness anew, and can now "remember" what I seem to have forgotten (even though I never knew it). Rather than this being burdensome and increasing a sense of being stuck and congealed, it has the opposite effect of feeling liberating, thrilling, a sense of lightness and light—like Gadamer's near-ecstatic image of the hermeneutic experience of words: "every word [has an] inner dimension of multiplication: every word breaks forth as if from a center [and] causes the whole of the language to which it belongs to resonate. Every word carries with it the unsaid" (Gadamer, 1989, p. 458). This is the "living met-aphoricity of language" (p. 432)—"the spontaneous and inventive seeking out of similarities by means of which it is possible to order things" (p. 432).

Ek-stasis, glimpsed, again. Joy.

What does this *mean*? It speaks against a sense of congealing and reifica-tion. It speaks about the practice of experiencing the world in light of what is *possible*—"*possible* ways of shaping our lives" (Gadamer, 1992, p. 59), ways which are offered with spaciousness around them in such a way that I must step in and decide what might now be best. It speaks about an experience of a slowly revealing sort of slipstream of ideas, full of life and vibrancy, spacious ("mean-ings are like a space in which things are related to one another" [p. 433]). It is an experience linked intimately to being connected to the life of the past and the living work of making our way in the world in a way that is conscious of our implicated-ness in this world and its inheritances. It is about ears popping, about waking up from a weird sleep. I can't tell you how many times I've said to myself, "Where have I been?" It is nearly hilarious that Gadamer, in linking this to an understanding of the phenomenon of play, cites two common German phrases that bespeak part of this experience: "something is going on (*im Spiele ist*), something is happening (*sich abspielt*)" (Gadamer, 1989, p. 104). I remem-ber well my first encounters with hermeneutics and saying that it involved the rather creepy experience of something going on behind my back and without me knowing it, something already in play, some game already afoot. Such is the profound and beautiful sense of humiliation that you have to get used to in this work.

Where *have* I been, indeed? And what have I been wasting my time and atten-tion and life on instead of this vivid joy?

That experience of spaciousness (of not being stuck inside oneself and one's own story or thoughts or ideas or history, but being out in the world which is constantly drawing me to venture [*Fahren*] beyond my congealed self) is one of the things that Philip Phenix (1975) means by "transcendence." This Latin term can be translated as "going beyond." Like this: going beyond being captured in the one congealed story of this or that and thinking that it is self-contained and final and finished and inevitable and not, instead, dependently co-arising, full of relations and relatives and moments of arising anew and needing to be addressed all over again.

So someone whispers how lovely families are and how we have to get back to all our relations, and I hear Maxine Greene's voice from a half-remembered video, saying that they are murderous.

The one voice prevents me from simply falling for the other, and vice versa. Both tales make the other tale more telling. Each uncongeals the other from the gumminess of believing and attachment. This simply means that murderousness is certainly possible as is loveliness, and reifying either (it *is* this or it *is* that) desecrates what "families" really are: full of possibilities beyond the ones I've come to assume and in which I might find (a false) comfort.

False? Yes. Congealing feels safe and good for a while, but, precisely *because of* such congealing, it becomes increasingly surrounded by threats to its safety and security, and the more it hardens, the more other possibilities become monstrous. It thus sets off a threat-retraction-terror us vs. them logic whose telos is only further retraction. It is not a coincidence that right as hermeneutics, ecology and Buddhism are emerging with this voice of fluidity, at the same time is arising, almost in identical proportion, talk of terrorism and threat and insurgency and zero-tolerance.

This dance, itself, is an instance of dependent co-arising.

In this way, when I release my own understanding of a phenomenon into its living array of possibilities, rather than simply being a piling up of alternatives and an exhaustion of effort, each liberates the other from itself and its intimate believe-ability. More strongly put, when poetry or careful scientific description is allowed to stand in the full array of the possibilities of human language, each becomes *more* understandable in its exquisite irreplaceability. Because, for example, scientific description is now experienced as possible but not necessary, the true nature of it can be grasped—what this possibility is for, where it is located, what to expect of it, where it came from, what beautiful instances are available, what its limits are, what *not* to expect from it, how one becomes practiced in it, what happens when it goes astray or too much is expected of it, or it is wielded as a weapon of power or suasion, and so on. This grasping fails only when it collapses into the stupidity of saying, for example, that poetry is always and everywhere a good idea.

So, we tell our differing and intertwining stories to each other, not to wallow or invite wallowing, but *to free each other*:

Buddhapalita's Commentary on [Nagarjuna's] "Fundamental Treatise" says:

> What is the purpose of teaching dependent-arising? The master Nagarjuna ... saw that living beings are beset by various sufferings and assumed the task of teaching the reality of things ... *so that they might be free.* [my emphasis] What is the reality of things? It is the absence of essence. Unskilled persons ... conceive of an essence in things and then generate attachment and hostility with regard to them. (Tsong-kha-pa, 2002, p. 210)

And then this:

> The aim of interpretation, it could be said, is not just another interpretation but human freedom, which finds its light, identity and dignity in those few brief moments when one's lived burdens can be shown to have their source in too limited a view of things. (Smith, 1999, p. 29)

CODA

These three roots of our work (hermeneutics, Buddhism, ecology) take this liberation as fundamental to the path itself and fundamental therefore to the venture itself. The path *and* the goal. All three take it as a practice that needs to be practiced in order to become practiced in it. With practice, it begins to yield and yield up "a hitherto concealed experience that transcends thinking from the position of subjectivity" (Gadamer, 1989, p. 100). Experiencing and gaining insight into these living lead-lines is a form of knowledge and a way of conducting ourselves, a way of being open to our surroundings and its life and ways.

Therefore, paradoxically, this story about stories is not just one more story among others but a recovery of the lived-experience of our storied lives. Hermeneutics, Buddhism and ecology would say that it is delusional to think otherwise, even though such delusions are full of their own stories and heroes and villains. That is why this work constantly feels like a knife-edge, because it involves maintaining oneself with an understanding of and sensitivity to the stories that have built our lives, but not simply falling for or falling into or falling in love or hatred with any of them. This is why Buddhism speaks about "detachment." And as our dear friend Thich Nhat Hanh said, only then, once we give up the dreams of things lasting forever, can we become effective workers for our environment. Detachment doesn't mean turning away from our lives and joys and woes, but turning towards our lives without congealing and attachment. It is the form of knowledge commonplace in the humanist tradition—the experience of being part of a living world and cultivating a strange and beautiful and earthly freedom. I cannot help but list some of the terms that define that tradition: eloquence, prudence, decorum, common sense, good judgment, thoughtful kindness, temperance, eloquence, prudence, a sense of proper proportionality, affection (see Bayer, 2008; Gadamer, 1989).

If I may exaggerate, not totally unlike the six perfections (see, e.g., Tsong-kha-pa, 2000): generosity, patience, perseverance, discipline, stillness and wisdom.

This freedom is the source of venturing and also its outcome. It is always "there" but always needing to be sought out anew. It rises up out of a child's comment, a text's leaping image, everywhere.

Everywhere.

So I'll end with the questions that David Loy (2010) leaves us with regarding becoming uncongealed:

> If delusion [and distraction] is awareness stuck in attention-traps, and enlightenment liberates awareness, does the spiritual path involve finding the correct story, or getting rid of stories, or learning to story in a new way? (p. vii)

CHAPTER SEVENTY-TWO

Ode to My Rabbit Teacher

JACKIE SEIDEL

You always appear when I most need you. Leaping and darting down the alley in front of my car. In the dark. You are terrified, desperately looking for a way out of that long tunnel—a hole in a fence, an open gate. I know your pounding heart and catching breath. This goddamn mammalian fleshfear adrenalin rush panic.

You remind me that I am also animal. That the predator is always just around the corner. I ran from a black bear once; in the night, its rumbling, throaty warning shook the forest. I just wanted to pee. Next thing I know, I am running, numb-minded to everything except terror, through the dark woods, and the oak scrub, looking for my tent. I was lost. Blood running down my legs from scratches that I couldn't remember getting. And so I know how it is that you can never remember where the safe place is, where there is a hole in the fence.

You ate my garden this summer. Over one hundred sunflowers sprouting, three rows of okra, all the edamame plants, most of the carrot tops, the first tender leaves of all the beets, most of the chard. But not the zucchini. I don't like those either. I was frustrated and so pissed at you. One day I was delighting in the seed-pods appearing on the okra; the next morning I was staring at twenty little leafless stalks sticking out of the ground. I schemed how to keep you away, if not this year, then next. What fences I could build. One million ways to make you unwelcome. To encourage you to move on. I'd wake up in the morning and see you out there in the morning sun, lying amongst the greens, nibbling the most tender. And I would curse you.

When you were running down the alley, there are clever things I wanted to tell you. Mostly this: You could be still. You could calm your heart and breath and mind. You could imagine yourself invisible and scentless. You do, after all, have the magical ability to turn yourself white in winter and brown in summer. What use is the power of camouflage if you don't use it? I tell myself this often: Be still, breathe quietly. It might be okay. Maybe no one will eat us and we can finally rest. For years you've appeared there in front of my car, doing your crazy leaping panicked run, and I thought this was the lesson. I congratulated myself on my cleverness and on 'getting it.' Until this summer of 2015 as hundreds of thousands of refugees, hungry and thirsty, their aching feet bleeding from the long walk, seeking shelter and sustenance and compassion wherever they could find it. Fences were built to keep them out. Words of violence spewed hatred and selfishness. Also words of love and compassion, acts of welcome and hospitality and safety.

Something shifted, Rabbit Teacher. Fellow traveler. I remembered that we are related, that you and me and also all those wanderers near and far, fleeing from fear, leaning towards safety—we are cousins in this fragile mortal life. We are connected through millions of years of soil, microbes, sunshine, bees, seeds and mammalian mother milk. I remembered that it is easy to curse and hard to love. I learned that it is easy to think you are my teacher when you are terrified in the alley, but hard to know you when you eat my garden. I don't feel very clever anymore. In the morning, you lie near my door in the warm sunshine. You have worn down a spot in the earth there, one place you feel safe. You made it through one more night and so did I. Your fur is turning white. You are a miraculous being. Cold and snow are coming. I greet you and say hello and wish you well on this day. It is a good day to be alive. I will plant more seeds for you next year. I will plant a place of refuge and sanctuary. Our garden is big enough for both of us.

CHAPTER SEVENTY-THREE

School Storage Bags

Not as Innocent as They Seem

STEPHANIE BARTLETT

Seen at the Dollar Store:

> SCHOOL Storage Bags: Perfect size for folders. Documents. Papers. Great to protect your documents.

Rushing through the Dollar Store, intent on my shopping list, I was suddenly jarred out of my multi-tasking state of mind. A gasp. A jolt. I found it strange that the nudge to return to mindfulness was triggered by a glance at a colourful box that was as busy and rushed as my thoughts. Blue, yellow, red and white collided with uppercase, lowercase, text boxes, images, cursive writing and different fonts. I stopped to take a photo. Michael Derby (2015) writes that "an ecohermeneutic approach to pedagogy thus encourages pausing momentarily in our tracks" (p. 4). Originally I took the photo because I wanted to document that individual moment; it wasn't until later that I realized the significance that photo would have on (re)defining my pedagogy, a reflexive process that evolves continuously.

The forced importance of leveled reading has permeated our culture to such a degree that we can now buy bags that are PERFECT to contain our precious documents (or leveled books.) Added to the irony is that there is an image of a Disney princess behind the box. Not noticing the princess in the background until later when I looked at the photo I'd taken gives way to an acceptance of "the way things are" simply because of the widespread reminders throughout our society. Stopping to pause for a moment here, I lament the loss of exploration and pure enjoyment in life for a child, free of gender-specific toys and competitive learning environments. As an educator, mother and woman, I must challenge this. How might we begin? Let's start with big beautiful picture books with atypical, magical stories and rich language that don't fit into those school storage bags.

CHAPTER SEVENTY-FOUR

Teaching, Practice, Wisdom

An Invitation to the Banff Centre

DAVID W. JARDINE AND JACKIE SEIDEL

At the conclusion of a four-course graduate certificate, we met for two days in June 2014 at the Banff Centre in Banff, Alberta, Canada, with two guests: Dr. Dwayne Donald (2009a and b, 2012a and b) and Dr. David G. Smith (1999, 2006, 2014), both of whose work we read over the course of our own ventures. A great part of our explorations involved an attempt to recover something lost in the world of schooling, that we have ancestors and fellow venturers whose work and words surround us and provide refuge, encouragement, warnings, support and reprimand, all at once. That many feel uprooted from this ancestry and rich ecopedagogical surrounding is why we called our first certif-icate "Two Roots of Classroom Inquiry" and also why we took great pleasure in what, over time, felt less and less coincidental: the Latin term for "roots" is radix. *It is itself the root of the word "radical." Radical. A rootedness that persistently, and with patience and perseverance, generosity and a certain discipline, needs to uproot the spells of our rootless-ness that have got us, not rooted but "bound without a rope" (Loy, 2010, p. 42).*

"Like a prisoner whose cell gate has never been locked" (Loy, 2010, p. 40).

This "never been locked" is part of the great and joyous humiliation that has been part of our work and why we've had to come to trust each other with the very frailties that hide and seek on the liminal outskirts of educational language and its sorrows and fretting. Now spoken, written, here, tattooed down the arms of embrace.

"Embracing brings you back" (Clifford, 2006). Pat Clifford is also the one who gave us that keen phrase in response to worries that such work is not possible in real schools: "If it actually exists, it must *be possible."*

What follows is an elaborated version of the invitation we sent out to all concerned about our upcoming retreat and refuge.

We are near to the end of a journey that has lasted one year for some of you, and two for others. No doubt, such things don't simply end, but how they continue is yet to be seen.

My [DJ's] dog Daniel just brought down another front deer leg from Cougar Ridge. He stood and waited again, just up at the skirt of the forest, facing the house. There's a pedagogy, here, but it is hard to tell who is the teacher and who is the student: the leg? The ridge? The dog? Domestication? Herd animals? Settlement? That bloody death and all its fears and chases and falling to gravity? Or perhaps the deaths of two of my other dogs at the very same cougar locale a few years back? Or the feeling of being already likewise pursued and those Buddhists who say that the only way to outrun what is coming is to stop running. Another old story: when you are chased by the Lord of Death and you trip and fall and your body scatters into blood and bone and air and earth and water, *who will the Lord of Death pursue?* Who was the Lord of Death pursuing before that trip and fall?

Or during that buzzer-driven race to cover the curriculum too often conceived in panic and regret? Who? Gary Snyder (1990, p. 175) cites Dong-Shan, a ninth-century Chan/Zen Master:

> One time when the Master was washing his bowls, he saw two birds contending over a frog. A monk who also saw this asked, "Why does it come to that?" The Master replied, "It's only for your benefit."

This leg, its blood, Daniel's waiting, is for our benefit, as are the little panics that schooling arouses without warning or recourse. But then we're left with the task of understanding, a path now not quite laid out, almost ready to be taken. Step.

We've come to know and let ourselves experience great depths of the troubles that surround us—not only our profession and our work but also our lives. Sometimes, for each of us in different ways and at different times, it is more than we can bear. We know that we've only scratched the surface of these woes, but we've scratched it enough to know that what lies underneath that surface is infinite and inexhaustible.

It is standing ready to exhaust us if we let it. It stands ready to uplift us if we practice.

"The way we treat a thing can sometimes change its nature" (Hyde, 1983, p. xiii).

And yet, perhaps not in spite of this insight but because of it, sometimes we've felt these things break apart and become obvious and foolish in the face of small and intimate beauties and insights, frail little things in which wisdom resides. The troubles don't disappear, but we can exercise a certain freedom where it is possible to do beautiful things with students and colleagues, finding patience and wisdom in what we see and hear and read. To coin a phrase, this is teaching as the practice of wisdom (with great thanks to one of our companions on this journey). We've caught glimpses of how wisdom has something to do with the life and well-being of the places we inhabit with other sentient beings, and, too, with water, with rocks, with spring sun arising, each of these, too, with their own spirit sentience: teachers, each of them (and this with great thanks to another companion). Sometimes we've found that we simply need to avert our gaze and, as Wendell Berry suggested (Berry & Moyers, 2013), look at what is right in front of us and ask what the right thing to do might be (this is asking us to practice wisely with our students over, say, this weird arithmetic, this map, this history, this voice, these concepts, even over these wonderfully difficult papers we've been reading for this long and luxurious while—study in *schola*, in leisure). In doing these things in concert with and in the face of the tough resistance of the world, we strengthen our ability to hold at bay the sirens of complaint and exhaustion, just for a moment. Wisdom and mindfulness are not grandiose but just this small and fleeting moment: sitting down and reading this beautiful book with young children *for absolutely no reason at all* except itself. This, too, is being caught up in the world we've inherited, but this, unlike strategic reading intervention schedules, makes—perhaps even *requires*—that our being caught up be precisely experienced as part of that gesture and the good of it part of our deliberations together. The promise of a final solution once and for all is merely one of the sirens. Like Berry said (Berry & Moyers, 2013), if you do that, consistently and with great patience, over and over again, you *might* become, not a savior of the world, but simply a good example.

One thing we've flirted with is how wrestling down our troubled circumstances and fixing them simply ends up fixing our gaze into a stare that is hard to break. Our troubles love our attention, and it is painfully easy to become caught in the gaze of what angers us and then become both aroused and paralyzed. What is that old story? I have two dogs inside me, a dark and angry one and one full of love and patience. Which one is the real one? The one I feed.

That's a rather bad re-telling, but it speaks to what we've heard over these courses from each of you. In full knowledge of our troubled lot, we seek a stillness that does not either ignore that lot or become transfixed by it.

Bite down little whisper, to cop a phrase from that lovely "nature poet" Don Domanski (2013), yet another dear companion we've grown to love.

Don't believe the lie of the University of Calgary's declarations of "Eyes High." It is just distraction spoken out of unpracticed, uprooted, unradical panic. Don Domanski published a new book since we started. So did David Smith. And us! Maxine Greene died. And four babies (so far) have been born nearby.

So here, then, is the purpose and imaginal locale of our upcoming days in Banff: Teaching, practice, wisdom.

CHAPTER SEVENTY-FIVE

"The Path AND THE Goal"

JACKIE SEIDEL AND DAVID W. JARDINE

It is somewhat difficult to establish, but once you are used to it, it will be like meeting an old acquaintance.

—JAMGON KONGTRUL, (2002, P. 67)

It's like making a path through the forest. At first it's rough going, with a lot of obstructions, but returning to it again and again, we clear the way. After a while the ground becomes firm and smooth from being walked on repeatedly. Then we have a good path for walking in the forest.

—AJAHN CHAH, (2005, P. 83)

The subject matter (Sache) is not merely an arbitrary object of discussion, independent of the process of mutual understanding (Sichverstehen), but rather is the path and the goal of mutual understanding itself.

—HANS-GEORG GADAMER, (1989, P. 180)

It is almost too easy to become suspicious of institutional demands for goals and outcomes. The merest glimpse at the logics of institutional accountability gives sway to clear and distinct examples of how such demands are often unconsciously disciplining. They are ways that audacity is pulled back into line and ways that, in such pulling, make what now falls outside of that line seem mere madness or petulance. That institutions are blessed with the ability to remain blissfully unaware of such matters and able at every turn to plead innocence to any intent whatsoever— all this is merely a sign, from outside the orbit of such dull-minded abusiveness, of their dominance. And all this can be at work without the slightest bad intent: we're just trying to be accountable. Yes, we all are, but the issue is then what counts as accountable to the work being done in relation to what counts as accountable institutional accounting. We all hope, too, for "quality assurance"—in all of our teaching, this is always our path and our goal. But such assuredness has to be grown with students and in their presence and under their witness and cannot be assured by a list of goals. Those asking us for program goals (inside our faculty and up through cold links of accountability in the university structure) know this, but none of us knows much of what to do or say in our circumstances.

The problem is this: Even though program goals are proffered as being merely informative, merely a way to offer information to others, they are not merely informative. They are, or certainly can be, deeply and silently *formative*. To the extent that such goals are not shaped into the right language and are not in the right pitch of thinking, they can seem suspect and those offering them can be deemed not to understand what is being asked of them. There is a silent and low-level suspicion that the purpose of writing up these things in this formative way, full of course outlines and bibliographies and descriptions of assignments written in a particular voice, is, in fact, so that one can ship off these packages around the world to be taught by anyone able to profit from doing so (thus profiting our institution at arm's length). In this way, the goal must be clearly and distinctly available without any foot being set on any path. The precious interiorities of refuge that define effective pedagogy as an intimate and sacred locale surrounding teachers and students—all this is now precisely that, too precious for words, silly, in fact, under the unforgiving glare of institutional accountability, legalities, objectivities and anonymities.

The authors discussed these dilemmas in our efforts to respond to requests for program goals for a series of M.Ed. courses we developed and offered over the past two years. We discussed how often it has arisen in our faculty (and beyond) how much *giving an account of what you are doing* has far and away outstripped, sometimes, it seems, even *replaced*, any substantive discussions about *what* anyone is up to, *what* our shared and contested work is therefore *about* and *for*. "Subject matter (*Sache*)" no longer holds any accountable sway.

So here, then, is the agonizing dance that followed. Do we fake it, and hand over what we think "they" want, given our overactive imaginations and understandings and well-founded experiences of how regime building and maintenance work? Giving the institution what we expect "they" want simply betrays our own having fully fallen for it. It demonstrates our own self-disciplining. Like this: we don't expect that "they" want us to write from the heart of our work, so we imagine producing program goals that are worded in ways we imagine are "acceptable." This hints at the psychopathological level of institutionalized *angst* that we see everywhere, how it can get inside of you and exhaust you from the core on out. It hints at a deep source of what is exhausting education itself and bleeding out the life of teaching and learning. (The great irony of our having even however briefly considered this route will be evident once you've read the goals of our program. Given the matters we were studying, it perhaps provides additional quality assurance of the program itself.)

But then and after all, there is no "us and them." There is no evil and under-handed perpetrator here except for our panic itself and how it can, if let hold sway, produce its own imagined enemy. We repeatedly explored and felt the agonies of this alluring logic in our classes. Moreover, we are colleagues and friends with those asking us for these program goals, and they themselves are good-heartedly doing the well-meant work being asked of them. We are all inside the beast and we all have the path and the goal of waking up more alert to our common lot, not just falling for it in real or feigned innocence.

We decided to take ourselves at our word and stand by our work and let matters unroll as they will. The following is what our program goals really have been, ones formulated and fashioned, through great and small episodes of suffering and joy, *with* our students. Of course, we took our students and our colleagues at their word, too, and they were all quite patient with us, and helped us understand how we must take this at-first-disturbing task at *its* word as well.

There is no assurance of quality except in such ventures.

One small hint of such things was a comment made in the class in which we discussed these goals and their measure of our work together. This exhaustion and a refuge from it are precisely what our program has been substantively and repeatedly *about*.

These dilemmas of pursuing good work in the surrounds of institutional logic have become like an old acquaintance.

A path was walked and re-walked and has become firmer under foot.

"The subject matter (*Sache*) is not merely an arbitrary object of discussion" (Gadamer, 1989, p. 180).

We have, over two years, roiled inside the beast often enough, and found our way out over and over again. In our class meeting over these goals, it was agreed that what follows is not precisely the goals we have reached but rather serves as repeated *reminders* of what is so easily forgotten in the confines of schools and their odd ways. To paraphrase Chogyam Trungpa (2013, pp. 56–57), we are not just journeyers who have reached a goal. We are building a path.

To wit, a draft of the path and the goal:

PROGRAM GOALS

Storytelling in the Ecological Heart of Curriculum

Program Description:

This four-course certificate program explores the relationships between ecological consciousness and storytelling in a vibrant, heartening understanding of curriculum. In contrast to some versions of "environmental education," we use the term "ecological consciousness" to point to a way of experiencing *all and any aspects of the living disciplines entrusted to teachers and students in schools* as constituted by relations of dependent co-arising and narrative patterns of interdependence, of gatherings, places, plots and ancestries. Parallels between ecological consciousness and both hermeneutics and threads of Buddhist epistemology/ontology will be explored in order to broaden their applicability to sustainable classroom practices.

Goals:

1) Study for the purpose of easing the burden of panic and distraction often found in contemporary schools and replacing these with wisdom, insight and contemplation.

2) Develop an enlightened understanding of the contemporary circumstances and contexts of curriculum practices.

3) (Re)learn the ancestry of educational thought and experience its practical, personal and community benefits.

4) Investigate diverse modes of educational inquiry and representation for the purpose of enacting one's own inquiries more skillfully and for reading the field in a nuanced and critical manner.

5) Create a refuge that provides community, space and time to reimagine and cultivate curriculum practices characterized by joy, freedom, hope, creativity, dialogue, reciprocity and respect for all beings.

6) Practice and strengthen the art of publicly speaking and writing about sustainable classroom practices so that the understanding/knowledge created together might be shared widely beyond this learning community with colleagues, through students publishing their work, etc.

7) Inquire into and document in diverse ways the transforming of our day-to-day pedagogical practices in such a way that our curriculum mandates and practices are more intellectually and spiritually in line with the forms of knowledge we have inherited, have been studying, and are inspired by.

8) As teachers, face the rising tides (literal, mythical and metaphorical) of Anthropocene life, that is, practice living with/in ecological crisis. Thus, our work is to understand the pedagogical meaning of this present and incommensurable loss of planetary diversity with courage and grace so that one's/our curriculum work becomes a healing gesture.

Bibliography

Abram, D. (1997). *The spell of the sensuous: Perception and language in a more-than-human world*. New York, NY: Vintage Books.

Abram, D. & Jardine, D. (2000). All knowledge is carnal knowledge: A conversation. *Canadian Journal of Environmental Education*. (5), 167–177.

Alberta Education. (2009). *The Alberta student assessment study: Final report*. Retrieved from http://education.alberta.ca

Aoki, T. (2005). *Curriculum in a new key: The collected works of Ted T. Aoki*. (W. F. Pinar & R. L. Irwin, Eds.). Mahwah, NJ: Lawrence Erlbaum.

Banks, P. (1980). Herbert Spencer: Victorian curriculum theorist. *Journal of Curriculum Studies, 12*(2), 123–135.

Barrett, K. (2015, January 10). Planted ID card exposes Paris false flag. *PressTV*. Retrieved from http://www.presstv.ir/Detail/2015/01/10/392426/Planted-ID-card-exposes-Paris-false-flag

Barthes, R. (1972). *Mythologies*. (A. Lavers, Trans.). New York, NY: Hill & Wang. (Original work published 1957)

Bayer, T. I. (2008). Vico's principle of sensus communis and forensic eloquence. *Chicago-Kent Law Review, 83*(3), 1131–1155.

Berk, A., & Long, L. (2012). *Nightsong*. New York, NY: Simon & Schuster Books for Young Readers.

Berry, W. (1986). *The unsettling of America: Essays in culture and agriculture*. San Francisco, CA: Sierra Club Books.

Berry, W. (2000). *Life is a miracle: An essay against modern superstition*. Washington, DC: Counterpoint.

Berry, W. (2001). *Life is a miracle: An essay against modern superstition* (2nd ed.). New York, NY: Counterpoint.

Berry, W. (2005). *The way of ignorance: And other essays*. Washington, DC: Shoemaker & Hoard.

Berry, W. (2010). *Leavings: Poems*. Berkeley, CA: Counterpoint Press.

Berry, W. (2014, April 23). *Who is watching the land? Wendell Berry and the resettling of America*. Retrieved from http://www.sagemagazine.org/who-is-watching-the-land-wendell-berry-and-the-resettling-of-america/

Berry, W. (Interviewee), & Moyers, B. (Interviewer). (2013, October 11). Writer and farmer Wendell Berry on hope, direct action, and the "resettling" of the American countryside. *Yes Magazine*. Retrieved from http://www.yesmagazine.org/planet/mad-farmer-wendell-berry-gets-madder-in-defense-of-earth

Blenkinsop, S. (2005). Martin Buber: Educating for relationship. *Ethics, Place and Environment*, *8*(3), 285–307.

Bly, R. (2005). *My sentence was a thousand years of joy: Poems*. New York, NY: HarperCollins.

Bodhi, B. (2012). Reflections on the fire sermon. *Parabola*, *37*(1), 82–88.

Bransford, J., Brown, A., & Cocking, R. (2000). *How people learn*. Washington, DC: National Academies Press.

Braverman, H. (1998). *Labor and monopoly capital: The degradation of work in the twentieth century*. New York, NY: Monthly Review Press.

Brown, M. (1980). *Witches four*. New York, NY: Parents Magazine Press.

Buber, M. (1964). *Daniel: Dialogues on realization*. (M. Friedman, Trans.). New York, NY: Holt, Rinehart and Winston.

Buber, M. (1967). *Encounter: Autobiographical fragments*. La Salle, IL: Open Court.

Callahan, R. (1964). *America, education and the cult of efficiency*. Chicago, IL: University of Chicago Press.

Campbell, J. (1988). *The power of myth*. New York, NY: Doubleday.

Caputo, J. (1993). *Against ethics: Contributions to a poetics of obligation with constant reference to deconstruction*. Bloomington: Indiana State University Press.

Caputo, J. D. (2000). *More radical hermeneutics: On not knowing who we are*. Bloomington: Indiana University Press.

Chah, A. (n.d.). *Everything is teaching us*. Victoria, Australia: Sangha Bodhivana Monastery. Retrieved from http://forestsanghapublications.org/viewAuthor.php?id=1

Chah, A. (2002). *The collected teachings of Ajahn Chah: Food for the heart*. Somerville, MA: Wisdom.

Chah, A. (2004). *Everything is teaching us: A collection of teachings by Venerable Ajahn Chah*. Victoria, Australia: Sangha Bodhivana Monastery

Chah, A. (2005). *Everything arises, everything falls away*. Boston, MA: Shambhala.

Chambers, C. (2012). Spelling and other illiteracies. In C. M. Chambers, E. Hasebe-Ludt, C. Leggo, & A. Sinner (Eds.), *A heart of wisdom: Life writing as empathetic inquiry* (pp. 183–189). New York, NY: Peter Lang.

Chambers, C., Hasebe-Ludt, E., Leggo, C., & Sinner, A. (Eds.). (2012). *A heart of wisdom: Life writing as empathetic inquiry*. New York, NY: Peter Lang.

Clifford, J., & Marcus, G. (1986). *Writing culture: The poetics and politics of ethnography*. Berkeley: University of California Press.

Clifford, P. (2006). *Embracing brings you back*. Regina, SK: Coteau Books.

Comprehend. (n.d.). In *Online etymology dictionary*. Retrieved from http://etymonline.com/index.php?allowed_in_frame=0&search=comprehend&searchmode=none

Costello, E. (1991). Couldn't call it unexpected No. 4. On *Mighty like a rose* [CD]. New York, NY: Warner Brothers.

Costello, E. (1993). The birds will still be singing. On *The Juliet letters* [CD]. New York, NY: Warner Brothers.

Dawkins, R. (2006). *The God delusion*. Boston, MA: Houghton Mifflin.

Dempsey, H. (1984). *Big bear: The end of freedom*. Vancouver, BC: Douglas & McIntyre.

Derby, M. (2015). *Place, being, resonance: A critical ecohermeneutic approach to education*. New York, NY: Peter Lang.

Descartes, R. (1901). *Descartes meditations: A trilingual HTML edition*. (D. B. Manley & C. S. Taylor, Eds.). (Original work published circa 1640) (Includes original Latin text of 1641, Duc de Luynes French translation of 1647, and an English translation by John Veitch from 1901.) Retrieved from http://www.wright.edu/cola/descartes/mede.html

Dillard, A. (1990). *The writing life*. New York, NY: First Harper Perennial Edition.

Doctor, T. H. (2014). Translators' introduction to *Ornament of the great vehicle sutras: Maitreya's Mahayanasutralamakara* (pp. vii–xvi). Boston, MA: Snow Lion.

Documentaryondemand. (2013, April 20). *Colisao: Ateu X Pastor* [Video file]. (This is a subtitled version of *Collision: Christopher Hitchens vs. Douglas Wilson*. LEVEL4 Studio, Phoenix AZ. Director: Darren Doane, October 27, 2009, ASIN: B002M3SHTO). Retrieved from https://www.youtube.com/watch?v=_JWySEcocc8

Domanski, D. (2002). The wisdom of falling. In T. Bowling (Ed.), *Where the words come from: Canadian poets in conversation* (pp. 244–255). Roberts Creek, BC: Nightwood Editions.

Domanski, D. (2010). *All our wonder unavenged*. London, ON: Brick Books.

Domanski, D. (2013). *Bite down little whisper*. London, ON: Brick Books.

Donald, D. (2009a). Forts, curriculum, and Indigenous Métissage: Imagining decolonization of Aboriginal-Canadian relations in educational context. *First Nations Perspectives, 2*(1), 1–24.

Donald, D. (2009b). *The pedagogy of the fort: Curriculum, colonial frontier logics, and Indigenous Métissage* (Unpublished doctoral dissertation). University of Alberta, Edmonton, Canada.

Donald, D. (2012a). Forts, curriculum, and ethical relationality. In N. Ng-A-Fook & J. Rottmann (Eds.), *Reconsidering Canadian curriculum studies: Provoking historical, present, and future perspectives* (pp. 39–46). New York, NY: Palgrave Macmillan.

Donald, D. (2012b). Indigenous Métissage: A decolonizing research sensibility. *International Journal of Qualitative Studies in Education, 25*(5), 533–555.

Dormer, D. (2014, February 10). Mayor calls the opponents to city hall's raising of the rainbow flag "the usual suspects," stands by decision. *The Calgary Sun*. Retrieved from http://www.calgarysun.com/2014/02/10/mayor-calls-opponents-to-calgary-city-halls-raising-of-the-rainbow-flag-the-usual-suspects-stands-by-decision

Dorrie, D. (2007). *How to cook your life: With Zen chef Edward Espe Brown*. Toronto, ON: Mongrel Media.

Egan, K. (1997). *The educated mind: How cognitive tools shape our understanding*. Chicago, IL: University of Chicago Press.

Egan, K. (2002). *Getting it wrong from the beginning*. New Haven, CT: Yale University Press.

Eisner, E. (2002a). *The educational imagination: On the design and evaluation of school programs* (3rd ed.). New York, NY: Prentice Hall.

Eisner, E. W. (2002b). What can education learn from the arts about the practice of education? *The encyclopedia of informal education*. Retrieved from www.infed.org/biblio/eisner_arts_and_the_practice_or_education.htm

Estés, C. P. (1992). *Women who run with the wolves: Myths and stories of the wild woman archetype*. New York, NY: Ballantine Books.

Evernden, N. (1993). *The natural alien: Humankind and the environment*. Toronto, ON: University of Toronto.

Fanon, F. (2008). *Black skin, white masks* (R. Philcox, Trans.). New York, NY: Grove Press.

Fawcett, L. (2002). Children's wild animal stories: Questioning inter-species bonds. *Canadian Journal of Environmental Education, 7*(2), 125–139.

Fidyk, A. (2012). Visitor, host and chrysanthemum: Hosting the unconscious through poetic form. In S. Thomas, A. Cole, & S. Stewart (Eds.), *The art of poetic inquiry* (pp. 347–360). Big Tancook Island, NS: Backalong Books.

Foucault, M. (2001). *Fearless speech*. Los Angeles, CA: Semiotext(e).

Fox, M. (2002). Interview with Matthew Fox. In D. Jensen, *Listening to the land: Conversations about nature, culture, and eros* (pp. 67–77). San Francisco, CA: Sierra Club Books.

Freire, P. (2006). *Pedagogy of the oppressed*. New York, NY: Continuum.

Friesen, S., & Jardine, D. (2011). *Guiding principles for WNCP/PONC curriculum framework projects: A report prepared for the Western and Northern Canadian Curriculum Protocol for Collaboration in Education/Protocole de l'Ouest et du Nord Canadiens de Collaboration Concernant L'Education*. Retrieved from http://www.education.gov.sk.ca/Default.aspx?DN=0583e277- 654d-45c5-98fec791c85a118b

Gadamer, H.-G. (1989). *Truth and method* (2nd ed.). (J. Weinsheimer, Trans.). New York, NY: Continuum.

Gadamer, H.-G. (1992). *Hans-Georg Gadamer on education, poetry, and history: Applied hermeneutics*. (D. Misgeld & G. Nicholson, Eds.; L. Schmidt & M. Reuss, Trans.). Albany: SUNY Press.

Gadamer, H.-G. (2001). *Gadamer in conversation: Reflections and commentary*. (R. Palmer, Ed. & Trans.). New Haven, CT: Yale University Press.

Gadamer, H.-G. (2004). *Truth and method*. (J. Weinsheimer & D. Marshall, Trans.). London, England: Bloomsbury Academic. (Original work published 1975)

Gadamer, H.-G. (2007a). *The Gadamer reader: A bouquet of the later writings*. (R. Palmer, Ed. & Trans.). Evanston, IL: Northwestern University Press.

Gadamer, H.-G. (2007b). Hermeneutics as a theoretical and practical task. In R. Palmer (Trans. & Ed.), *The Gadamer reader: A bouquet of later writings* (pp. 246–265). Evanston, IL: Northwestern University Press.

Gibran, K. (1923). *The prophet*. New York, NY: Knopf. Retrieved from https://soulgatherings.wordpress.com/tag/kahlil-gibran/

Glieck, J. (1987). Chaos: *The Making of a New Science*. New York: Penguin Books.

Godless UK. (2011, October 8). *Christopher Hitchens—last public appearance—Dawkins Award* [Video file]. Retrieved from https://www.youtube.com/watch?v=ud973COUVYs

Goo Goo Dolls. (1995). Flat top. On *A boy named Goo* [CD]. Buffalo, NY: BearTracks Studio.

Goyette, S. (1998). *The true names of birds*. London, ON: Brick Books.

Grant, G. (1998). *English-speaking justice*. Toronto, ON: House of Anansi Press.

Greene, M. (1978). *Landscapes of learning*. New York, NY: Teachers College Press.

Greene, M. (1995). *Releasing the imagination*. San Francisco, CA: Jossey-Bass.

Greene, M. (2001). *Variations on a blue guitar: The Lincoln Center Institute lectures on aesthetic education*. New York, NY: Teachers College Press.

Guiney Yallop, J. J. (2012). Emotions, identities, and communities: Some stuff that really matters. In S. Thomas, A. Cole, & S. Stewart (Eds.), *The art of poetic inquiry* (pp. 98–108). Big Tancook Island, NS: Backalong Books.

Halfe, L. (1994). *Bear bones & feathers* (No. 12). Regina, SK: Coteau Books.

Halper, S., and Clarke, J. (2004). *America alone: The neo-conservatives and the global order*. New York, NY: Cambridge University Press.

Hardon, J. (1985). *Pocket Catholic dictionary*. New York, NY: Doubleday.

Heidegger, M. (1968). *What is called thinking?* New York, NY: Harper & Row.

Heidegger, M. (1971). *On the way to language*. New York, NY: Harper & Row.

Heidegger, M. (1972). *On time and being*. New York, NY: Harper & Row.

Hesse, H. (1984). *Bäume: Betrachtungen und Gedichte* [Trees: Reflections and poems]. Frankfurt, Germany: Insel Verlag. Translation retrieved from http://www.brainpickings.org/index.php/2012/09/21/hermann-hesse-trees/

Highway, T. (2003). *Comparing mythologies*. Ottawa, ON: University of Ottawa Press.

Hillman, J. (2006). *City and soul*. Putnam, CT: Spring.

Hitchens, C. (2007). *God is not great: How religion poisons everything*. New York, NY: Twelve Books.

Hodson, J. (2004). *The Eastern origins of Western civilization*. Cambridge, England: Cambridge University Press.

Hoggan Public Relations. (2011, August 17). *David Suzuki & Thich Nhat Hanh: Despair* [Video file]. Retrieved from https://www.youtube.com/watch?v=RWqB4-em308

Hongzhi, Z. (1991). *Cultivating the empty field: The silent illumination of Zen master Hongzhi*. (T. D. Leighton & Y. Wu, Trans.). San Francisco, CA: North Point Press.

hooks, b. (1994). *Teaching to transgress: Education as the practice of freedom*. New York, NY: Routledge.

Hyde, L. (1983). *The gift: Imagination and the erotic life of property*. New York, NY: Vintage.

Inhelder, B. (1969). Some aspects of Piaget's genetic approach to cognition. In H. Furth (Ed.), *Piaget and knowledge: Theoretical foundations* (pp. 9–23). Upper Saddle River, NJ: Prentice-Hall.

Jardine, D. (1998a). Student-teaching, interpretation and the monstrous child. In D. Jardine, *"To dwell with a boundless heart": On curriculum theory, hermeneutics and the ecological imagination* (pp. 123–134). New York, NY: Peter Lang.

Jardine, D. (1998b). *To dwell with a boundless heart: Essays in curriculum theory, hermeneutics, and the ecological imagination*. New York, NY: Peter Lang.

Jardine, D. (2005). *Piaget and education: A primer*. New York, NY: Peter Lang.

Jardine, D. (2008a). Foreword: The sickness of the West. In C. Eppert & H. Wang, *Cross-cultural studies in curriculum* (pp. 9–14). Mahwah, NJ: Lawrence Erlbaum.

Jardine, D. (2008b). On the while of things. *Journal of the American Association for the Advancement of Curriculum Studies, 4*, 1–16. Retrieved from http://www.uwstout.edu/soe/jaaacs/vol4/Jardine.html

Jardine, D. (2011). Birding lessons and the teachings of cicadas. In D. Stanley & K. Young, (Eds.), *Contemporary studies in Canadian curriculum: Principles, portraits and practices* (pp. 343–350). Calgary, AB: Detselig Enterprises.

Jardine, D. (2012). *Pedagogy left in peace: On the cultivation of free spaces in teaching and learning*. New York, NY: Continuum.

Jardine, D. (2013a). Morning thoughts on application. *Journal of Applied Hermeneutics*. Retrieved from http://jah.synergiesprairies.ca/jah/index.php/jah/article/view/52

Jardine, D. (2013b, May 4). Time is [not] always running out. *Journal of the American Association for the Advancement of Curriculum Studies*. Retrieved from http://www.uwstout.edu/soe/jaaacs/upload/2013-05-4-Jardine.pdf

Jardine, D. (2014a). *Pedagogy left in peace: On the cultivation of free spaces in teaching and learning*. New York, NY: Bloomsbury.

Jardine, D. (2014b). Story-time lessons from a dog named Fideles. In J. Seidel & D. W. Jardine (Eds.), *Ecological pedagogy, Buddhist pedagogy, hermeneutic pedagogy: Experiments in a curriculum for miracles* (pp. 57–90). New York, NY: Peter Lang.

Jardine, D. (2014c). One fell swoop. Retrieved from: https://www.academia.edu/9314364/One_Fell_Swoop

Jardine, D. (2015a). *An ode to Xmas present*. Retrieved from https://www.academia.edu/10101433/An_Ode_to_Xmas_Present

Jardine, D. (2015b). In praise of radiant beings. In D. Jardine, C. Gilham, & G. McCaffrey (Eds.), *On the pedagogy of suffering: Hermeneutic and Buddhist meditations* (pp. 231–249). New York, NY: Peter Lang.

Jardine, D. (2015c). On hermeneutics: "What happens to us over and above our wanting and doing." In K. Tobin & S. Steinberg (Eds.), *Doing educational research: A handbook* (2nd ed., pp. 235–254). Rotterdam, the Netherlands: Sense.

Jardine, D., Clifford, P., & Friesen, S. (2006). *Curriculum in abundance.* Mahwah, NJ: Lawrence Erlbaum.

Jardine, D., Clifford, P., & Friesen, S. (2008). *Back to the basics of teaching and learning: Thinking the world together* (2nd ed.). New York, NY: Routledge.

Jardine, D., & Novodvorski, B. (2006). Monsters in abundance. In D. Jardine, S. Friesen, & P. Clifford (Eds.), *Curriculum in abundance* (pp. 103–106). Mahwah, NJ: Lawrence Erlbaum.

Jensen, D. (1995). *Listening to the land: Conversations about nature, culture, and eros.* New York, NY: Context Books.

Judson, G. (2010). *A new approach to ecological education.* New York, NY: Peter Lang.

Kanigel, R. (2005). *The one best way: Fredrick Winslow Taylor and the enigma of efficiency.* Cambridge, MA: MIT Press.

Kant, I. (1964). *Critique of pure reason.* London, England: Macmillan. (Original work published 1797)

Keller, C. (1996). *Apocalypse now and then: A feminist guide to the end of the world.* Boston, MA: Beacon Press.

King, T. (1992). *A Coyote Columbus story.* Toronto, ON: Groundwood Books.

King, T. (2003). *The truth about stories: A native narrative.* Toronto, ON: House of Anansi Press.

Kinnell, G. (2002). St. Francis and the sow. Retrieved from http://www.poetryfoundation.org/poem/171395

Klagge, J. C. (Ed.). (2001). *Wittgenstein: Biography and philosophy.* New York, NY: Cambridge University Press.

Kohn, A. (2012). The case against grades. *Education Digest, 77*(5), 8–16.

Kongtrul, J. (2002). *Creation and completion: Essential points of Tantric meditation.* Somerville, MA: Wisdom.

Kumar, S. (2014). *Satish Kumar on the new story* [Video file]. Retrieved from https://www.youtube.com/watch?v=GjgdwI6p9Ks

Latremouille, J. (2014). *Feasting on whispers: Life writing towards a pedagogy of kinship.* (Unpublished master's thesis). Werklund School of Education, University of Calgary, Canada. Retrieved from http://theses.ucalgary.ca/bitstream/11023/1704/2/ucalgary_2014_latremouille_jodi.pdf

Lavoie, R. (Host). (1997). *When the chips are down … strategies for improving children's behavior* [Educational DVD]. United States: PBS Video.

Leach, W. (1994). *Land of desire: Merchants, power, and the rise of a new American culture.* New York, NY: Vintage Books.

Lee, H. (1982). *To kill a mockingbird.* New York, NY: Warner Books.

L'Engle, M. (2001). *Madeleine L'Engle {herself}: Reflections on a writing life.* (Compiled by C. F. Chan). Colorado Springs, CO: Shaw Books.

Leggo, C. (2012). Where the wild words are: Provoking pedagogic imagination. In S. Thomas, A. Cole, & S. Stewart (Eds.), *The art of poetic inquiry* (pp. 378–394). Big Tancook Island, NS: Backalong Books.

LeGuin, U. (1987). *Buffalo gals and other animal presences.* Santa Barbara, CA: Capra Press.

Lilburn, T. (2002). The provisional shack of the ear. Tim Lilburn interviewed by Shawna Lemay. In T. Bowling (Ed.), *Where the words come from: Canadian poets in conversation* (pp. 174–183). Roberts Creek, BC: Nightwood Editions.

Lopez, B. (1990). *Crow and weasel.* Toronto, ON: Random House.

Loy, D. (2010). *The world is made of stories*. Somerville, MA: Wisdom.

Lui, W. C., & Lo, I. (1990). In the seventh month. In *Sunflower splendor: Three thousand years of Chinese poetry* (pp. 87–111). Indianapolis: Indiana University Press.

Martusewicz, R. (2014). Letting our hearts break: On facing the "hidden wound" of human supremacy. *Canadian Journal of Environmental Education, 19*, 31–46.

Marx, K. (1978). The eighteenth brumaire of Louis Bonaparte. In R. Tucker (Ed.), *The Marx-Engels reader* (pp. 594–617). New York, NY: Norton. (Original work published 1852)

Marx, K. (1990). *Capital* (Vol. 1). (B. Fowkes, Trans.). London, England: Penguin Books. (Original work published 1867)

Marx, K. (1993). *Grundrisse: Foundations of the critique of political economy*. (M. Nicolaus, Trans.). London, England: Penguin Classics. (Original work published 1858)

McLeod, N. (2007). *Cree narrative memory: From treaties to contemporary times*. Saskatoon, SK: Purich.

Miller, A. (1989). *For your own good: Hidden cruelty in child-rearing and the roots of violence*. Toronto, ON: Collins.

Minh-Ha, T. (1994). Other than myself/my other self. In G. Robertson, M. Mash, L. Tickner, J. Bird, B. Curtis, & T. Putnam (Eds.), *Travellers' tales: Narratives of home and displacement*. London, England: Routledge.

Molnar, C. (2014). Life and mortality: A teacher's awakening. *In Education, 20*(2). Retrieved from http://ineducation.ca/ineducation/article/view/165/674

Montessori, M. (2009). A critical consideration of the new pedagogy in its relation to modern science. In D. J. Flinders & S. J. Thornton (Eds.), *The curriculum studies reader* (pp. 22–33). New York, NY: Routledge.

Moss, C. (2014). Now you can buy a bulletproof blanket specifically made for kids to use during school shootings. *Business Insider*. Retrieved from http://www.businessinsider.com/bodyguard-bulletproof-blanket-for-kids-2014-6

Moules, N., McCaffrey, G., Field, J., & Laing, C. (2015). *Conducting hermeneutic research: From philosophy to practice*. New York, NY: Peter Lang.

Moyers, B. (Producer). (2013). (2013, October 4). Wendell Berry, poet & prophet [Television series episode]. In B. Moyers (Producer), *Moyers & Company*. New York, NY: PBS. Retrieved from http://billmoyers.com/episode/wendell-berry-poet-prophet/

Nadeau, S. (2011, March 1). Grandin mural about living in harmony: Artist. *Edmonton Journal*. Retrieved from http://www2.canada.com/edmontonjournal/news/letters/story.html?id=7f30618e-711b-48f5-9f21-c7564f58376c

Nancy, J-L. (2003). *A finite thinking*. Stanford, CA: Stanford University Press.

Nhat Hanh, T. (1975). *The miracle of mindfulness: An introduction to the practice of meditation*. Boston, MA: Beacon Press.

Nhat Hanh, T. (1991). *Peace is every step: The path of mindfulness in everyday life*. New York, NY: Bantam Books.

Nhat Hanh, T. (2008). *The world we have: A Buddhist approach to peace and ecology*. Berkeley, CA: Parallax Press.

Nhat Hanh, T. (2012). *Handful of quiet: Happiness in four pebbles*. Berkeley, CA: Plum Blossom Books.

Nietzsche, F. (1975). *The will to power*. New York, NY: Random House

Nishitani, K. (1982). *Religion and nothingness*. Berkeley: University of California Press.

ObjectiveBob. (2010, July 5). *Christopher Hitchens makes a shocking confession* [Video file]. Retrieved from https://www.youtube.com/watch?v=E9TMwfkDwIY

Okri, B. (1997). *A way of being free*. London, England: Phoenix House.

O'Leary, K. (2012). *Dragon's den*. Produced by the Canadian Broadcasting Company. Series 6, Episode 19. Retrieved from www.cbc.ca/dragonsden/pitches/ukloo

Online etymology dictionary. (2014a). Retrieved from http://www.etymonline.com/index.php?term=poet&allowed_in_frame=0

Online etymology dictionary. (2014b). Retrieved from http://www.etymonline.com/index.php?term=scoff&allowed_in_frame=0

The Oxford dictionary of English etymology. (1966). New York, NY: Oxford University Press.

Perlmutter, A. H., & Konner, J. (Producers). (2002). *Joseph Campbell: Power of myth* [Television series]. New York, NY: PBS.

Phenix, P. (1975). Curriculum as transcendence. in *Curriculum theorizing: The reconceptualists* (pp. 321–340), ed. W. Pinar. Berkeley, CA: McCutchan, 1975.

Picciano, A., & Spring, J. (2012). *The great American education-industrial complex: Ideology, technology, and profit*. New York, NY: Routledge.

Pope, D. (2015, January 7). "Can't sleep tonight. ..." [Twitter post]. Retrieved from https://twitter.com/davpope/status/552844593046097920/photo/1

Richardson, L. (1994). Writing: A method of inquiry. In N. Denzin & Y. Lincoln (Eds.), *Handbook of qualitative research* (pp. 516–529). Thousand Oaks, CA: Sage.

Richardson, L., & St. Pierre, E. A. (2005). Writing: A method of inquiry. In N. Denzin & Y. Lincoln (Eds.), *Handbook of qualitative research* (3rd ed., pp. 959–978). Thousand Oaks, CA: Sage.

Rodé, M. A. (2012). How to grow a mandala. *Undivided, 1*(3). Retrieved from http://undividedjournal.com/2012/12/06/how-to-grow-a-mandala/

Ross, S. M. (2004). Gadamer's late thinking on *Verweilen*. *Minerva*, 8. Retrieved from http://www.ul.ie/~philos/vol8/gadamer.html

Russell, C. (2005). "Whoever does not write is written": The role of "nature" in post-post approaches to environmental education research. *Environmental Education Research, 11*(4), 433–443.

Russell, J. (in press). Animal narrativity: Engaging with story in a more-than-human world. In J. Castricano & L. Corman (Eds.), *Animal subjects 2.0*. Waterloo, ON: Wilfrid Laurier University Press.

Sartre, J. P. (1970). Intentionality: A fundamental idea in Husserl's phenomenology. *Journal for the British Society for Phenomenology, 1*(2), 3–5.

Sartre, J. P. (2004). Existentialism. In G. Marino (Ed.), *Basic writings of existentialism* (pp. 340–367). New York, NY: Modern Library.

Scofield, G. A. (1993). *The gathering: Stones for the medicine wheel*. Vancouver, BC: Polestar Press.

Seidel, J. (1999). *Heavy work: Living with children in schools* (Unpublished master's thesis). University of British Columbia, Vancouver, BC. Retrieved from https://circle.ubc.ca/bitstream/handle/2429/9262/ubc_1999-0383.pdf?sequence=1

Seidel, J. (2006). Some thoughts on teaching as contemplative practice. *Teachers College Record, 108*(9), 1901–1914.

Seidel, J. (2014a). Hymn to the North Atlantic right whale. In J. Seidel & D. Jardine (Eds.), *Ecological pedagogy, Buddhist pedagogy, hermeneutic pedagogy: Experiments in a curriculum for miracles* (pp. 111–112). New York, NY: Peter Lang.

Seidel, J. (2014b). Losing wonder: Thoughts on nature, mortality, education. In J. Seidel & D. W. Jardine (Eds.), *Ecological pedagogy, Buddhist pedagogy, hermeneutic pedagogy: Experiments in a curriculum for miracles* (pp. 132–152). New York, NY: Peter Lang.

Seidel, J. (2014c). Meditations on contemplative pedagogy as sanctuary. *The Journal of Contemplative Inquiry, 1*(2), 141–147.

Seidel, J., & Jardine, D. W. (Eds.). (2014). *Ecological pedagogy, Buddhist pedagogy, hermeneutic pedagogy: Experiments in a curriculum for miracles.* New York, NY: Peter Lang.

Sekida, K. (1976). *Zen training.* New York: Weatherhill.

Sewall, L. (2012). Beauty and the brain. In P. H. Kahn & P. H. Hasbach (Eds.), *Ecopyschology: Science, totems, and the technological species* (pp. 265–284). Cambridge, MA: MIT Press.

Shepard, P. (1996). *The others: How animals made us human.* Washington, DC: Island Press.

Sheridan, J. (2001). Mythic ecology. *Canadian Journal of Education, 6*(2), 194–205.

Sheridan, J., & Longboat, R. D. (2006). The Haudenosaunee imagination and the ecology of the sacred. *Space and Culture, 9*(4), 365–381.

Silverstein, S. (1964). *The giving tree.* New York, NY: Harper & Row.

Smith, D. G. (1999). *Pedagon: Interdisciplinary essays in the human sciences, pedagogy, and culture.* New York, NY: Peter Lang.

Smith, D. G. (2006). *Trying to teach in a season of great untruth: Globalization, empire and the crises of pedagogy.* Rotterdam, the Netherlands: Sense.

Smith, D. G. (2008). "The farthest West is but the farthest East." The long way of Oriental/Occidental engagement. In C. Eppert & H. Wang (Eds.), *Cross-cultural studies in curriculum: Eastern thought, educational insights* (pp. 96–128). New York, NY: Taylor & Francis.

Smith, D. G. (2009). Engaging Peter McLaren and the new Marxism in education. An essay review of Peter McLaren's "Rage + hope: Interviews with Peter McLaren on war, imperialism + critical pedagogy." *Interchange, 40*(1), 93–117.

Smith, D. G. (2012). Spiritual cardiology and the heart of wisdom. In C. M. Chambers, E. Hasebe-Ludt, C. Leggo, & A. Sinner (Eds.), *A heart of wisdom: Life writing as empathetic inquiry.* New York, NY: Peter Lang.

Smith, D. G. (2014). *Teaching as the practice of wisdom.* New York, NY: Bloomsbury Academic.

Snyder, G. (1977). *The old ways.* San Francisco, CA: City Lights Books.

Snyder, G. (1990). *The practice of the wild.* Berkeley, CA: Counterpoint Books.

Solnit, R. (2014, December 12). Are we missing the big picture on climate change? *The New York Times.* Retrieved from http://www.nytimes.com/2014/12/07/magazine/are-we-missing-the-big-picture-on-climate-change.html?_r=0

Stevens, W. (1990). *The collected poems of Wallace Stevens.* New York, NY: Vintage Press.

Stiggins, R. (2007). Assessment through the student's eyes. *Educational Leadership, 64*(8), 22–26.

Suzuki, D. (Host). (2014, November 14). Chasing snowflakes [Episode video file]. *Nature of Things.* CBC. Retrieved from http://www.cbc.ca/natureofthings/episodes/chasing-snowflakes1

Suzuki, D., & Ellis, S. (2003). *Salmon forest.* Vancouver, BC: Greystone Books.

Taylor, F. W. (1911). *Scientific management, comprising shop management, the principles of scientific management and testimony before the special house committee.* New York, NY: Harper & Row.

Thoreau, H. D. (1963). *Walden.* New York, NY: Washington Square Press.

Travers, P. L. (1989). *What the bee knows: Reflections on myth, symbol and story.* London, England: Penguin Books.

Trungpa, C. (2013). *The profound treasury of the ocean of dharma: The path of individual liberation.* Boston, MA: Shambhala.

Tsong-kha-pa. (2000). *The great treatise on the stages of the path to enlightenment* [Lam rim chen mo] (Vol. 1). Ithaca, NY: Snow Lion.

Tsong-kha-pa. (2002). *The great treatise on the stages of the path to enlightenment* (Vol. 3). Ithaca, NY: Snow Lion.

Tsong-kha-pa. (2004). *The great treatise on the stages of the path to enlightenment* [Lam rim chen mo] (Vol. 2). Ithaca, NY: Snow Lion.

Tsong-kha-pa. (2005). *The six yogas of Naropa*. Ithaca, NY: Snow Lion.

Wallace, B. (1987). *The stubborn particulars of grace*. Toronto, ON: McClellan and Stewart.

Wallace, D. F. (2005). *This is water: Some thoughts, delivered on a significant occasion about living a compassionate life* Commencement address, Kenyon College, Gambier, OH. Retrieved from http://web.ics.purdue.edu/~drkelly/DFWKenyonAddress2005.pdf

Warren, J. (2012, July). Whales are people too. *Readers' Digest Canada*. Retrieved from http://www.readersdigest.ca/?q=magazine/true-stories/derrid-whales-are-people-too

Weinsheimer, J. (1987). *Gadamer's hermeneutics*. New Haven, CT: Yale University Press.

Werner, M. (1994). *Managing monsters: Six myths of our time* [Transcriptions of the Reith Lectures, BBC Radio]. London, England: Vintage Books.

West, C. (2015). *Black prophetic fire*. New York, NY: Beacon Press.

Wilson, E. O. (2012). *The social conquest of earth* [Kindle version]. New York, NY: Norton. Retrieved from https://read.amazon.ca. 2012

Wintergreen. (2015). Corporate website. Retrieved from http://www.wintergreen.ca/en/furniture/wintergreen-classroom-colours/classic-guided-reading-tables-swt968ye_group

Wolf, E. (1982). *Europe and the people without history*. Los Angeles: University of California Press.

Yolen, J. (1988). *Favorite folktales from around the world*. New York, NY: Pantheon Books.

Zwicky, J. (2003). *Wisdom & metaphor*. Kentville, NS: Gaspereau Press.

List OF Contributors

Khatleen Alnas is a Filipino native who immigrated to Canada in 2008. She has a degree in Education (from the University of the Philippines) and she is currently finishing her last semester as a graduate student at the University of Calgary. Her areas of interest include (but are not limited to) the Reggio Emilia Approach, ecology, poetry, early childhood education, hermeneutics, pedagogy, critical literature, and arts-based research

Deirdre Bailey wants to live in a world where pedagogy is patient, stories are sacred and wild things are free. As an educator and writer, she is a passionate and vocal advocate for inquiry, ecology and experience in education. When she's not experimenting, deconstructing or philosophizing with students, you can find her running trails around town, re-reading the collected works of Jane Austen, or escaping to the mountains in a tent.

Stephanie Bartlett is pursuing her master of education degree at the University of Calgary, specializing in Curriculum and Learning. A long-time supporter of environmental issues, her efforts to teach sustainability begin with teaching her students the importance of loving their local community. She enjoys writing poetry and connecting with nature.

Hannah Blades is an elementary and middle school teacher in Calgary, Alberta. Her pedagogical interests include worthwhile task design, collaborative practice and classrooms for social justice. Other interests include her large blended family, vegetable gardens and inflatable pool chairs. She has great difficulty speaking of herself in the third person.

Lori Bonanno is an elementary teacher in Calgary, Alberta. She is also a graduate student at the Werklund School of Education at the University of Calgary.

Michael W. Derby is a teacher, an educational researcher, and occasionally a poet. He is a member of the Imaginative Education Research Group and assistant director of Imaginative Ecological Education at Simon Fraser University. His research considers ecocritical, lyric and place-based pedagogies that imaginatively engage students and inspire caring relationships with the more-than-human world. He also aspires to build a bee sanctuary one day.

Dwayne Donald Ph.D., is a descendent of the amiskwaciwiyiniwak and the Papaschase Cree and is an associate professor in the Faculty of Education at the University of Alberta. His work focuses on ways in which Indigenous philosophies can expand and enhance our understandings of curriculum and pedagogy.

Towani Duchscher is a doctoral student in the specialization of Curriculum and Learning, in the Werklund School of Education at the University of Calgary. Her research interests include exploring the rituals of schooling, as well as arts based educational research through movement and poetry.

Holly Gray is an assistant principal and teacher who actively involves children in their learning through literature, the arts, the environment and their community. Her experience is in second language learning in elementary school.

Jennifer Gray is a passionate teacher and dedicated mom who describes herself as a curious explorer of life. Inspired by experiential learning, mindfulness and creativity, she sees writing as a way of making sense of the world.

Scott Hassett is a middle school teacher with a passion for teaching grounded in the heart of community and purpose. A father of two he tries to find balance between being a father, husband, and avid sports fan, always trying to remind himself to live one moment at a time.

Miranda Hector is an elementary school teacher living in Calgary. She adores spending time with her husband, twin daughters and her dog. Miranda enjoys traveling and learning new things. She hopes to continue to explore local and international spaces to absorb a variety of diverse cultures with her family.

Judson Innes is a teacher in Calgary, Alberta. In education, he looks for ways that his students can explore ecological issues within curriculum in a thoughtful and interconnected manner. Away from school he enjoys a variety of outdoor pursuits.

L. A. James's childhood dreams of being a writer gave way to a decade in banking. Her curious children showed her the way back. Today she spends her days playing and learning alongside children outdoors sharing the goodness the natural world offers in helping them stay true to their own paths.

David Jardine is a recently retired full professor who did not apply for emeritus status. He is the author of the forthcoming collection *In Praise of Radiant Beings: A Retrospective Path Through Education, Buddhism and Ecology.*

Carole Jones is a dedicated teacher and lifelong learner. Every day she strives to inspire a joyful love of learning in children and adults. In her work she knows that deep learning happens when we connect in authentic ways with the world around us.

Jessica Kelly is a teacher from Calgary, Alberta. She is passionate about education, drama and dance. Some of her interests include running, yoga, theatre and tirelessly trying to make people laugh. She spends most of her time with her wonderful husband, lovely daughter and playful dog.

Tanya Kowalchuk is an educator in Calgary.

Jodi Latrmouille is a doctoral student and sessional instructor with the Werklund School of Education at the University of Calgary. She is interested in the ways in which ecological pedagogy, holistic and poetic ways of knowing, and hermeneutic inquiry may influence conversations in education.

Derek Lawson is a graduate student at the University of Calgary.

Paul Le Marquand is thankful for the support of his colleagues as a graduate student in chemistry and education, as a clean energy scientist in the Canadian federal government, and as a Catholic teacher in the province of Alberta.

Megan Liddell is a middle school teacher passionate about doing meaningful, important and worthy work with kids. She is also a keen learner in her other roles as quilter, runner, writer, reader, wife and mother of two wonderfully curious children.

Neelam Mal is a teacher in Calgary who is passionate about picture books, storytelling and, most important, her young daughters. In her work and in her life, she explores issues of gender equality, social justice and living authentically.

Sandra McNeil longs for children to follow their questions with wonder and awe. Teaching children a range of disciplines, Sandra is drawn to the minutiae of a moment, a concept, a curriculum and strives to uncover the connections between them. Her love of teaching comes from her deep respect for children of all ages.

Jennifer Meredith is a teacher in Calgary who loves helping her students find their passions through inquiry-based education. Through her master's work, she developed a love of writing and enjoys spending time reflecting on her work and life in general, while enjoying the outdoors and bird watching.

Carli Molnar is an elementary teacher in Calgary, Alberta. Carli has taken a number of graduate studies courses in the field of Curriculum and Learning at the University of Calgary. She is deeply concerned with contemplative, hermeneutic and Buddhist pedagogies and curriculum reconceptualization.

Margeaux Montgomery is an MEd student at the University of Calgary and an educator. Her teaching and research interests focus on the importance of place-conscious pedagogy, holistic education and how to live well in the world with her students.

Kyria Pires teaches elementary students in Calgary. She loves being surprised by her students' creativity every day. When she is not teaching she enjoys backpacking and hiking with her husband and her dog, crocheting, playing the guitar and sailing.

Erin Quinn works for the Calgary Board of Education and believes, above all, that the purpose of education is for learners (teachers included!) to think, wonder and discover together.

Elisa Rapisarda is a teacher in the Calgary, Alberta, area.

Peter Rilstone based his master of education studies in the 1980s on studying the effects of elementary students' use of computers as a writing tool. After teaching for forty years, in his retirement he continues to pursue his passionate interests in teaching and learning. He is currently enrolled in education and religious studies courses, reads Latin every day, participates in a philosophical discussion group every Friday afternoon, and sings with the Calgary Philharmonic Chorus.

Trish Savill's career in education focuses on moving the classroom into the community and the ways students make sense of and pay attention to the world around them. After hours, much of her time is spent outside: operating a small family farm, in the mountains, on the water, and perhaps most important, enjoying those spaces as much as possible with her husband, children and grandchildren. Trish's professional passions continue in home life as she tries to make sense of the world around her through journaling.

Kate Schutz, Education Manager at the National Music Centre, is both a visual artist and an arts educator with more than a decade of experience in community and museum education. She holds a BFA in Painting and is currently completing her master of education degree with a focus on arts-based learning. Kate is a yoga teacher whose mindfulness practice infuses every aspect of her work.

Karen Schweighardt has been teaching for twenty-nine years. Her career started in Saskatchewan, moved to Toronto and has settled in Calgary. She shares her passion for music and the environment with her students. Her greatest and favourite teachers have been her own children.

Jackie Seidel is an Associate Professor, Werklund School of Education, University of Calgary. Her teaching and research focus on ecological consciousness, ecopsychology, education and climate change in relation to curriculum and learning. She is passionate about beekeeping, reading fiction and poetry.

Lauren Sele is an education student at the University of Calgary. She believes firmly in the power of storytelling to connect us across time and place, attune us to different voices, and guide us through multiple grounded truths. Speaking pedagogically and from the classroom, she thinks storytelling gets to the root of engagement and, when you get right down to it, is a whole lot more fun.

Kari Sirup is an elementary and middle school teacher from Calgary, Alberta. She is interested in art and mathematics and enjoys thinking about almost anything with children. When she isn't teaching, Kari loves spending time with her family outdoors.

David Geoffrey Smith, Ph.D., is Emeritus Professor of Education, University of Alberta, Edmonton, Alberta, Canada. He was born in China during the Maoist revolution but grew up in Northern Rhodesia (now Zambia), experiences that have always made him see Western culture as something odd, indeed worthy of study. His essays have been collected in three volumes: *Pedagon: Interdisciplinary Essays in the Human Sciences, Pedagogy and Culture* (Peter Lang, 1999); *Trying to Teach in a Season of Great Untruth: Globalization, Empire and the Crises of Pedagogy* (Sense, 2006); and *Teaching as the Practice of Wisdom* (Bloomsbury, 2014).

Lesley Tait is an educator and student in Calgary, Alberta. She loves life and attempts to get everything out of every day that she can. She has a passion for teaching and is looking forward to what the future may bring.

Lisa Taylor is a teacher and a mom. She loves spending time with her family and getting outdoors as much as possible. She enjoys mountain biking, hiking, camping and skiing. She also enjoys creating things with her hands and has been relearning how to sew and quilt.

Darren Vaast is an educator with ten years' experience being mindful and intentional in his teaching with young children. He has recently completed his master of education degree under Dr. David Jardine, focusing on educational philosophy and a more hermeneutic approach to teaching.

Kirsten Varner is a graduate student in the Werklund School of Education at the University of Calgary, Canada. Her passion lies in teaching the natural sciences through a practice of inquiry and exploration. Her broader interests include curriculum studies, hermeneutics, ecopedagogy and poetic inquiry.

Ian Walsh was born, raised and educated in Thunder Bay, Ontario. He currently lives in Calgary, Alberta, with his wife and daughter and is a middle school teacher.

Studies in Criticality

General Editor
Shirley R. Steinberg

Counterpoints publishes the most compelling and imaginative books being written in education today. Grounded on the theoretical advances in criticalism, feminism, and postmodernism in the last two decades of the twentieth century, Counterpoints engages the meaning of these innovations in various forms of educational expression. Committed to the proposition that theoretical literature should be accessible to a variety of audiences, the series insists that its authors avoid esoteric and jargonistic languages that transform educational scholarship into an elite discourse for the initiated. Scholarly work matters only to the degree it affects consciousness and practice at multiple sites. Counterpoints' editorial policy is based on these principles and the ability of scholars to break new ground, to open new conversations, to go where educators have never gone before.

For additional information about this series or for the submission of manuscripts, please contact:

Shirley R. Steinberg
c/o Peter Lang Publishing, Inc.
29 Broadway, 18th floor
New York, New York 10006

To order other books in this series, please contact our Customer Service Department:

(800) 770-LANG (within the U.S.)
(212) 647-7706 (outside the U.S.)
(212) 647-7707 FAX

Or browse online by series:
www.peterlang.com